OPTIMAL

OPTIMAL

---

*How to Sustain Personal and
Organizational Excellence Every Day*

DANIEL GOLEMAN &
CARY CHERNISS

HARPER
BUSINESS

An Imprint of HarperCollins*Publishers*

HarperCollins books may be purchased for educational, business, or sales promotional use. For information, please email the Special Markets Department at SPsales@harpercollins.com.

FIRST EDITION

Designed by Kyle O'Brien

Library of Congress Cataloging-in-Publication Data has been applied for.

ISBN 978-0-06-327976-6

23 24 25 26 27 LBC 5 4 3 2 1

Contents

PART IV | The Future of Emotional Intelligence

Your Optimal Zone

Imagine how you would feel if you were in Ajla Tomljanović's shoes in the fourth round at the 2022 U.S. Open Tennis Championships. She was the one who defeated Serena Williams in what was to be Williams's last match. Williams was a legend: she'd won a Grand Slam championship twenty-three times, and that day was playing at her peak. Plus she was the clear favorite of the twenty-four thousand fans crammed into the largest tennis stadium in the world.[1]

Nearly all of those fans were "screaming for Williams to win," with millions more watching online. Imagine "all the noise, the roars for Williams, the indecorous cheers when Tomljanović missed a serve, all the celebrities in the stands, the video tributes to Williams."

But Tomljanović had a secret weapon. Her father, a former professional handball champion and her first coach, taught her how to calm her nerves by focusing. "He showed her what the pitcher in the film *For Love of the Game*, played by Kevin Costner, did in the midst of a perfect game. He focused explicitly on the catcher's glove and ignored everything else in the stadium." Tomljanović followed her father's advice and kept a keen focus.

After her match, she said, "From the first moment I walked on court, I didn't really look around much. I was completely in my own little bubble." Tomljanović maintained that focus for more than three hours and went on to play the best tennis of her career, defeating Williams in three sets.

Her remarkable tennis game exemplifies flow, that state of full immersion where someone performs at their ultimate peak. Such superb focus helps anyone do their best, as we'll explore in detail. And your emotional state matters greatly, too, since upsetting thoughts are distractions from full concentration. That's why world-class athletes talk so much about the "mental game": they are competing with other athletes who have mastered their sport at the highest levels. So their internal states and focus emerge as keys to winning.

But because most often "flow" refers to rarified, even elusive, events in our lives, we prefer a more realistic, attainable goal: feeling satisfied that you've had a good day, productive by whatever standard works for you. That's what we mean by "optimal."

We argue that spotlighting supreme accomplishments like Tomljanović's overlooks the clues and the conditions—in particular, her hawklike focus—that make it possible for each of us to enter our optimal state where we perform at our best.

Holding ourselves to our highest standard—whatever our personal equivalent of Tomljanović's perfect tennis fame might be—we suspect, makes us prone to a perfectionism that can easily bring exhaustion and burnout. We just can't be at our peak in every moment all the time—but we can always strive to do our best. The relentless pursuit of flow points us toward extremes, while doing our best offers a more realistic goal.

Our optimal model offers the performance equivalent of the notion in parenting that we don't have to be the perfect mom or dad every moment, but rather do the best job we can. While the flow ideal holds us to a too-high standard, to that perfectionist's view of "our best," the optimal standard lets us relax and enjoy what we're doing without constant self-judgment. Just quiet that critical voice inside your head and focus on the task at hand.

In Part One of this book we'll sketch what an optimal state feels like, based on journals kept by hundreds of people that outline the inner architecture of having a good day. Then we'll see how that private edifice looks from the outside, using the lens of outstanding workplace performance.

Since we're both psychologists we look for hard research findings to guide our thinking. Following the research leads us to see a critical component of an optimal state in being intelligent about our emotions—in other words, emotional intelligence.

Seeing how workplace metrics for excellence map from the outside what people report from their inner experience was for us an epiphany, one that points to how emotional intelligence offers a doorway to personal excellence. Though the abilities of emotional intelligence go by many names these days, we conclude that the active ingredients in optimal performance hinge on emotional intelligence.

We draw on decades of scientific discoveries bearing on emotional intelligence, with direct implications for that optimal state—and what keeps us out of it. Having a satisfying day, rather than some mind-blowing peak experience while in flow, offers a key to achievement and fulfillment—not to mention avoiding burnout.

We see many ways emotional intelligence offers each of us the inner resources to more readily access this optimal state. In this book you'll find practical methods for entering your optimal state more readily, rather than having to await those elusive elements that will pitch you into a flow moment.

Why This Now?

For Dan, this book represents a culmination and confirmation of a hunch he had almost three decades ago: that emotional intelligence offers a map for being at our best. This, his fifth book on the topic, harvests a rich bounty of research affirming his original hunch.

Cary and Dan were cofounders of the Consortium for Research on Emotional Intelligence in Organizations a few years after the first scholarly article on the topic appeared in 1990, and were cochairs for the Consortium's first twenty-five years. The Consortium's mission: encourage sound research that integrates the standards of academic methodology with the practical needs of operating organizations.[2]

The Consortium was meant to bring together practitioners who are trying out applications of emotional intelligence in organizations like business and schools, with academic researchers who can apply their methodological skills to such studies.

Now, more than a quarter century later, there are such studies galore. While in the early years of the concept several critiques complained (justifiably) that there was scant evidence to support how emotional intelligence matters for, say, job performance or leadership, by now a substantial case can be made for its importance for effectiveness of all kinds—especially when self-mastery and empathy, social skills or stress resilience matters, which is all too often.

We came together to harvest this rich research bounty. In Part One of this book we'll delve into the ingredients of what's happening when we shine and how emotional intelligence can help get us there.

In Part Two we'll update our understanding of the competencies that translate emotional intelligence into effective action. We'll unpack the basic ingredients of emotional intelligence in our self-awareness, how we manage ourselves, in attuning to other people, and in putting that all together for effective relationships.

In Part Three we'll explore a particularly important aspect of our lives: working at our best. We'll look at ways emotional intelligence helps us perform optimally, whether as an individual, as a leader, or as a team member. In all these cases emotional intelligence boosts effectiveness, with a remarkable similarity between the optimal state and the ways research shows emotional intelligence boosts our individual performance in the workplace. We'll detail ways to help anyone upgrade these abilities. And we'll look into what it means to have an emotionally intelligent organization—one where emotional intelligence has become embedded in the DNA of an organization's culture.

Finally, in Part IV we explore the future of emotional intelligence, suggesting how these competencies—combined with other mental and emotional capacities—can better prepare us for the uncertain tomorrow we all face.

There's a new urgency to this exploration. Rudeness seems to have spread like a virus in recent years; witness the drumbeat of reports of unruly airplane passengers being arrested as their flight lands. Voices of hatred have become hard to ignore on social media. Children and teens in schools are showing rising rates of fights, bullying, depression, and high anxiety.[3] And as we'll see in Part III, the emotional intelligence skill set offers a crucial advantage in today's tough business climate. The need for emotional intelligence not just in our individual lives but in society at large seems greater than ever.

PART I

The Emotional Intelligence Path to Optimal Performance

1

Optimal You

Consider you at your best. What's your inner condition during peak effectiveness, where whatever talents you have are manifest at full force?

This range of excellence goes beyond the confines of the all-too-rare moments like "flow" to the more general experience of having a very satisfying day, one where we feel we did well in ways that matter to us, were in a mood that facilitates what we did, and felt ready to take on whatever challenges came along—our optimal state.[1]

There are several ways to tell if you are in such an optimal state. People in this zone are more creative, able to come up with novel and useful solutions.[2] Their productivity at turning out high-quality work stays high. They feel committed to their work, despite any difficulties. And their inner state reveals itself in how they treat the people around them: they are positive, supportive, fun.

We can think of this state as one of "maximum cognitive efficiency," where your mind operates on all cylinders. That cognitive personal best in our mental life depends, in turn, on our emotional state. The brain areas that allow us to use our talents at peak flourish when we can keep our disturbing emotions in check and our engagement high.

Our cognitive strengths operate at full force when the brain's alarm systems stay quiet, and with positive motivational circuitry active. As we get more calm, our thinking becomes sharper and more clear. We can exhibit whatever talents we may have at our best.

Being in a good mood underlies the signs of high performance, and enhances both attention and intention—for instance, being better able to see the big picture rather than getting caught by details, and feeling energized to take on a wider range of projects and tasks.[3]

A survey of over 5,000 managers and executives by McKinsey consultants found that some said they were in their best state of mind as much as 50 percent of the time, while others said just 10 percent.[4] More telling, in this same McKinsey survey, executives and managers reported that when they were in this best state, their productivity was 5 times greater than when they were just in an "average" or neutral state. While this relatively soft data can't be taken as scientific proof, it indicates how highly effective we feel while in our optimal state.[5]

Having a Really Good Day

Many specific ingredients in personal experience while having such a really good time emerged when researchers at Harvard Business School asked several hundred men and women to journal about the events of their workday, their feelings during those events, and their accomplishments.[6] Those accomplishments were all signs of cognitive effectiveness—mental challenges like solving a knotty problem in computer programming, coming up with new and useful kitchen gadgets, or managing the manufacture and distribution of tools.

At the end of their working day each person filled out a survey reviewing the events just past—a total of almost 12,000 accounts of their inner life. This trove of data yielded the ingredients of those highly satisfying days.

For everyone, being in their best state paid off in how well they performed at work.[7] Of course, there is no single measure of productivity; each of us needs to find our own yardstick, depending on what outcomes matter to us. Consider, for example, "small wins" that move you toward a larger goal. For a software code writer a small win meant finding a way to clone some old code, which cuts many hours off the time needed to finish a group software project.[8] Or, for example, Shannon Watts, who founded a nonprofit organization and tells of the sort of small wins that matter for her.

"I want to put a win on the table every day," she says. "That could look different every day, and it might seem small in the eyes of some. It could be a good editorial," for instance, or an effective conversation.[9]

She adds, "A win may not always look like a great triumph, but what counts is that you really put your heart into it."

And, of course, your wins need not be toward some grand goal, but rather aligned with what matters to you. If you've got five kids and you're their main caretaker, it may simply be folding the laundry, getting a costume together for a play one of the kids is in, or seeing that they all do their homework. If you're a manager or executive, accomplishing the task at hand, besting a KPI (or "key performance indicator"), or taking a small step toward an organizational goal may give you the sense of a win.

On their good days people felt more positive about those around them, about their organization and the nature of their work, and were more committed to it. These were days when, for example, they felt most creative in solving the problems of that day. Whether a software coder finally getting rid of a "bug," or a stay-at-home parent getting buy-in from a group of parents to form a car pool, cognitive sharpness ups the likelihood of such small wins—what feels like a victory on a task at hand.

People often recalled feeling buoyed by such wins—these minor victories put them in a good mood. Reports on what they felt was a good day showed small wins about three-quarters of the time, with setbacks rare on up days (and being "up" can make a setback easier to take). People felt good about their day in particular if people or events supported them—for instance, they felt respected and encouraged by people around them.

When we can easily resolve the problems and challenges that come our way, we naturally feel in a more upbeat mood; our perceptions take on a positive hue, so we see "problems" as invigorating challenges, and the people around us seem more friendly—and we are to them.

Conversely, on hard days, when it all seems more difficult, people report feeling frustrated and anxious, even sad. And the people they count on to get their tasks done seem less supportive and the resources at hand appear insufficient. Brain studies tell us that too-high levels of the neurochemicals secreted under stress can torpedo our cognitive abilities—uncontrollable stress, for instance, impairs our attention and our ability to suppress inappropriate responses.[10]

And, of course, there's a feedback loop here. While positive feelings enhance the likelihood of a good day, solving problems and the like in turn can make us feel great. A sense of accomplishment can mean not just satisfaction, but even elation.

By the same token, while a bad mood can make solving problems harder, being unable to resolve problems can lead to frustration, even self-pity, and disgust. On their worst days people said they felt thwarted by, for example, a lack of emotional support from other people or outright discouraging turns of events—both of which had toxic effects on their moods. If you end up drained of all joy, the odds are you've had an upsetting setback that day; setbacks lean into feelings of sadness, fear, or just frustration.

Rethinking Flow

Pick from all your good days the very best ever, one punctuated by a singularly spectacular accomplishment. What's your personal equivalent of that spectacular tennis match where Ajla Tomljanović defeated Serena Williams?

For example, a neurosurgeon told of a very difficult operation, one that, going in, he was unsure he could perform. But he succeeded, despite his initial uncertainty. Once he finished the surgery, the neurosurgeon noticed some rubble in the corner of the operating room.

"What happened?" he asked a nurse.

"While you were operating," the nurse replied, "the ceiling caved in—but you were so focused you didn't notice."

This tale exemplifies the thousands gleaned by a research group at the University of Chicago who first captured that fleeting event, the flow state, where we are at our absolute best.[11] A moment of flow spotlights our peak achievement in a given domain—surgery, basketball, ballet, you name it.

In the original research on flow, the researchers asked a wide range of people about times they had outdone themselves—when even they were surprised at how well they did. The domain of expertise of the people asked varied widely; chess champions, surgeons, basketball players, and ballet dancers, for instance, were among them.

No matter the specifics of that remarkable performance—an artist absorbed in her work, a master playing chess, a surgeon during an operation, a basketball player making a really tough shot, or a dancer whirling—the inner experience for the performer was the same. This inner state the researchers dubbed "flow."

In popular usage "flow" has become synonymous with the times we are at our peak. Companies are encouraged to help create flow states in people who work there.[12] But here's the problem with flow: it's by definition a rare event, that one time when we are at our absolute best.

Experiences of flow are wonderful, even semi-miraculous—but you can't count on them. They seem to happen out of the blue, apparently when crucial elements—like that surgeon's superfocus—line up. That's why we favor an optimal state, one that can occur as a result of our own efforts, and far more of the time than such peak flow events.

This widening of the target helps us all by making our expectations for ourselves more realistic. We don't have to be at our very, very best on any given day. Instead we can feel good by making steady improvement toward a larger goal rather than berating ourselves for not getting that peak experience (one that we can't sustain, let alone produce at will). Having a good day means we've done well enough to quietly congratulate ourselves. Unlike a flow moment, a good day may be nothing to brag about, but can still be highly satisfying.

Flow vs. Optimal

The extensive research on flow pinpoints several crucial dimensions of us at our best. But that flow-focused lens meant only the topmost events were captured (though, to be sure, some research on flow shades into what we see as an optimal state). But here's the key distinction we make between flow and optimal performance: we see the ingredients of peak performance not as a single event but rather as points on a wider spectrum. And that spectrum itself offers key elements of a recipe for having a day where we feel a well-earned sense of satisfaction.

The flow research names these specific elements:

» A balance between the challenge and our skills
» Absence of self-consciousness
» Time collapses, lengthening or shrinking in our experience
» Feels great
» Seems effortless

But consider how these very elements need not be confined to that rare "flow" event, but rather how each points to a dimension that can be part of our more prevalent optimal times.

Take, for instance, that absence of self-consciousness about how well we are doing, with little or no self-doubt or thoughts about how others may see us. Such lack of self-consciousness bespeaks the abandonment of our usual focus on our self—I, me, and mine. Such absence of worried judgments about how we are doing signals the lessening of the sense of self that we typically spend so much of our energy protecting, inflating, and defending.

Such self-preoccupation dissolves as we become absorbed in our actions. Absorption in the activity at hand lets us discard our emotional baggage—full concentration demands we leave that baggage at the door. In such focused moments our ordinary stream of thought becomes a distraction. We need to let go of thoughts of the future—for example, worries about what will happen—as well as memories of the past, particularly regrets, and bring our mind back to the present task at hand.

A rock climber, for instance, told us that one reason he loved climbs was that they forced him to pay full attention to his every move; he forgot his worries. To the extent we forget about ourselves—our to-do lists, troubles of the day, personal hopes and fears—our attention gets freed up to focus on the task at hand.

Perhaps the most telling sign of this optimal state: *feeling great.* "Autotelic" was the technical jargon the researchers used for this kind of pleasure.[13] We are in such a positive mood that we love the very act of doing whatever we are involved in (pay, for instance, seems less relevant as a motivator at these moments).

Then think of that sense of effortlessness. What looked from the outside like a tremendous effort was for those in flow relatively effortless. This aspect of our optimal state, we suspect, indicates that we are applying a well-learned skill.[14] One intriguing finding about the brain in someone who has mastered a skill: while performing that sequence, whether as a chess champ or basketball player, that person's brain uses *less* energy during that activity than does the brain of someone just learning, say, the Queen's gambit in chess or shooting baskets for the first time from the penalty line. The effortless actions of masters of a domain mean their brain has created a habitual sequence they are following.

The science of habit formation tells us this effortlessness marks a neural shift, where the sequence of actions involved has become a habit, one that happens automatically and unconsciously. Such habitual sequences are activated in the basal ganglia, one of the more primitive areas toward the bottom of the brain. Once the basal ganglia takes over a learned sequence, we can perform that new habit effortlessly, without having to think about it. Sounds like flow, no? But what it really indicates is a well-honed skill.

Then there's *full concentration.* We are utterly absorbed in the task at hand, indistractable. We lose track of time—it speeds up or slows down—we are so lost in what we are doing. Virtually nothing can tear us away from this full absorption. As we'll detail, we see this one-pointedness as a pathway to the optimal zone rather than a side effect, contrary to what the original flow theory proposed.

Beyond Flow

In mapping the inner landscape of our optimal zone we question the need to include each and every dimension the Chicago group identified as elements of flow. In addition, we don't see the recipe for "optimal" as being either-or (you have it or you don't) but rather as being on a spectrum, shading into the larger region of our inner states. So on our good days we experience, say, feeling good, agility in solving dilemmas as they present themselves, and full attention on what we're doing. That doesn't mean we are in the vaunted "flow" state—just that it's all going well. The optimal state can emerge in a larger scope of our life than does flow.

Plus we wonder about some of the basic premises of the flow paradigm. The key to entering flow, the researchers postulated, was that a person was being challenged at the peak of their ability, and so had to call on the top of their skill set (whatever that might be for the particular challenge). The person in flow, they said, was also agile in handling the challenge, no matter how demands changed moment-to-moment. The rule of thumb: match a person's ability to the challenge. In the business realm or in school this might mean giving a person an assignment that stretches their abilities a lot—but not too much.

But we see it differently. Whereas others have argued that the chances of getting into flow are greatest when the demands of a challenge draw on our peak set of skills, we suggest that this challenge-skill matchup may not be sufficient for entering an optimal state. In our view, how well you can display your best talents depends not just on whether the situation draws them out and how well you have sharpened them, it also depends on your inner state. If you are in the wrong state of mind—uninterested in the challenge or highly stressed, say—you are unlikely to be at your best, no matter what your potential might be.

For instance, when students in a school of architecture kept diaries of their moods and performance each day, being in a positive mood and feeling free to choose how to do their work rather than a specific match between skill and challenge was associated with their being absorbed.[15] Another review of flow studies found it had less to do with the ratio between skills and the challenge than it did with how important to someone's goals the task at hand seemed.[16] In our view, full concentration, perhaps boosted by a sense of meaning in what you do and feeling some control over how you do it, emerges as more crucial to our optimal state than does matching our skills to a given challenge.

While the original flow research saw such absorption as an effect of flow, we see concentration—being undistracted—as itself a ticket into our optimal state. In other words, concentration begets a good day's work, not the other way around. The other elements, like lack of self-consciousness, are side effects of such full absorption in the task at hand. This reframing of flow as accessible through our powers of concentration reveals a doorway into our optimal zone that does not depend on serendipity or a once-in-a-lifetime moment.

Here's a list of the subjective elements of being in an optimal state—having a really good day:

» More creative, seeing obstacles as challenges
» More productive, turning out high-quality work
» Feeling good, in an upbeat mood
» Mentally sharp, making small wins toward a larger goal
» A positive outlook, committed to your efforts
» Giving and getting support in relationships

These ingredients of our subjective experience of the optimal state reveal a view from inside. But as we'll see in the next chapter, viewing from outside how we operate while in this state maps, to a surprising degree, the benefits of emotional intelligence.

2

___

Emotional Intelligence
and the Bottom Line

How much does emotional intelligence help someone thrive at work? When Dan's first book on emotional intelligence (or EI, the shorthand we'll use here) appeared more than twenty-five years ago, we couldn't answer that question. There was very little research on the direct link between EI and meaningful results like work performance and engagement. There was also considerable skepticism among both business leaders and academic researchers. But in science, as in business, skepticism can be useful. It can spur us on to do the hard work of proving what we think is right, or giving up our beliefs in the light of good data.[1]

Many popular topics on how to be successful in business never receive much scrutiny from dispassionate researchers. They are just fads, the "flavor of the month," soon to disappear as a new fad emerges. Fortunately, that did not happen with emotional intelligence. Thanks to the efforts of the Consortium for Research on Emotional Intelligence in Organizations (CREIO), along with many others in both universities and the corporate world, there has been a steady flow of research since the mid-1990s. It shows that EI can make a big difference for the performance of people at all levels of an organization.

One of the more compelling studies followed a large group of college students from a university in the midwestern United States.[2] The students took an emotional intelligence test prior to graduation and then completed a survey ten to twelve years later. The study found that their scores on the EI test while in college predicted their salaries at the follow-up, even above their IQ, personality, grades, and gender.

In an academic career, influence is measured, for example, by the number of other academics who cite your peer-reviewed articles. Your braininess matters greatly here. In the academic world you need an MA or PhD, so you train to become a professor. You find the topic you want to focus on, and you do independent work on it—that's what you are rewarded for.

Ground rules in academics differ greatly from business. If you join a business you need to focus on what that company deems essential for its strategy and to work as part of a team, not independently. Unlike with tenure in academia, in the business world your place is only as secure as your performance—and the fiscal health of your outfit—allow. There's an entire industry that resocializes PhDs so they fit better into corporate reality.

Salary, of course, roughly measures success in climbing the company's ladder more than it measures performance. People who earn high salaries are not always the most effective at doing their jobs. (You can likely think of some glaring examples!) But much research now looks directly at EI and performance.

Sales professionals are a particularly good group to study not only because their sales data offers a hard measure of their performance, but because selling itself demands EI skills. At a major national real estate company, for example, agents who scored high in emotional intelligence generated more sales revenue than those who scored low.[3] The same with insurance agents: higher EI meant greater sales revenue and customer retention.

In sales, the researchers suggested, EI can help in several ways. For instance, EI helped them keep their composure when interacting with anxious or frustrated clients. EI also helped the agents understand why clients might feel the way they did, which enabled them to focus their sales messages accordingly and address any underlying feelings that might be getting in the way. Maintaining emotional balance in combination with empathy—two EI abilities—made the difference.

The implications of this research go far beyond real estate and insurance sales. There are many occupations where one must "sell" something. Consider Martha, the head of a program for people who had lost a loved one. In her role as the executive director, the most important "selling" occurred when meeting with potential donors. Early in her career, during one of those meetings, she shared her own story of how she had lost her father to cancer when she was eight years old.

As Martha told the story, she noticed that the atmosphere in the room changed. Her audience suddenly became more attentive. One or two people began to tear up. Martha also noticed that she began talking about the program with more passion. She realized that telling her personal story was a powerful tool to use in connecting with potential donors. Martha's EI—her ability to perceive, understand, and manage her emotions and those of others—boosted her effectiveness in winning donors for her program.

Emotional Intelligence in STEM Occupations

It's not difficult to see how emotional intelligence can help bring about optimal performance in work that involves selling of some kind. But what about the many fields where that may not be the case, such as engineering? Richard Boyatzis and some of his students at the Case Western Reserve University's Weatherhead School of Management studied engineers working in the research division of a large automobile company.[4] The engineers rated each other on their effectiveness as engineers. Result: the engineers' emotional intelligence was a significant predictor of their effectiveness, but their IQ as measured by general mental ability was not, nor were any personality traits.

Emotional intelligence has become more important for engineers and others in STEM (science, technology, engineering, and mathematics) fields in recent years because increasingly engineers are working in teams where their performance depends in large part on how well they manage those relationships. Working in teams can be a challenge when people with different personalities, cultural backgrounds, and specialties come together with different ideas for how to do things. Emotional and social competencies such as emotional balance, adaptability, empathy, and teamwork can help manage difficulties in ways that lead to more innovative solutions to challenging problems.

Cognitive intelligence is still important. Just to be hired for an engineering position, someone needs a relatively high level of intelligence. But once they get in the door, differences in IQ don't have much impact on performance. So cognitive intelligence is necessary, but not sufficient; EI becomes especially important.

Take another STEM profession, information technology (IT). Almost every medium- or large-size company now has at least one IT person whose sole responsibility is to keep computers, phones, and other electronic systems running. So how is EI important for them?

Several years ago Cary worked in a university department that had two IT people. Both were qualified. One of them had a stronger tech background, but whenever something went wrong with a computer, the staff usually called on the other person. Why? Because he was friendlier. And he was more reassuring when anxious users worried about whether they had "broken" their device. If the more emotionally intelligent IT person wasn't available, the staff tended to put off calling in the other IT person and tried to fix the problem themselves.

Perhaps surprisingly, giving financial advice is another field where EI plays a large role. A poll by the Harris organization found that in selecting a financial advisor, people considered advisors' emotional intelligence more important than their digital literacy.[5] The poll was commissioned by the Million Dollar Round Table, an association of insurance agents and financial advisors whose sales amount to more than a million dollars in a year.

More than 2,000 people were polled and more than half said they "would be more likely to trust advice from advisors who 'Listen to and acknowledge their clients' needs,' 'Communicate in easily understood ways,' 'Follow through on their word,' and 'Show they care about their clients as people.'"[6]

In contrast, just 30 percent of those polled said they would be more likely to trust the advice of advisors with up-to-date websites; only a quarter said the same for advisors who regularly recommend relevant content. It's not that an advisor's technical competence is unimportant. But when it comes to trust, which is crucial in choosing a financial advisor, people care more about EI. As the report noted, "While digital literacy makes business operations more efficient and helps bring clients in the door, it does not by itself communicate trustworthiness."

Studies like these can be persuasive, but the outcome of any single study could be an anomaly. To better assess the relationship between EI and optimal performance across a wide variety of roles and occupations, we can turn to meta-analysis, a technique that combines the results of many different individual studies. This method takes into account the fact that one study might have positive results while most others are negative—a difference that could be due, say, to disparate ways of measuring results, or some unique feature of those being measured, or how well an intervention gets done—or an endless list of such factors. Even the time of day or year that a study was done can make a difference. But when a meta-analysis combines results from a large number of studies, each assessing a different group and even using different measures, the impact of one or two anomalous findings gets nullified.

In one such aggregation of 99 studies with a total of over 17,000 participants, EI was a significant predictor of performance.[7] The measures used to gauge performance in these studies varied widely. In some performance was assessed by supervisors' ratings; in others the metric was financial outcomes or direct measures of work performance. The link between EI and performance also varied from one occupation or industry to another. For instance, EI was a particularly strong predictor of excellent performance among bankers and police officers.

At least five other meta-analyses have resulted in similar findings: EI consistently emerges as a significant predictor of people's performance on the job.[8] When the researchers looked more closely at the data, they found that EI was particularly important in jobs that required employees to regulate their feelings or involved a high frequency of social interactions.[9] However, even in jobs that involved less such emotional self-management and relationship skills, higher EI was associated with better performance.

The Engaged Worker

Imagine a personal assistant who is sitting at a computer and typing emails composed by his boss. As a skilled keyboardist he can perform well enough even while thinking about other things, such as what a jerk his boss is. The PA is not *engaged* in his work, but his performance is satisfactory.

There are all too many situations like this when our output might be adequate, but our attitudes and feelings aren't. Optimal performance involves more than just how well we do our work. Imagine how much better that assistant might be if he were not only technically adept, but also engaged enough to give his best effort. One expert described work engagement as "a positive, fulfilling work-related state of mind that is characterized by vigor, dedication, and absorption."[10] That definition describes a worker in an optimal state.

Consider the experience of high school teacher Eugenia Barton. She enjoyed teaching her vocational education classes, but after a few years she felt a bit bored, and began to look for something that would engage her more. She came up with the idea of a student store. Students would run the store under her supervision, and they would learn about the world of business in the process. The store proved very successful, and the hours when she worked on it with her students were the high point of her day. She described it as "the most wonderful thing I ever thought of."

Engagement not only contributes to our job satisfaction, it also enhances our performance. A meta-analysis found that employees' engagement was linked to how satisfied their customers were, their productivity, and even company profit, as well as lessened employee turnover and fewer accidents.[11]

Unfortunately, employee engagement has been declining steadily in recent years. In 2016, the Gallup organization reported that the global rate was only 32 percent; by 2022, it had dropped to 21 percent.[12]

Numerous studies have shown that more emotionally intelligent workers are more engaged in their work, such as research on over 2,100 nurses.[13] Likewise, emotional intelligence in teachers linked to their engagement, which in turn led to higher achievement by their students.[14] And among police officers, those with higher emotional intelligence were more engaged in their work and less likely to quit.[15]

One reason that EI might lead to greater engagement and job satisfaction is that it helps us to seek out situations that are a good fit for us. People high in emotional self-awareness are better able to identify when a certain job possibility will be satisfying and meaningful, or find ways to make the job they have more engaging.

Take Maggie, a lawyer, who worked in the legal department of a large city.[16] Her job was tedious and unfulfilling—until the day she discovered a stack of old bankruptcy cases that no one in the office was working on. When she looked through them more closely, she discovered that the city was entitled to hundreds of thousands of dollars in money. Maggie focused on those cases and became a star performer, bringing millions of dollars into the city treasury.

Maggie thrived on recognition and admiration, and loved highly analytical and challenging work. Several of the cases were more mentally stimulating than anything she had worked on before. The high point came when she brought one of the cases to the federal circuit court and argued it in front of some of the best judges in the country. She was finally in her element, in her optimal state.

Maggie was both highly satisfied with her job and highly engaged. Though job satisfaction is closely related to engagement, they are not quite the same. Workers can be satisfied with their jobs but not particularly engaged. That had been the case for Maggie; at a previous job for a legal aid office and before she stumbled on the bankruptcy cases, she was rarely in an optimal state at work.

People with higher emotional intelligence tend to be both more satisfied with their jobs and more engaged. A meta-analysis combining

120 studies with a total of 29,119 workers found a significant relation between job satisfaction and emotional intelligence.[17]

That study also found that workers with lower emotional intelligence were more likely to leave their jobs. Employee turnover can have a big impact on a company's bottom line.[18] The costs of replacing just one worker can be considerable. According to a Gallup Workplace Report, "Replacing exiting workers costs one-half to two times the employee's annual salary. Assuming an average salary of $50,000 that replacement cost translates to between $25,000 and $100,000 per employee."[19] For a high-level executive that cost can be several times greater.

Then there's the lost productivity of those who stay, due to anxieties about what might happen to them. Plus the intangible but invaluable loss of expertise, gaps that have long-term costs. In addition, when an organization replaces someone who left with a new worker, the "on-boarding" period can put a strain on colleagues for a considerable period of time. So it's not surprising that low turnover has been connected with better business outcomes like return on investment, return on assets, and profit.[20]

As a person's organizational commitment declines, so does her optimal performance. A meta-analysis finds that committed workers perform at a higher level—and emotional intelligence boosts commitment.[21]

The Good Organizational Citizen

Who at your workplace went out of their way to help you recently? That person represents something beyond ordinary kindness—he or she typifies the person who goes beyond their own job description to lend a hand when others at work need it.

Sometimes called being "a good organizational citizen," its definition highlights any helpful activity outside the standard reward system for a given position.[22] Being a good citizen at work means you help out your coworkers in ways beyond the demands of your own job—for instance, offering to help a coworker who is swamped by taking over part of their tasks, or helping clean up after an internal company event. This, too, links to EI. Understandably, going out of your way to help someone else—especially if done by many people—also boosts how your group or entire organization performs.[23]

A meta-analysis of more than 16,000 employees showed that those with higher EI were more likely to be good organizational citizens.[24] Worse, people with lower EI were more likely to engage in problem habits such as loafing, bullying, and lateness.[25]

Then consider the impact of being ill on getting into your optimal state. Imagine you wake up one morning and feel a headache coming on. You have an important meeting at the office later that morning, and you need to finish up a report for your boss. So you drag yourself out of bed and dress. You skip breakfast because you feel nauseous. You manage to get into the office and do what you have to do. But you feel "off" all day. You contribute little at the meeting, and your report is not very good. Imagine this happening a few days every month.

Headaches, difficulty sleeping, or mild stomach problems, as well as more serious maladies, can all prevent workers from being at their best. Although there are many factors that contribute to physical and mental illness, research has shown a significant link with emotional intelligence.[26] One reason that people with high EI may be healthier is how EI helps us cope with stress, being more resilient, as we will see in Chapter 6.[27]

Self-awareness, along with emotional self-regulation, helps people identify stress before it becomes overwhelming, and so manage it more effectively. Many anger management programs, for example, help people recognize the first signs of frustration and irritability. They then teach people ways to respond that reduce their arousal rather than allow it to reach a full-blown outburst.

Self-management also helps people get healthier through exercise, following a nutritious diet, and sleeping well—and they more often comply with what their doctor tells them to do.[28] In addition, people with EI competencies such as empathy and teamwork are more likely to have strong social support networks, which are a buffer against a number of illnesses.[29]

El Benefits, Capsulized

The wide range of benefits that research has found for having higher levels of emotional intelligence can be seen as the optimal state viewed from the outside, through the lens of what matters to an organization.

To be more specific, the empirical evidence from workplace research suggests that greater levels of EI make you:

- More productive, engaged, and have higher performance in any job, at every level
- Go further in your career
- Be better at sales, in every sense of the word
- Generate more revenue for your organization
- Be more effective, even in STEM jobs like engineering and IT
- Be seen as more trustworthy
- Feel more satisfied with your job and committed to your work
- Be less likely to leave your job
- Help out others when they need it
- Less likely to be a bully, chronically late, or loaf
- Have better health

We see all these, taken together, as external views of being in our optimal state. To highlight just a few: one sign of the optimal state was positive relationships, which shows up on this list as helping workmates out. Or take the optimal zone indicator of feeling highly involved in the task at hand; from the outside that can be seen as high engagement, a valued quality in the workplace. A strong sense of commitment, as well as a sense of satisfaction, shows up on both lists.

To be sure, the workplace indicators that correlate with a person's high EI were not designed with the optimal state in mind, but rather reflect measures that matter most to an employer. All the more reason that the resonance is striking between the signs of high EI seen from the outside and the more private experience of someone in their optimal zone.

In Part Two we explore in more depth the competencies of emotional intelligence, which we now see as active ingredients of our optimal zone. Each part of emotional intelligence helps us in its own way enter and stay in that best state for our personal performance. Self-awareness offers an inner platform from which we can better manage our inner state. Empathy—tuning in to the emotions of the other person—does the same for our relationships.

PART II

Emotional Intelligence: The Details

3

Emotional Intelligence, Redux

Bobby's mom was Dan's fourth-grade Sunday school teacher; Bobby was a few grades ahead of Dan. He disappeared from Dan's life only to resurface decades later, shortly after Dan's book *Emotional Intelligence* was published in 1995. By then Bobby had emigrated to Israel and changed his name to Reuven Bar-On. He contacted Dan to say he had just completed a doctoral dissertation that overlapped with emotional intelligence. The topic: well-being.

Though Reuven's thesis at the University of South Africa was on well-being, he reshaped his measure for those qualities into an assessment of emotional intelligence—at the time a hot, new approach to talking about people's personal and interpersonal abilities. Reuven's research captures one of many ways to view emotional intelligence, and his measure—among several others—has spawned a multitude of studies. So when it comes to what, exactly, the benefits of emotional intelligence might be, answers can now be found in a well-researched and detailed mapping.

If you type into a search engine the term "emotional intelligence" you'll get millions of hits. That's because the term (or the slang "EQ" for short) has entered common parlance and gets used quite loosely these days. Because of the ambiguity of meaning this reflects, and due to the proliferation of so many theories of emotional intelligence, we feel it's time to revisit what we mean by the term—and to help the reader clear up confusion over what, exactly, EI refers to here.

There are more than a dozen influential models of emotional intelligence, all created since a Yale psychologist, Peter Salovey (who eventually became president of Yale University), and his then grad student John (Jack) Mayer wrote their first article on the concept in 1990.[1] They went on to design a measure of emotional intelligence by now widely used in scholarly research on the topic.

A few years later, as Dan was finishing his book *Emotional Intelligence*, he and Cary formed the Consortium for Research on Emotional Intelligence in Organizations. Many experts in the field joined, including Reuven.

Over the last quarter century we have welcomed as Consortium members a wide range of practitioners and researchers, who draw on various models of emotional intelligence that have been proposed since the original Salovey and Mayer article. This proliferation means that from the get-go there's the question "What do you mean by 'emotional intelligence'?" Despite the controversies over this within the field, there are some basic agreements.[2] In a survey of members of the Consortium, who represent most major schools of thought on EI, the following model was acceptable to most everyone:

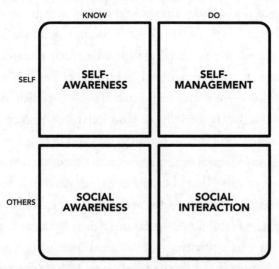

Figure 1. The basic template for emotional intelligence acceptable to all schools of thought sees four domains: Self-Awareness; Self-Management; Social Awareness; Social Interaction. Each EI approach then maps these domains in its own way.

The EI quadrants represent one of innumerable ways to slice and label this essential personal and interpersonal skill set. Self-awareness gives us an ongoing sense of what we are feeling, why we have those emotional reactions, and how they shape our thoughts, feelings, and urges to act. Self-management lets us use that inner awareness to handle our emotions effectively: keep disturbing emotions from disrupting our activity, enhance positive feelings, bounce back from upset, keep our eye on our goals despite distraction, and be agile in our responses to changing challenges. These abilities help us stay in our optimal zone.

Then empathy lets us tune in to others—to sense how they see a situation, how they are feeling, and to care about their welfare. This fosters the positivity in relationships typical of "good days." Finally, managing relationships and interactions well lets us guide and persuade, even inspire others to do their best. We can mentor and coach them, be an effective team member, surface and settle simmering conflicts. All this means we can help others get and stay in *their* optimal state.

Though most all emotional intelligence theories agree on the import of these four domains, how a given EI thinker fills in each of those domains varies greatly. The dozen or so different models and definitions of EI (and about as many different tools for assessment) each build on differing assumptions about what they are measuring.[3] The plethora of models signifies the intensity of scientific and practical interest—a good sign.

A Radical Proposal

David McClelland, Dan's mentor in graduate school at Harvard, made what was in those days a radical proposal: he wrote an article in the main psychology journal that argued it would be better to hire people for their competence than any other talent indicators. Test job applicants for competence, he argued, not for intelligence.[4]

What McClelland meant was this: If you want to know the best person for a given job, don't look at their IQ scores or at how well they did in school. Look, instead, at people who hold that position in your organization who perform in the top 10 percent—those with the highest competence—by whatever metric makes sense for their job. Compare them with people in the same role who are only average performers. Then do a systematic analysis to determine the abilities or competencies that you find in the stars that you don't see in the average performers.[5]

That gives you a "competence model." Today, most organizations that have high-quality people operations use a competence model for their key positions. The model helps them in decisions on who to hire, who to promote, and what strengths to help those in midcareer develop further.

There are two kinds of competencies. *Threshold* competencies are the abilities everyone needs to get and hold a given job. Cognitive abilities like IQ or business expertise turn out to be largely a threshold competency: When you apply for a job you want to show you have the intelligence and experience to handle the cognitive complexity of that particular position. But once you're hired, you're working with and competing with people who are as smart as you are, creating what's called a "floor effect" for IQ. That is, some specific cognitive abilities are the basic skills that everyone must have who holds that position.

The other kind of competency is called a *distinguishing* competency, one that sets the outstanding performers apart from the average ones at any given job. It's the distinguishing competencies that count (or should count) in terms of promotion, in terms of being a star performer or an outstanding leader.

When Dan gave a talk at Google about the EI competencies he heard a lot of pushback: one executive insisted that some competencies Dan called "distinguishing" had become threshold there—that is, just to do the job everyone needed to exhibit them. So exactly what competencies matter most for outstanding performance depend on the norms of a given organization.

Still, the EI competencies offer a map anyone can find useful, akin to a physical where medical tests give you highs and lows on a range of biological indicators like cholesterol and triglycerides. Your EI profile can help you spot where to start working on getting better, as we'll detail in Chapter 12.

The Hidden Role of Emotional Intelligence

In his first semester of college Cary was about to sit for the final exam in a course on Plato's dialogues. The stakes were high: this exam would determine students' grades in the course. The demand was high, too: repeat verbatim three of the eight Platonic dialogues the course had covered.

Cary, preparing for the final, had pretty much memorized all those dialogues. But when the professor handed out the exam for the three-hour final, Cary froze. His mind went blank. He started sweating profusely, his heart racing.

After what seemed an eternity (but probably lasted five minutes at most) his nervous system gradually quieted. As his nerves calmed down, Cary's mind started working again. He still felt stress, but his mental mechanics kicked in. Once he began to remember the first dialogue, he was off and running. The more Cary wrote, the calmer and more confident he felt that he could perform well on the exam.

How Cary was able to calm himself made all the difference in how well he could access his academic knowledge; he aced the exam rather than failing it. That interplay between his cognitive abilities and his turbulent emotions points to why emotional intelligence matters so much for life success.

The importance of emotional self-mastery for academics (or any field where cognitive skill counts) may be difficult to see during our school years. But consider this: school grades rarely reflect a student's abilities when it comes to teamwork or leadership, let alone creativity. Instead grades generally reward talent at mastering new knowledge—or a knack for cramming for tests. For success in a career, though, such cognitive abilities (amply rewarded during our school years) may be necessary, but they are not sufficient for becoming a leader, or being an outstanding team member.

Many organizations evaluate how well employees are doing on their job with a measure called a KPI, or "key performance indicator." These are perhaps the closest parallel in a business to grades in school. But consider what a KPI measures: metrics that matter most for the strategic success of the organization. Examples of KPIs: how many new clients signed up in a given period or how many old clients you retained; or how many people visited a store and how many of those made a purchase, or the number of downloads an online link got.

Doing well on such measures demands a threshold of the relevant cognitive abilities, but they also require emotional intelligence in various ways. Going into the future this may be much more true. Take, for example, the ability to sense a customer's experience of a brand. This empathic ability, arguably crucial for a direct-to-consumer company's survival, goes beyond the way KPIs are typically formulated today.

The interplay between cognitive abilities and emotional intelligence can be complex. Both matter for success and for entering the optimal zone—but they matter differently.

Our GMA, or "general mental ability," another label for what we often think of as IQ or cognitive skills, has been shown over and over to be the best predictor of a student's school grades, eventual income, and job success in general.[6] But there's one big exception to this rule: when life or work becomes an emotional roller coaster. Another exception: in our relationships, where empathy matters enormously. In these cases our self-management and interpersonal abilities make a huge difference.[7]

Data suggests the IQ and emotional intelligence skill sets are lodged in differing brain circuitry. Our cognitive abilities—determined by, for example, our working memory and the speed with which our mind processes information—tend to wane as we age. Emotional intelligence, on the other hand, seems well preserved, or even to improve with age, as indicated by greater positivity, emotion control, and stability.[8]

For now, let's get more specific about the basic building blocks of this skill set. For our purposes we'll use the model shown below in Figure 2, developed by Dan with Richard Boyatzis, professor of management at

Case Western University, built on decades of research on the EI competencies that nest in one or another of the four domains of emotional intelligence. We'll use this template to explore aspects of emotional intelligence that are less appreciated or newly prominent—and that are helpful for reaching the optimal zone.

This version of emotional intelligence was based on specific competencies within the EI domain that distinguished star performers at work from those who were just average.[9] Though originally derived from data on what distinguishes top 10 percent stars in the workplace, these abilities can benefit any of us, no matter what shapes our days.

That generic table of EI generated by our Consortium members, when filled in with the competencies based on proficiency in each of the four domains, looks like this:

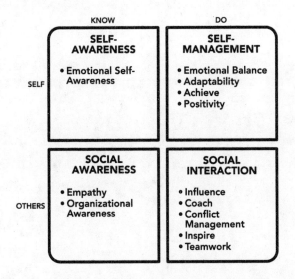

Figure 2. The generic emotional intelligence domains with the competencies nested within. Each EI competence depends on the underlying domain.

The list of a dozen emotional intelligence competencies in Figure 2 was often (though not exclusively) applied to leaders. But let's expand our idea of who, exactly, can be called a "leader." The essence of leadership boils down to influencing other people in one way or another. In that sense, each of us is a leader: we have our own sphere of influence, whether a small group or a wider reach. Teachers, heads of households, circles of friendships—all of us are in one way or another a leader. So the emotional intelligence competencies apply to each of us.

The chapters that follow map a dozen key EI competencies and explore facets that seem most timely. We take a fresh look at the competencies of emotional intelligence and in some cases highlight underappreciated benefits. We review the basics of these competencies, both as a refresher for those already familiar with them and to rethink these building blocks of emotional intelligence as they operate in ourselves, in leaders, in teams, and in organizations as a whole. And, of course, these competencies each help ease our way into an optimal state.

4

Self-Awareness Applied

What gets most athletes' attention is the idea of being in the 'zone'—the mind-state where they are playing at their best, they can do no wrong, and no matter what happens they are always a step ahead. There's a lack of self-consciousness, a relaxed concentration, and a sense of effortlessness. . . ."[1]

That summary of the optimal state comes from George Mumford, who has worked with champion athletes for many years, including the Chicago Bulls and the Los Angeles Lakers basketball teams. Mumford uses the promise of getting into an optimal state to invite athletes to begin an attention-training course.

"I let them know that if they pay attention, the zone will happen as a by-product," Mumford told them. "When they are in the moment and absorbed in the activity, they play at their best."

While the flow researchers saw utter absorption in the activity at hand as an *outcome* of flow, we consider the ability to tune in fully to what's at hand as a doorway *into* the optimal state. Concentration demands that our distractions be at bay; the more concentrated we are, the fewer distracting thoughts and feelings we have—and during our best efforts we are indistractable.

Neuroscience refers to this brain state, when we are at our best, as "neural harmony." Neural circuits demanded by the task at hand activate more fully, while those irrelevant to the task remain relatively quiet. This lets us be utterly concentrated on what we are doing. If a finely focused attention can become a doorway into being at our best, then distraction—which shows up in the brain as the activation of circuitry irrelevant to what we are doing—represents a quick exit from that zone. That's seen, for instance, in multitasking (or worse, doomscrolling on social media), when we get lost in activities irrelevant to what's most urgent and important. At its worst we are swept away in frazzle.

Consider someone rapt in a video game where they are furiously dodging asteroids while trying to capture crystals floating through space. While they play this video game, their brains are being scanned by an MRI; the more absorbed they become in the game, the stronger a particular brain pattern becomes: their circuitry for attention fires up and connects to their brain's network for pleasure.[2] It feels good to be utterly concentrated. This full-concentration entryway for our optimal state has other benefits: as we quiet neural networks for worry and self-doubt, we feel more confident and free of self-consciousness.

Good news here: our ability to fully concentrate, decades of research shows, can be learned and improved by practice.[3] Of course sports coaches and yogis have known this all along. As George Mumford said to his professional ballplayers, learning to focus and stay calm pays off in performing from their optimal state.[4] Yogis, of course, practice similar attention skills, but in a spiritual context.

Amishi Jha, an attention researcher at the University of Miami, taught breath focus to members of that college's football team just as they were starting their grueling preseason combination of aerobics and strength-building—a stressor in itself.[5] Those athletes who put the most time into the attention training did best on measures of both attention and mood at the end of that stressful training period. This is but one of a host of studies demonstrating that we can upgrade attention skills such as concentration, with the right practice. That practice exercises a muscle of emotional intelligence.

The foundational skill in emotional intelligence is an awareness of our own emotions and how they shape our thinking, perceptions, memories, and impulse to act. Such self-awareness requires that we tune into our inner experience.

With self-awareness, a basic definition tells us, "You know what you are feeling and why—and how it helps or hurts what you are trying to do."[6] Other key points: you can align your self-image on how others see you; you have an accurate sense of your limits and strengths, and so a more realistic self-confidence; you are clear about your sense of purpose and values, which helps you be more decisive.

Cognitive scientists call this self-reflexive attention "meta-awareness." We can watch our thoughts and feelings as they come and go, and know where our attention focuses—and change that focus if we want. This deliberate control of the beam of our attention is a mental skill. Think of our mind as a sort of gym, a place where we can practice in ways that will bulk up our mental capacities.

The research on flow, you may recall, revealed that the person's focus while in flow was 100 percent. They were one-pointed, fully present to the moment. Such absorption indicates meta-awareness, that ability to monitor and manage your own focus. But we don't need that diamond-like beam of focus all the time: a stronger muscle for attention boosts the odds that we can get into an optimal state.

Focus—paying attention where and when we want to—has endless uses. Deliberate concentration on whatever may be important to us at the moment lets us do our best; being distracted worsens our effort. Having control of our attention is for the mind what cardiovascular fitness is for the body; just as a fit heart enhances any physical task, full focus enhances whatever we do.

Self-Awareness Helpers

Be Mindful. There's a simple mindfulness exercise that strengthens focus; many people, especially in the workplace, and even kids in school already practice the method. It goes like this: Bring your attention to your breath, being aware of the full in-breath, the pause between breaths, and the full out-breath. Stay with your focus on your breath as long as you can. But be mindful: when your mind wanders off (and we guarantee it will) and you notice it wandered, bring your focus back to your breath and pay full attention to the next inhalation or exhalation. Keep practicing this. That's it. Very simple.

Maybe not so simple, actually: as you keep practicing you'll inevitably find a mental tug-of-war for your attention between breath focus and your thoughts. A key to sustaining concentration on the breath occurs when we notice our mind has wandered off, and so bring focus back starting with the next breath again. This demands self-awareness; indeed, such mindfulness can be seen as self-awareness in action.

Neuroscientists tell us that the more we repeat a sequence like this, the stronger the neural circuitry for that sequence becomes. Here we are practicing paying attention and letting go of distractions, and the elements of focus that let us do this become stronger.[7]

Inner Check-in. We can use routine moments, like brushing our teeth or waiting for our computer to get up to speed, as a reminder to ourselves to assess our inner state. This inner check-in can take the form of naming the predominant emotion we feel, or scanning our entire body's sensations to find the places that need more attention and, perhaps, relax them.[8]

Check Your Self-Talk. A public health nurse had been visiting an elderly patient at home who suffered from a number of chronic ailments. During their last contact, the patient said, "I don't know why you're bothering with me. I just want to die." Many nurses would attribute the patient's words to depression or some other flawed thinking. But Sarah saw it as a personal failure, saying, "I thought, 'Gee, what's wrong with me? What did I do?' I might have done something wrong."

There's a simple antidote to such self-judgment: shift to more realistic expectations. Teachers who understood they couldn't always inspire every student and the lawyers who realized losing a case was just part of the job fared far better. They still set ambitious goals and believed success was possible—but they were prepared for failure, too.

The strongest distractions come from our upsetting emotions. Challenging the thoughts that power those feelings can help us let go of upset and stay focused.

Stay Focused. The opposite of keen focus, of course, is mind wandering. A classic study found that people's minds were wandering during the day around half the time.[9] The highest rate of mind wandering was in three situations: during a commute, while looking at a video monitor, and while at work. While our minds wander off from what we are doing at the moment—no surprise here—our performance suffers.[10] But training our attention to notice when our mind wanders lets us stay on task, handle distractions better, and perform at our best.[11]

Research on this kind of one-pointed attention finds:[12]

- *We become more calm.* We can "just say no" to agitation and worry, and even to emotion-driven impulses. The data show that the circuitry in the prefrontal cortex that can inhibit emotional impulse gets stronger with mindfulness practice. Those who have a daily habit of mindfulness become less reactive emotionally, less likely to be triggered in the first place, and recover more quickly from upset if they do get triggered.
- *We are more concentrated.* Training attention lies at the heart of every meditation and mindfulness practice—but such systematic improvement of our ability to focus need not be based in any particular belief system. The improvement of concentration with practice follows the basics of every other skill training regimen.
- *Multitasking gets easier.* Cognitive scientists tell us the popular notion of "multitasking" is a fiction—we can't do several separate tasks at once. Instead, research reveals, we switch rapidly from one task to another. A landmark study at Stanford University found that if someone had practiced the breath exercise, they more readily regained focus on an important task, even after their mind wandered off for a while.[13]
- *We learn better.* One marked benefit of enhanced concentration: it strengthens working memory, what we can hold in mind at any one moment.[14] The more distracted we are, the poorer our working memory; the more focused, the better. A big payoff here: all learning requires we pay attention so the

new knowledge registers in working memory. Such attention training seems to make sense as a standard part of education.[15]

- *We think better.* Attention training enhances cognitive abilities beyond attention itself, such as memory, and lets us be at our mental best even under high stress.[16] This expands the range of our optimal zone, making such training appealing in any role where cognitive abilities are part of selection criterion, from law and medicine to accounting and special forces.

When our focus is rock solid we are immune to distractions, which is a precious asset in this age of information flooding and digital seductions. This concentration also means we can stay homed in on our goals—what's important—despite the multitude of attentional off-ramps that come our way. And so self-awareness, the very foundation of our ability to concentrate, serves as a doorway to our optimal state.

Our Inner Rudder

Mark Connor knew from an early age that he wanted to work with kids, and so he took a job in an inner-city school after graduating from college.[17] He found talking with troubled kids one-on-one was the best part of the job.

But his first job as a school psychologist was a disaster. He spent almost all of his day administering tests, writing reports, and attending meetings. And his boss was really a pain. The job had little meaning for him, along with its high stress. It didn't take much self-awareness to tell he felt awful, day after day.

So Mark went to school part-time to train as a psychotherapist, and found a new job as a school psychologist to pay the bills. To his surprise, the new job was highly rewarding. His testing load was light, leaving him plenty of time to do counseling and therapy with the kids—the work that made him happiest. His boss was very supportive. Mark sensed himself being in an optimal state more often.

Those feelings of an optimal state grew. After a few years, Mark began to supervise interns, which he loved. He initiated a district-wide internship program, which gave him even more time to do what he found most meaningful. He said that his work in the public schools, working with a diverse group of students and supervising the next generation of psychologists, with a supportive boss and congenial colleagues, was even more rewarding than seeing clients in private practice.

Mark's ability to recognize the best work situation for him guided him into a rewarding career. His career path illustrates how emotional self-awareness, the core of EI, can be especially helpful in our career choices, leading us to work where we can operate in optimal states more of the time.

Consultants at McKinsey analyzed the inner recipe of people in their optimal state—showing remarkable levels of energy, self-confidence, and effectiveness, and being highly productive.[18] Their conclusion: driving all these outstanding performances is an ironclad sense of meaning— that what the person is doing truly matters, whether to themselves or to those they care about.

Along with focus, another underappreciated function of self-awareness is how it helps us find what matters to us, our sense of purpose.

Listening to Our Inner Voice

When Apple cofounder Steve Jobs learned he had the liver cancer that was to cause his death, he gave a heartfelt talk to Stanford students. "Don't let the voice of others' opinions drown out your inner voice," he told them. "And most important, have the courage to follow your heart and intuition. They somehow already know what you truly want to become."

That sage advice gets support from neuroscience. The wiring of our brain, it turns out, can make it hard to articulate that "inner voice," the internal compass that points us to our sense of meaning and purpose in life. It can point us in the right direction, but doesn't give us the words to name where we are heading.

The brain stores our life wisdom—the sum total of every experience we've ever had—in circuitry deep in its lower reaches. These deep-down circuits connect to a midbrain structure, the insula, that monitors feelings throughout our body. These are the circuits, as Jobs put it, that "already know what you truly want to become."

But this deep circuitry has zero connection to the part of our brain that thinks in words, our verbal cortex in the brain's topmost layers. In addition, these bottom-up circuits respond faster in brain time than do the reasoning circuits in the neocortex, the brain's top layers. When it comes to thinking fast and slow, to put it in terms coined by Daniel Kahneman in his bestselling book on our mental life, intuitions come more quickly than our rationality.[19]

While this intuitive circuitry can't "talk" directly to the verbal cortex, it has strong connectivity to the gastrointestinal (GI) tract. Take that all-important question, *Is what I am about to do in keeping with my sense of values and purpose?* Because of the brain's wiring, we don't get that answer in words. We get it in a felt sense, a "gut feeling."

For instance, very early in her career Oprah Winfrey was a news reader on the six o'clock news show of a Baltimore TV station. But she never felt fully comfortable in that job; rather, she felt out of place. Then she was transferred—actually demoted—to being host of the station's daytime talk show, *People Are Talking*.

From the very first time in that slot, as she recalls, "I felt lit up from inside, like I had come home to myself. When the hour ended, there was a sense of knowing resonating within my heart and radiating to the hairs on the back of my neck. My entire body told me this was what I was supposed to do."[20]

Neuroscientist Antonio Damasio calls the sensations in our body that tell us if a decision feels right or wrong "somatic markers." These internal signals guide us in every major decision in life, from whom to marry to putting our sense of purpose into action. But the feelings come first, the action after. It's not to dismiss the rational pros and cons of decision-making, but rather that this felt sense gives us compelling data, too.

Take, for example, a business consultant who had just become a mother, and was feeling exhausted and overwhelmed. She took a course on emotional intelligence that showed her how to tune in to the feelings in her body—and when she paired that with an exercise about her "best self" she realized that she felt at her best at work; she often found herself in her optimal zone.[21] While she had considered quitting, she decided to talk to her boss about her feelings. He turned out to be surprisingly understanding and supportive and they worked out a way she could stay engaged in the work she loved while also being attentive to her family's needs and her own health.

On the other hand, tuning in to your feelings can have quite different consequences. In that same EI course another woman with a similar burden—family, kids, and a full-time job—did that feelings exercise. "She was feeling burnt-out and frustrated with her job, but it was sensing her bodily feelings that led her to the decision to leave that job," according to Michael Stern, who led her group through the EI course.

The better we are at reading our gut feelings, the better we can draw on our life experience in making a decision. Self-awareness gives you clarity on your values and sense of purpose, so you can be more decisive when you set a course of action. Of course some people might well make mistakes when they think they are following their gut feeling. Self-awareness helps us read those feelings more accurately.

Self-Awareness: The Added Value

A new lens on self-awareness sees its benefits as going far beyond the standard understanding, that knowing what we are feeling and why we feel it helps us see how those feelings help or hurt what we are doing. Beyond this, the optimal model values two other advantages of self-awareness. The first comes down to applying self-awareness to strengthen the beam of our concentration, helping us spot and turn away from distractions.

The second application of self-awareness: sensing the subtle sensations in our body that tell us whether what we are doing gives us the feelings of an optimal state—or not. Think again about that estimate reported by McKinsey consultants that being in our optimal state can result in feeling we are as much as five times more effective as we are in our usual state. Fundamental to entering and staying in that zone, the McKinsey consultants found, was that the very effort people were making resonated with their felt sense of what mattered most to them, their sense of meaning and purpose.

There's still another crucial capacity stemming from self-awareness that helps us stay or get into that optimal zone: managing ourselves well. Take, for example, how Seth handled his high-stress job and the challenge of sleepless nights with a newborn by using a system for enhancing self-awareness that was developed by Consortium member Marc Brackett, who directs Yale's Center for Emotional Intelligence.[22] From time to time during his day Seth would check on his feelings of the moment, pegging them by using a "mood meter" that laid out the names of dozens and dozens of feelings along two grids: pleasant–unpleasant, and high–low energy. That grid helped him name his emotion, such as "drained" (low energy) or "despair" (really unpleasant).

Labeling an emotion is one of five steps in Brackett's system, RULER. Labeling (the L) relies on first recognizing what you feel in the moment and understanding why you feel that way and what it moves you to do. Then there's expressing the emotion.

"If I'm happy with my son," Seth noted, "I might express that by laughing and playing with him. But if I'm frustrated at work—that's a combination of high energy and feeling unpleasant—I might decide to take a walk to cool down or put a conversation on hold, giving me a chance to pause and consider what's going on. You can't always control what happens to you, but you can always control your own response."

The final step, regulating, suggests how much handling our emotions well depends on first being aware of them, as we'll see in the next chapter.

5

Manage Yourself

Picture a snowy, wintry day in New England. A five-year-old wants to go out and play in the snow. His mom says, "Sure—just put on your snowsuit."

At that the five-year-old melts down into a tantrum. "No, I won't!" he yells defiantly, crying and shouting at the same time.

Then suddenly he stops and quietly goes to his room. After a few minutes in his room he comes out, snowsuit on, and starts to go outside.

His mom, startled, says, "Hey—what just happened?"

"Oh," explains the five-year-old, "my Guard Dog got upset so I had my Wise Owl talk to it."

That five-year-old was explaining rudimentary brain science to his mother. The Guard Dog, he had learned in school, refers to emotional and attentional circuitry that acts as a sentinel for danger and alerts us to prepare for an emergency. Too often in modern life that means getting upset—angry or frightened—out of proportion to the actual danger. Even symbolic threats—your mom making you put on your snowsuit before you can go out to play—can trigger the Guard Dog.

Our very ability to place our attention where we want and when we want depends on a closely related mental skill called "cognitive control."[1] Cognitive control lets us focus on a given task and ignore distractions—especially those that come wrapped in strong emotions.

Psychologists use the term "cognitive control" for a set of mental self-management abilities, including the capacity to inhibit your first impulse so you don't just do whatever comes to mind immediately, but rather what makes the most sense. Others include keeping repetitive negative thoughts—the most disturbing kind of distractions—in abeyance.

Each of us has our own set of triggering events—and that's when we might best use cognitive control to manage our negative thoughts and impulses. Take, for example, an infamous moment during the 2022 Academy Awards when comedian Chris Rock made a cringe-worthy joke about Will Smith's wife, Jada Pinkett-Smith. His joke was about her being bald—but he did not mention that her struggle with alopecia was the reason. That joke triggered Smith, who leapt to the stage and slapped Rock.

But—and here's the point—Rock somehow kept his composure after being slapped. Rock, who was hosting the awards, was in the middle of a mini stand-up routine when Smith slapped him, and, keeping the mood light, Rock immediately made a meta-comment about the incident: "That was the greatest night in the history of television." Rock calmly went on to announce the winner for Best Documentary, Ahmir (Questlove) Thompson for *Summer of Soul*.

Rock's unflappable reaction might well be due to the Wise Owl, the brain's executive centers in the prefrontal cortex and beyond. This circuitry helps us rethink our upsets and find a more reasonable way to act. That seems to have been at play both with Rock and that five-year-old.

When it comes to our private emotional life, much of the action revolves around the interplay between these two brain regions, the impulsivity stemming from our emotional centers and the prefrontal area which can just say "No" to impulse. The key lesson at the brain level comes down to not reacting on our first impulse when we have an emotional hijack.

In emergencies our overrehearsed habits surface, as the amygdala and related circuits take over from the prefrontal areas. We fall back on habit, acting before we can think what to do. For instance, in a tragic incident a newly hired police officer meant to reach for her Taser to subdue an unruly suspect. But instead she reached for her pistol and shot him, even as she yelled, "Taser, taser . . ."

Tellingly, helicopter pilots need to relearn how to unfasten a seat belt, for a simple reason: in a helicopter the seat belts are designed differently than those in a car—the pilots are strapped in across their chests. While we've unfastened auto seat belts thousands of times, clicking them open as they reach across our waists, this habit could be fatal in a helicopter emergency, taking precious seconds before the pilot realizes the need to open the seat belts crossing the chest. So new pilots are drilled over and over in this new habit, which could save lives.

Cognitive control matters enormously in such moments—but also anytime we need to manage disruptive impulses and unruly thoughts. This talent is the basis for maintaining our focus where we want it—helping us stay in our optimal zone—as well as for all self-regulation abilities.[2]

Turbulent emotions, as we all know, interfere with being at our best. Research shows that some emotional arousal—say, an engaging story from a teacher—boosts learning and intellectual performance. But when our emotions become disruptive they torpedo our efforts.[3]

We can't control what emotions come to us, how strongly we feel them, nor when they arise. But we have a choice point once we feel them; we do not have to act them out. Some define maturity in terms of increasing the gap between that first impulse and our subsequent reaction.

You can see the difference in comparing preschoolers, who are notoriously impulsive and chaotic, and third graders, who can be far more focused and well-behaved. In developmental science this change is called the "five-to-seven shift," and refers to the burgeoning of circuitry in the prefrontal cortex that can inhibit emotional impulse during those years of life. That self-regulation ability has countless advantages for a child, not the least of which comes in the form of paying attention to what the teacher is saying.

This crucial self-control skill lies at the heart of all the emotional intelligence competencies for self-management: maintaining our emotional balance, striving toward our goals, being flexible in the face of shifting challenges, and staying positive in our outlook. Lacking cognitive control, each of these would suffer. Self-management, in essence, depends on cognitive control.

Marshmallows Again

Perhaps the best-known measure of cognitive control has been the "Marshmallow Test" done by a group led by psychologist Walter Mischel while he was a professor at Stanford University (and our apologies to those readers familiar with this famous study . . . but still, for the benefit of those new to this crucial research, here goes).[4] Four-year-olds were given the choice of a marshmallow now, or waiting until the experimenter ran an errand, and getting two then. Fourteen years later, those who had waited (and got two), compared to those who just grabbed the marshmallow, got along better with peers, still could delay gratification in pursuit of their goals, and—to the researchers' surprise—did far better on achievement tests as they finished high school.[5]

Even better, this tool for life success can be taught; four-year-olds less adept in cognitive control who had acquired this mental ability by age eight showed the same benefits as those who always had it. Middle schoolers with better cognitive control got better grades than their IQ would predict, likely because their teachers based grades not just on test scores, but also factors like class participation, attendance, completing homework, and effort—all non-IQ skills.[6]

The benefits of childhood cognitive control seem to persist through the life span. Tracked down in their thirties, those who at age four had impulsively eaten the marshmallow were less likely to have sound financials and were in poorer physical health compared to those who managed to stifle the impulse to grab. And, remarkably, waiting to get the two marshmallows at age four (or acquiring this ability by age eight) predicted slower biological aging and a younger brain some forty years later.[7] Cognitive control in adults was found to be independent of the wealth of their family of origin and their childhood IQ.

The good news: it's never too late to master this inner skill. Any time you control your impulses and wait for a better choice you are strengthening the brain's circuits for cognitive control. This strategy—boosting self-control—is, for example, at the heart of addiction treatments, from alcoholism to binge eating to compulsive gambling. Anger management treatments use the same step. Even counting to ten before you act from impulse-promoting emotions like anger or fear points to the identical pause.

If you didn't master this skill in childhood but managed to gain more cognitive control by life's middle years, that shift enhances your readiness for old age biologically, financially, and socially—you would likely live longer, and be in better health than people your age who were more impulsive.

Cognitive control matters in other ways. For instance, in adults poor cognitive control seems a neural feature of later-life clinical depression, according to a meta-analysis of studies with a total of 16,806 adults.[8] Those with better cognitive control had better function in the prefrontal cortex, which helps us make more thoughtful decisions than the impulses that lead to problems like addictions (all of which are signs of poor cognitive control). And, more generally, the more often our thoughts drift to what upsets us—that is, we ruminate and worry—the more prone we will be to full-blown emotional problems like anxiety disorders.[9]

On the other hand, whether in business, sports, the arts, or elsewhere, a singular state of mind facilitates great performance. One of the components that facilitates our optimal state is emotional mastery: the ability to keep emotions in balance and be resilient despite difficulties.

One sign of that state shows as being agile in adapting to changing demands. Our mood stays or returns to positive no matter what befalls us. And, of course, peak performance gives us a pleasant emotional buzz. All of these bespeak an emotional self-mastery, adult versions of that Wise Owl.

Self-Discipline

The year: 1905. A circle of serfs huddle deep in the Russian woods, on the lookout for soldiers of the czar, who would kill them on sight. At the center of the circle a twelve-year-old girl reads aloud from a pamphlet; unlike most girls her age in those parts, she had been taught to read by a tutor. She's urging them to rise up and overthrow the landowners for whom they toil in indentured servitude—an abortive, failed revolution against the czarist government.

That twelve-year-old girl was Emma, Dan's mother's mother.

Fleeing for her life from Russia, she somehow made her way to America. Her husband, Jacob, an immigrant, too, whom she met on the ship to Philadelphia, wanted to be an engineer but never could afford to get the education he needed. The same with Dan's father's parents, also immigrants; so far as Dan knows (they passed away before he was born), they had little or no formal schooling.

But Dan's American-born mother and father—like all the other kids of immigrants they knew—labored very, very hard at their schoolwork, putting in hours and hours poring over homework, like other achievement-driven family members of their generation.[10] Dan's mother graduated from the University of Chicago, then got a master's in social work from Smith College; her brother also studied at Chicago, then became a physicist and eventually director of a national laboratory. Dan's father, likewise the child of immigrants, received an advanced degree in philology from Yale. Dan's parents were typical of so many children of poor, uneducated newcomers to the United States who saw excelling in school as their children's path to economic security.

There's no question that studying harder and longer than other kids do will raise a student's grade point average. That's exactly what a huge meta-analysis of IQ and school performance found: conscientiousness—like doing schoolwork beyond just the assigned homework—paid off in school grades only slightly below the advantage of a high IQ.[11] The power of sheer hard work explains another finding, that students who do not have the highest IQ can get better grades than their cognitively gifted peers if they work at it.[12] In other words, even if you are not the brightest kid in your class, grinding away at schoolwork can get you high grades (though being IQ-smart means you might get those grades without the sweat). We don't need peer-reviewed research to know this; it's common knowledge.

Seen through the lens of emotional intelligence, this drive to succeed, to work harder than others, indicates the "Achieve" competence. The backstory of this ability starts with Dan's grad school mentor David McClelland and his seminal research on what he called the "achievement motive." This emphasis on motivation led Dan to include motivation as one of five parts of emotional intelligence. But now Dan sees the way we motivate ourselves as a type of self-management, the cluster of competencies where Achieve sits today.

The hallmarks of high achievers include an intense focus on their goal, an awareness of the steps needed to get there, and an openness to measures showing how they are doing toward that goal. This includes doggedness, persisting toward the goal despite setbacks and obstacles. That's the part of the drive to achieve that has been the focus of the concept of "grit," a driver of success studied by psychologist Angela Duckworth at the University of Pennsylvania.[13]

Grit demands stamina, perseverance, and passion for a goal, letting us keep our eye on reaching that distant goalpost even when the going gets tough. Duckworth has found that the presence of grit identifies the high school students with the highest grade point averages (and, conversely, the least hours spent watching TV), the cadets least likely to drop out of the U.S. Military Academy at West Point, and champions in spelling bees. To win a spelling bee, for instance, takes years of persistent practice.[14]

Duckworth got her first inkling of the power of this drive for success when she was teaching seventh graders. She saw that, just as was true of Dan's parents' child-of-immigrants generation, the intense push to achieve and persist despite whatever difficulties may come made some of her students succeed while others who had equal intellect floundered.

Grit lets someone pursue their long-term goals with resilience, confidence, and the courage to keep going despite the occasional failure along the way. While Duckworth does not particularly acknowledge McClelland's earlier work on the achievement drive, her findings echo his. McClelland's research found, for instance, that successful entrepreneurs were high on the "Need to Achieve," as he called it. Likewise, Duckworth has identified grit as the underlying ability that makes for excellence. The common theme underlying such outstanding performance boils down to keeping your eye on a long-term goal—that drive to achieve.

That research team at Harvard investigating good workdays discovered that the most potent benefit comes from making progress toward a goal that matters to you.[15] That's a key sign of the optimal state. By contrast, on their worst days people said they felt thwarted, which had a toxic effect on their moods; the setbacks left people feeling sad, fearful, or just frustrated.

The fear of not doing well in one's work affects young people as well. Their workplace is school, and the pressure to excel there is a major source of stress for them. A paradox: students from wealthier, more privileged families who attend high-achieving schools suffer from anxiety, depression, and other stress symptoms at anywhere from three to seven times more than do students at less high-pressure schools.[16]

Why? More than half of such students name pressure from their parents to do well in school. Those same parents, though, will say they want their kids to have loving marriages, to be happy and healthy, and somehow to give back to the world. Yet their children see the path to this flourishing through a narrow gate: being high-achieving in school so as to get into one of the best colleges, with the hope of getting a high-paying job after graduation.

Some child therapists see this problem in how parents praise their children for their achievements, sending the message that being loved depends on their doing well in school.[17] Parents, too, are stressed by all this; in one survey 70 percent of parents reported that they were under extreme stress about their children's academic, social, and emotional development.[18]

So a strong achievement motive, like many positive traits, can be carried too far. But a healthy goal-orientation, when combined with good stress management skills, offers another kind of advantage.

Studies of those with high levels of achievement—such as successful entrepreneurs—reveal another trait that will have great value in years ahead: seeking feedback in order to continuously improve. People with the achievement drive love to get hard metrics on how well they are doing. They use those metrics to experiment with how to do even better; they build a learning curve into their efforts.

There are specific signs of this drive to achieve.[19] For one, people high in achievement typically strive to meet or even exceed a high bar, a standard of excellence greater than most others. This leads them to seek out metrics for and feedback on their performance, always looking for ways to do things better. They set themselves challenging goals and take calculated risks, while balancing their drive to achieve personally with the goals of their organization.

Cognitive control comes into play here.[20] That ability to regulate our attention, our emotions, and our impulses allows us, for instance, to keep focused on our long-term objectives despite the distractions of the day, week, or year. Grit requires cognitive control—to an extent.

While having a goal in mind matters greatly, a mental goalpost in itself may not be sufficient. Adventurer Colin O'Brady completed the Three Poles challenge (reaching the North and South Poles and climbing Mount Everest) and now trains athletes "to relate to their goals wisely."

He adds, "As soon as they notice they've been caught up in over-rehearsing, strategizing, or focusing on a future outcome, they can bring themselves back into the moment."[21] This presence to the moment, he says, allows their years of training to take over and gets their mind out of the way.

One other sign of the achievement competence: taking "smart risks." They are "smart" because the person taking the risk knows he or she has a particular strength—say, having practiced a skill—that is not so apparent to other people. This gives the risk-taker confidence about what they are about to do; entrepreneurs often experience this. But people who just see the risk-taking but not the expertise behind it may think it's not so smart.

Positivity, or Growth Mindset

Just as "grit" seems to a large extent to be a relabeling of the Achieve competence in the EI model, other EI competencies have gotten renewed attention for the same reason—old wine in new bottles. Take "positivity," an EI competence where you have an optimistic attitude about what happens to you, about developing your own abilities—and seeing other people as able to grow further strengths, too.

The attitude that "I can learn and grow better," a fundamental axiom of positivity, lies at the heart of what Stanford's Carol Dweck calls a "growth mindset."[22] Dweck argues that how we think about our abilities can become a self-fulfilling prophecy. If we have a rigid, "fixed" mindset, we take our failures and setbacks to be due to an innate lack of ability—and give up.

Dweck's concept of a growth mindset combines the Achieve and Positivity EI competencies. She adds to positivity about your own potential the notion that setbacks and failures are learning opportunities, not showstoppers. Grit, or the Achieve competence, and growth mindset, or Positivity, support each other, though they are distinct.[23]

As psychologists have long known, attributing our setbacks to some unchangeable flaw in ourselves leads to giving up in the face of difficulties. Martin Seligman at the University of Pennsylvania identified this way of thinking as a cause in many cases of depression. He called it "learned helplessness." Seligman went on to reverse that approach by helping people develop more positive outlooks, which he called "learned optimism."[24]

Changing a mindset means learning to think differently. For instance, one method to switch from a fixed to a growth mindset: put the word "yet" with a limiting assumption: "I can't do that *yet*." Another such mindset-changer, as Seligman found, challenges the idea that our abilities are fixed and limited, by reminding ourselves that we can learn and develop new strengths.

With a growth mindset you see yourself able to learn from failures and setbacks, and develop further strengths. This principle operates everywhere from coaching sports to parenting to teaching and business; it offers a motivation to keep going (supporting grit). Our beliefs about our abilities and what's possible for us add energy to what we do and, in fact, open the way to success. This "I-can-do-it" attitude works synergistically with the Achieve competence, creating an inner orientation toward getting better and better—essential for attaining any goal, and particularly for upgrading your EI skills.

Learn to Do Better

When Tom, a successful engineer, was faced with blistering criticism early in his career, his stress levels went off the chart. But he was able to calm himself by focusing on what he might learn from the criticism. As his sympathetic nervous system cooled off, he was able to ask questions and explore the nature of the problem. We can learn from even the most dire situation, so long as we get useful feedback—and criticism, if it's grounded in specifics, is a form of feedback.

The Positive Outlook competence gives you the ability to see the best in yourself, in other people, and in events so that you can persist in pursuing your goals despite any setbacks or obstacles you might encounter.[25] Rather than being stymied by setbacks, you seize opportunities that others might find devastating. You expect that the future will be better.

People with a positive, growth mindset find challenge exhilarating, which predisposes them to experiencing their optimal zone more frequently than those with a fixed mindset. If they have a setback or fail, they see that as an opportunity to stretch their abilities, grow, and develop. Those with a fixed mindset, on the other hand, take a failure as a judgment on their abilities—they've flunked life's tests yet again.

Those with a fixed mindset see every test of their abilities as an assessment of their value; they hunger for the approval that comes from doing well. But a growth mindset brings a different lens to such challenges, where a passion for learning—and the deep belief that *I can learn to do better*—propels them forward.

Even positivity can be carried too far if not tempered with other qualities. The late British psychiatrist R. D. Laing describes a "knot" that can make people feel comfortable by ignoring unhappy facts, through being tied up in a shared collusion. The knot comes from the denial to oneself and everyone else that we are unhappy, which ends up in keeping that unhappiness secret, so that we can maintain the charade that we are all happy. Laing calls this the "game of happy family," and of course this can occur not just in families, but in any organization.

Adaptability = Agility

Just as in Laing's "game of happy family," psychologist Susan David sees that just being harmonious despite our real feelings can stifle beneath-the-surface unhappiness. Her approach views uncomfortable feelings as important, saying they can indicate significant problems that are not surfaced or otherwise cannot be addressed.

This speaks to the distinction between being "nice" and being "kind." If you're just nice then you do whatever keeps everything harmonious—you play the game of happy family (or some variation, like "happy workplace"). But kindness can lead you to say what might rock the boat in order to address problems that "niceness" hides: that is, saying what's not comfortable to address seething troubles. That's another sign of emotional agility.

What David calls "emotional agility" looks a lot like the EI competence "adaptability."[26] David also argues that *every* emotion has its place and message for us, an idea that dates back at least to Charles Darwin. So effectiveness at work may not mean a feeling of happiness—if you're checking a spreadsheet or proofreading text, picking up fine detail may be facilitated by a more somber mood rather than a manic one.

In some ways "agility" overlaps with the Achieve competence. For instance, one mark of agility can be seen in people who use feedback on their performance to quickly alter what they do in order to improve. That same instant use of feedback stands as one of the hallmarks of Achieve.

In terms of emotional competence, adaptability means "having flexibility in handling changes, being able to juggle multiple demands, and adapting to new situations with fresh ideas or innovative approaches. It means you can stay focused on your goals but easily adjust how you get there.

"An adaptable leader can meet new challenges as they arrive and not be halted by sudden changes, remaining comfortable with the uncertainty that leadership can bring."[27]

A course that helps people develop further strengths in EI competence points out that adaptability takes a mindset that sees change as an opportunity rather than something to be avoided.[28] Guided reflections like "What's it like to step out of your comfort zone?" prepare the learner to take action. So Laxman, who had suffered for years in a toxic climate as a tech director for a large corporation, set out to find a new position. The adaptability course helped him realize he was thinking too narrowly about his options, and that just the thought of taking on a different kind of job made him anxious. He started spotting the stories he was telling himself that made him fearful of new possibilities, and with this more open mindset started reaching out to his network with wider possibilities in mind.

IN SUM, EACH OF THE SELF-MANAGEMENT COMPETENCIES BUILDS on self-awareness; lacking this fundamental ability to recognize our feelings and thoughts of the moment, we are unable to take the next step, managing them well. Each of the EI self-management competencies has entered the popular lexicon under new names: "growth mindset" for positivity; "grit" for achievement; and "agility" for adaptability. Our ability in each of these can be improved with the appropriate learning, such as adapting our mindset for positivity or embracing change for adaptability.

All of these come into play in handling the inevitable stresses that life and work bring our way.

6

From Burnout to Resilience

Ashley Harlow, a nurse practitioner, couldn't take working in her hospital's intensive care unit during the peak of a Covid surge anymore. The last straw was seeing her own grandmother die there. She, like the other nurses on the ICU, were only able to keep working because of adrenaline surges. But after those surges passed, Ashley felt depleted—it was just too much. So she quit.[1]

That progression from constant stress to emotional exhaustion to burnout became all too common among the one in five health care workers who walked out on their job during the Covid pandemic. From restaurant employees and warehouse workers to senior executives in the C-suite, stress and burnout seem to be more prevalent than ever: survey after survey shows people are increasingly stressed.[2] An annual report on the status of workplace burnout found that 30 percent of the people in their survey reported experiencing high levels of burnout in 2020. In 2021 that number increased to 35 percent. In 2022 it rose once again to 38 percent.[3]

Stress blocks us from the optimal state, leading to burnout and quitting, not to mention poor health, unhappiness, overeating, and drinking too much.[4] The now-familiar litany of the negative impacts of stress range from emotional depletion and torpedoed performance to untimely death.

The emotional intelligence ability that makes a huge difference between being at our best and at our worst has been called "emotional self-control," or "emotional balance."[5] We can keep our intense emotions and impulses in check so they don't disrupt our effectiveness, even under stressful or hostile circumstances. We have resilience, the capacity to bounce back from stress and upset.

This does not mean suppressing our upsetting emotions, but rather managing them well so we can stay clearheaded and calm. In this chapter we'll not just detail the arc of stress and burnout, but offer several methods for resilience, which lets us come back to this essential inner balance.

From Stress to Burnout

The path from stress to burnout usually starts when we're under constant stress. For example, the demands of a job are high and the resources for meeting those demands are too low, as was the case with Ashley Harlow. The same path to burnout can occur anywhere else, from a single parent overwhelmed by too many kids, to a manager given a bigger and bigger workload as her company fires other managers.

How we appraise what's happening—our own thoughts—can make it worse. For instance, unrealistically high expectations for ourselves can become an internal stress. This happened to many ICU nurses who felt their duty was to care for very sick patients, many of whom might not make it. But those expectations were all too often shattered by the overwhelming numbers of sick patients brought about by the Covid pandemic. And they were not used to running out of essential equipment like ventilators, masks, and even beds for patients.

As Epictetus, a Greek philosopher, put it, it's not what happens to us but rather how we *react* to it that matters. To put that a bit differently, how severely we undergo stress depends not just on the stressful events, but also on how we appraise them.[6]

Rethinking our initial appraisal can help. If we perceive that a potential stressor is a harmful threat then we need to handle our turbulent feelings. So the first appraisal might be something like, *I have a project due tomorrow and I'm way behind—I'm in big trouble!* That leads to a feeling of panic and frazzle.

But rethinking the situation could lead to a reframing like this: *Wait a second—I don't think it will be the end of the world if I'm a day or two late.* This approach to handling the turmoil of stress has many variations, many of which we will share later in this chapter. Both of these appraisals in steps two and three occur almost instantaneously and usually without our conscious awareness.

If we continue on the trajectory to emotional exhaustion, we're prone to burnout. Our bodies were built to handle short bouts of intense stress, followed by periods of recovery. Emotional balance includes resilience, the ability to recover. But if stress stays high for a long time, with no chance to recover, burnout can begin to set in. One of the first signs is emotional exhaustion, where we find it hard to motivate ourselves, even in jobs that we once found engaging. Understandably, we grow to dislike our work and even the people with whom we work. What once gave us pleasure now evokes cynicism.

Take Connie, who attended one of the nation's top law schools.[7] She wanted to work with the disadvantaged—and to change the world. So she passed up interviews with recruiters from the big firms and took a job at a neighborhood legal aid office. But after eight months of working with incessant demands and almost no support, spending most of her time on the phone doing work someone with far less than a law degree could do, and dealing with unappreciative clients who lied to her, she had become cynical and was ready to quit. She even considered going to work for the prosecuting attorney's office, to put many of her clients "behind bars where they belong."

Such cynicism is a sign of burnout; when someone who had been idealistic about their work turns cynical, a low point in the stress-burnout cycle, we start seeing long-term consequences. These can include a host of somatic problems, like frequent headaches, gaining weight, gastrointestinal problems, trouble sleeping, and heart disease; for instance, burnout among industrial workers predicted serious heart trouble ten years later.[8] Stress may prematurely age your immune system.[9] Mental consequences can include depression, social isolation, and using drugs or alcohol to dull the emotional pain. In one survey three-quarters of respondents said stress at work negatively impacted their personal relationships, and two-thirds lost sleep due to work stress.[10]

Small wonder burnout lowers productivity and impairs work quality.[11] Other signs include absenteeism—just not showing up—and (understandably perhaps) wanting to leave your job, not caring about your organization, and job dissatisfaction in general. A small but significant number of people, 16 percent, say they've had to quit a job due to stress.[12] Forget optimal performance.

Your Brain Under Stress

Has this ever happened to you? You're making an important presentation to a group you want to impress. But suddenly you can't seem to get your PowerPoint to work. Your talk stops in midsentence as you fiddle with your laptop, and there's silence while everyone waits for you to fix the problem. But your mind has gone blank—a small glitch you'd ordinarily fix without blinking now seems insurmountable. You feel yourself unravel; your hands start to shake, your breathing gets shallow and your neck damp. All you can think of is how stupid you must look as you fumble.

Something similar happened to Deborah, Cary's wife, when she was making a Zoom presentation. It turned out all right—but she can still recall those tense moments even years later.

That unforgettable scenario of fumbling some tech trouble captures many of the changes in our brain and mind in the throes of stress. We become distracted and disorganized, can't remember the simplest thing, and seem unable to do anything other than operate from habit; never mind troubleshooting a tech glitch. And our memory for these awkward moments lingers.

Brain science tells us that these signs of a stress attack are due to a family of brain chemicals call catecholamines—dopamine, norepinephrine, and epinephrine. These trigger the famed "fight-or-flight" reaction that prepares us for an emergency: our heart and muscles amp up as our digestion and immune systems (among others) slow down, shifting energy to where it's needed in the short term. At the same time the brain hands control over to our emotional circuitry instead of our executive centers in the prefrontal cortex.

Paradoxically, the catecholamines also make sure we remember what was so upsetting by enhancing memory consolidation. All of that, no doubt, helped our ancient ancestors survive threats to their lives—but today that same biological reaction to stress is triggered too often or too out of place to be helpful, especially when we need prefrontal efficacy to come up with the best response.

As stress increases so does another brain hormone, cortisol. During the height of stress, cortisol levels are also at their highest. This cortisol jump brings stress signs like more rapid breathing and faster heart rate along with an increase in blood pressure and blood sugar levels. With these bodily shifts come reactions such as heightened fear, anxiety, irritability, or sadness. Mentally we might find it hard to focus or remember key points—the mental lapses associated with frazzle.

Anxiety and peak performance, brain science shows, are reciprocally inhibiting: when one ascends, the other drops. So when we are in frazzle our performance plummets as our cognitive capacity narrows. During the peak of an emotional hijack our attention fixates on the perceived threat, not on what we need to be doing. We become rigid in how we respond, relying on overlearned reactions rather than what works best now.

Dan used to call such moments of frazzle an "amygdala hijack," but he now thinks about it differently. While a simplistic view of brain function sees a specific brain area as "causing" an emotion, neuroscientists will tell you that a state like frazzle activates widespread circuitry in the brain, not just one node.[13] So when we say that the amygdala acts as the brain's radar for threat, for example, we mean that the amygdala is an important part of a larger network that activates when we detect something that inspires fear.[14]

Closely linked to our fear circuits is the brain's "salience network," which decides moment-to-moment what is most relevant for us, and so shifts our attention there. The intertwining of our circuits for threat and for focus result in our attention riveting on what makes us frightened. In human prehistory, no doubt, this tight link between threats and focus helped our ancestors survive a dangerous world. Today, however, we can endure fairly constant "threats"—the things we worry about. And so our worries and anxieties become continual sources of distraction, narrowing our attention.

Put more positively, engagement and attention flow together: we pay more attention to what matters most to us and what we love doing. The optimal zone requires that we be calm and clear.

The antidote to the stress of a threat lies in becoming more relaxed, shifting from sympathetic nervous system arousal to the body and brain's recovery mode, the parasympathetic. This physiological pivot draws on emotional balance, the key to managing our emotions well.

Although cortisol is one of the neurochemicals triggered by stress, at its lower levels cortisol helps us—for instance, it's what gets our body clock going in the morning and gives us the mental energy we need for the day. When we are challenged mentally, cortisol gives us the ability to rise to the demands. A moderate level of cortisol can leave us humming with the pleasure of a good mood in that optimal state where we can tick off a list of challenging tasks with ease.

Excitement or nervousness "can be a good thing," says a college teacher, adding, "my life is a cycle of deadlines. As I approach the due date for an article or the start of class, the experience heightens and intensifies. Once I finish, that energy quiets down and relaxes. I think we benefit from that kind of stress-relaxation cycle. It gives us an edge."[15]

Such nervous system arousal, sometimes called "eustress," or good stress, gets us going, charged up for whatever tasks await us. From a biological point of view this mounting mobilization tracks an increase in the brain hormone cortisol. Our cortisol levels start rising around dawn, getting us ready for a new day's activities.

When we feel that we have work to do that we enjoy, cortisol primes our brain and body to get it done. The optimal state for most of us occurs when cortisol readies us for the challenge at hand. But past the point of cortisol's optimal levels, as we experience a continued rise in cortisol—

with another stress hormone, adrenaline, kicking in, too—we suffer what we typically call "stress," the bad kind.

Indeed, that college teacher who described being energized by challenge goes on to note that higher levels of anxiety do not help us: "The more anxious and cautious we become, the more we attract disaster," she admits, noting that when top gymnast Simone Biles "experienced extreme anxiety during her Olympic performance, she realized how dangerous it would be to continue in that state." So Biles dropped out of the Beijing Olympics in 2022.

We associate stress with negative emotions like anxiety. But every emotion has its uses, as we noted before. Salovey and Mayer's group often cite research showing that being sad, for instance, enhances accuracy in detail work.[16] In those situations where the relevant information comes from a narrow range—like proofreading a text, or doing the math for our taxes—then negative emotions that put us in a more serious frame of mind are better.

Positive emotions tend to let us take in a wider array of information, and enhance cognitive efficiency; negative emotions lead to narrowing. That may be why we do better at solving our day-to-day problems and challenges when we are in a better mood. "If information comes from diverse sources," University of Wisconsin neuroscientist Richard Davidson tells us, "the positive emotions enhance" how we do cognitively. That complexity is the usual case in the challenges of our lives.

Feeling good—having positive emotions—has an unexpected benefit. Rather than making us complacent (the "fat and happy" theory of life), it turns out that feeling good makes people more likely to take action on big issues, like climate warming.[17]

What Makes a Stressor?

Perhaps the most widespread source of stress in the workplace: too much to do and too little reward. Oddly, though work overload is one of the most common sources of stress, it does not always have bad effects;

not *enough* work can be worse than too much. In one workplace survey 79 percent of respondents said not having enough work is more stressful than having too much work. And 74 percent would be happy to take on more work if they got paid more.

But it's not just pay that matters. There's also a lack of status, recognition, or appreciation. Even worse: having no intrinsic rewards; the sense that your efforts have no meaning.[18] Take, for example, a lawyer who rarely has a chance to do real legal work. Most of her time gets spent doing what to her seemed mundane tasks like making phone calls and doing paperwork. She's a ripe candidate for burning out.

Being treated unfairly is another source of stress. Imagine a young woman who is smarter than any of her male team members. But she's ignored whenever she tries to contribute an idea during a meeting. More frustrating for her, if one of the male members suggests the same idea a few minutes later, the group responds with enthusiasm. This sexism, of course, epitomizes unfairness, and could easily lead her to be angry and bitter. And if this unfair treatment goes on and on she would become ripe for burnout.

Such bias can take many forms at work, from who is and who is not promoted, to how pay raises are allotted, and even who gets disciplined and who does not. When Americans in 2019 were asked to indicate sources of stress during the past month, 25 percent cited such discrimination. In 2021, that number had increased to 32 percent, and in 2022 had leveled off at a still too-high 28 percent.[19]

Stress from bias multiplies when a negative stereotype is in the air. For instance, when a group of women volunteered for an experiment where they would do math problems, some of them were primed with the thought that (as one stereotype has it) women are not good at math.[20] This "stereotype threat" triggered distractions like the thought they would do poorly—which became a self-fulfilling prophecy.

Such stereotype threats have been shown to have a powerful and detrimental impact on members of any group so targeted.[21]

A third major source of stress comes from within: the hidden fear that we lack what it takes to do well. This fear of failure occurs often when someone starts a new job or assignment and has an underlying sense of inadequacy. Our sense of identity and self-worth is strongly linked to how well we perform in our key roles, whether it be at work, at home, or in some other domain of our lives that matters to us. For instance, professionals who have no family life tend to see their self-worth as depending on how well they do at work—and so they up their expectations for their performance.

When Cary interviewed professionals during their first year on the job, he found concern about their ability to meet expectations to be widespread among them. That's no surprise. But twelve years later his research team found that many of the professionals were still worried about doing well enough. As one veteran high school teacher admitted, "I still have nightmares in the fall about telling a class to do something, and then they all look at me and say, 'NO!' The anxiety is still pretty high."

Such self-imposed stress amplifies with perfectionism. Expecting ourselves to score a goal every time creates immense stress. Like the ideal that we should get into flow continually, this way of thinking creates internal stress over and above whatever pressures a job poses. You can see this in new teachers who believe they need to inspire every child in their classes and new lawyers who beat themselves up whenever they lose a case.

Pathways to Resilience

Consider the nurse in a Boston hospital who had to spend long days in the intensive care unit during a Covid surge. She found this heartrending— she was working with patients who were suffering the most, and too many of her patients died. Her work made her feel awful.

But she made an intentional decision not to let this destroy her own well-being. She got up earlier so she could start her day with a long run. She went out of her way to organize get-togethers via Zoom with close friends in which they would not talk about what had happened that day for them, but fun memories or positive things they were looking forward to once they could travel again. She meditated daily. She would call family members that she hadn't seen in a long time, just to reconnect. She felt she was spreading joy.

The nurse has found ways to connect with her emotional balance, the competence that, in particular, lets us lessen the ravages of stress. As Richard Boyatzis, who interviewed her about how she had found such emotional balance, put it, despite the enormous stress in her workday, "Her spirits were great."

There are many routes to finding our emotional balance in the face of stress. Here are some:

Find meaning. Having a sense of purpose helps buffer stress because we are able to reappraise negative life events in light of that deeper sense of purpose. In a study of several thousand men and women at midlife and beyond, those with a purpose-focused life were less likely to brood and ruminate about setbacks, losses, and failures, and quicker to recover their inner equilibrium.[22]

Focus on the task at hand even in the face of toxic levels of stress. A daily practice of meditation—whether "mindfulness" or some other variety—can help here. If we get upset, a mounting body of research shows, these mental exercises tend to make us less reactive to stress and more resilient—able to recover more quickly.[23]

Manage the tug-of-war between work and family. Anyone with a family knows those needs can conflict with work demands.[24] There has always been a certain tension between work and the rest of our lives. Fully meeting the needs of one typically means skimping on the other; most of us find it impossible to adequately meet all the demands all the time.

Consider a single mom with two young kids. She's got to work to support her family, but working means she's just not available to her sons as much as she wished. That's a stress.

On the other hand, if you're lucky sometimes family life can lower work stress, not raise it. For instance a teacher was married to a midlevel manager in a large multinational company who had no aspirations to move up further—and who was so supportive of her teaching career that he not only took over many domestic chores but also gave her a sympathetic ear whenever she had a particularly stressful day at school.

Change what you can. "Grant me the serenity to accept the things I can't change, courage to change the things I can, and the wisdom to know the difference," implores theologian Reinhold Niebuhr's Serenity Prayer. That insight applies in spades to how we can handle what stresses us. Sometimes we can better cope by handling our own reactions better (if the stressor is something we can't change) or by, say, changing a worrisome deadline by getting an extension or enlisting help.

Resilience can require a midcourse correction, like changing careers or taking jobs elsewhere. A lawyer who found her job too stressful went back to school part-time, got a master's in urban planning, and found a job in the planning department of a large city. It wasn't what she had hoped for at the beginning of her career, but it was much more rewarding than her previous job.

Or resilience can be helped by adjusting how someone did their work. Take, for example, Charles, the president of a wholesale food distributor. He always dreaded meeting with one customer, who seemed to know how to push all of Charles's buttons. But one year he sent one of his executives to meet with that customer instead of going himself. Problem solved. Charles avoided the stress, and his executive came back with an excellent new contract.

Find a sense of control. At the end of her first year of teaching, Eugenia Barton was among the most burned-out teachers. Looking back on that year, she said, "I thought I'd died and gone to hell!" But twelve years later she was at the same school, and remarkably resilient. She pointed to the autonomy her job provided. As she put it, "I like the independence. We can mumble and complain about principals and superintendents and all sorts of boards of education. But when you close that door to your room, you really are independent. . . . And I like that."

Take a break. Research tells us the human body can take only so much stress, pressure, and deadline tension. We need to give ourselves a break, time off from *doing* to enjoy just *being*.

That's what our Consortium colleague Richard Boyatzis found when he made a thorough search of scientific findings about the common sources of stress in our lives, and the ways we can renew.[25] The physiology of stress and renewal comes down to how stress pumps the sympathetic nervous system, designed to help us survive in an emergency via the fight-flight-or-freeze shift in our body's metabolism.

When this arousal system boots up incessantly, reacting to one crisis after another—*The baby's sick! The car won't start! I'm missing that important meeting!*—we edge toward a state of emotional exhaustion. If such stress gives us little or no time to recover, we end up in a frazzled state. If it continues and becomes chronic, it can lead to burnout.

But, Boyatzis found, there's a simple way to counter this vicious downward struggle: pace our days and weeks with periods of renewal. This activates the parasympathetic nervous system, the body's mode of restoration and recovery. Renewals can be as simple as a walk in nature, a talk with a good friend, or time with a pet. As a top executive in a high-pressure job told us, "Playing with my cat saved my life."

Working with Dan, Boyatzis designed a simple self-assessment that lets you see the ratio of stresses-to-renewals in your life.[26] The assessment lists the main well-researched ways to renew ourselves, giving you options for what you might insert into your day to get the right balance. And when it comes to lessening stress itself, there is a specific tool: emotional balance.

Deep breathing. Our breathing can reflect the state of our autonomic arousal: quick and shallow when we are in the fight-or-flight zone, and deep and slow when we are in the body's recovery mode (or sympathetic and parasympathetic arousal, to be technical). We can shift from the stressed state to a more relaxed mode—at least temporarily—by intentional deep breathing. Sometimes this is done to a 4-4-4 count: Take a deep breath into your lower diaphragm, so your belly expands, to the count of four (or as long as you can comfortably). Hold your breath in to a count of four, or as long as you find comfortable, and exhale slowly to a four-count or longer. Try this several times in a row for best benefit. It's a quick, on-the-spot way to shift toward more resilience.

Gratitude. One way to shift negative thinking (like the cynicism that emotional exhaustion breeds) to a more positive track can be intentionally bringing to mind people or aspects of your situation you are grateful for. In one version of this practice, people daily wrote down three people or things they were thankful for in their life, and their stress levels declined.[27]

Self-Focus: What's Missing

The sources of stress in our lives and work are everywhere. We can't avoid it. Because stress activates parts of the brain that distract us from the task at hand, it can torpedo our effectiveness. Stress seems the enemy of our optimal state.

But we're not helpless; there are many ways to better handle life's inevitable stresses. From changing the situation if we can, to having a more positive mindset, to shifting our physiology toward resilience, the options are great. We do not have to be victims.

Emotional balance—or call it "stress resilience"—along with the other self-management competencies, gives us key ingredients for high performance, for success in a career, and for "winning." But are these enough? A narcissist—someone completely self-absorbed— could embrace these competencies as aids to their individual fulfillment. In our way of thinking being adept in these paths to personal success does not necessarily make you someone who will care about other people, who would be an asset on a team, or embrace an organization's greater purpose.

While the self-awareness and self-management competencies give us more control over how we manage ourselves, they are not sufficient in themselves to improve our relationships. Being excellent for your own ends does not necessarily mean you will care about other people, let alone be compassionate. And forget being the kind of person people love to work for or be around, someone who offers an inspiring vision and purpose that people resonate with, or who helps others develop further strengths toward their own effectiveness.

Widening your goals beyond your personal success opens the way to better relationships, to being a valued team member, and to becoming an asset to your community or organization. All that begins with empathy.

7

Empathy

A three-year-old answers the phone and in reply to her aunt's question "What are you doing?" says, "I'm playing with *this*."

"This" is her dolly, and the toddler does not realize that her aunt cannot know what "this" might be. The reason: at three she has not yet developed the capacity for what psychologists call "theory of mind," the ability to know what someone else perceives, thinks, or feels. By age five most children have mastered this ability to sense what's in the mind of someone else.

Having a theory of what's going on in someone else's mind represents an essential skill in our social world, one that makes our interactions smoother. We are constantly surmising what other people experience, and implicitly deploying our guesses in our interactions.

Knowing what someone else might be thinking represents a key element in *cognitive* empathy, one of three varieties of tuning in to the people around us that make us more emotionally intelligent. The brain lodges the three main strands of empathy in different sets of neural circuitry.[1]

Cognitive empathy, largely based in the thinking brain, or neocortex, lets us know how the other person thinks and sees the situation at hand. We can read another person's perspective, unpacking their mental models to get a sense of their language, in order to make our own message spot-on. This means we can be a highly effective communicator.

The idea of such effectiveness in communication has a long history.

Many traditions, for instance, have for centuries lauded the capacity to understand how a given people think and the ability to address them in terms they find compelling.[2]

Emotional empathy, nested primarily in the brain's emotional circuitry, lets us know immediately what the other person feels because we feel it, too. Emotional empathy depends on a brain-to-brain linkage, where the emotional circuitry in one person resonates with that in another. This makes emotional empathy both quick and powerful—we immediately feel the joy or sadness of the person we are with. A danger here is when another's toxic state—panic, rage—floods us, causing empathy distress. This pathology of empathy has become a severe problem in jobs like nursing, where burnout and quitting result from being continually flooded by contact with angst-ridden patients.

Emotional empathy lets us feel the other person's emotions through a cascade of nonverbal channels like facial expression, tone of voice, and gestures. This emotional nuance shades the person's words with a particular meaning that our emotional empathy lets us pick up. It turns out that there are many circuits in the forebrain designed to create this automatic, instantaneous, and unconscious link to the brain of the person we are interacting with—a bridge for emotional traffic. Knowing how the other person feels moment-to-moment lets what we say and do be more on-target.

Dan once gave a talk at a huge annual gathering of marketers in which he pointed out that cognitive and emotional empathy are what it takes to hone a powerful marketing message. There was uneasy laughter—uneasy because he went on to point out that the third kind of empathy means that message won't be solely in the service of self-interest (or a given brand's market share), but will also be for the target person's best interests.

Caring Matters

Dan's wife was frustrated when a home delivery service left her groceries at a UPS store instead of bringing them to her home. The delivery had some key ingredients for dinner that night. So she called the customer service line of that delivery outfit. From the moment that call was answered she started to feel better.

For one, the rep immediately gave her the feeling he was there to help her. Though she started out very upset, the rep stayed calm and really listened to her. He understood the problem right away, agreeing that the delivery never should have been made to a UPS office. He empathized with her feelings of frustration. He not only put in her order all over again to be delivered to the proper address, but even gave her a gift certificate to cover the cost.

Although Dan's wife began the call feeling upset, she was thrilled by the end of it. Where she had felt down before, she felt happy afterward—and wished there were more people like that rep.

That customer service rep was outstandingly empathic in the usual ways, cognitively and emotionally. But what was even more compelling: he clearly was on her side.

The third kind of empathy means *caring* about the person you are tuning in to. This variety of empathy opens the way to compassion, to considering what might be in the other person's best interests, not just your own. Every major religion has fostered such caring, whether under the guise of "charity" or "kindness" or compassion itself. The Dalai Lama has famously said, "My religion is kindness," and he sees this emphasis on caring as common to all spiritual traditions.

Religion aside, such caring has come into the scientific world as "empathic concern," caring about the other person.[3] We not only sense what the other person thinks and feels, but feel concern for their well-being. This concern for the other seems to reside in the same circuits as a parent's love for their child, and gives us a felt basis for altruism, even compassion. An early critique of emotional intelligence held that the concept had no room for a moral dimension. Empathic concern refutes that charge, putting caring for others squarely within the emotional intelligence domain.

Showing concern matters in every sphere of our lives, from our closest connections to where we do business. There seems to be a below-the-radar thirst for this caring quality among people in corporate settings. "The emotional intelligence course here is immensely popular," a manager at one of the world's largest retailers says. "It's the first time anyone in this company has used the word 'compassion.'"

Just as we might love a four-year-old having a tantrum (we feel ongoing affection for the child, though not for her behavior), with empathic concern, research shows, maintaining our love for the person as we attune to their suffering and pain lets us stay present to them rather than turning away. This defuses "empathy distress," where people tune out of another person's pain in order to ease their own discomfort. Staying present to their pain allows us to take the next step, which is to act compassionately. This lets us be kind, not just calm and clear—and this is the kind of empathy we want in our partner or spouse, our boss, our friends, and the people we love.

As a competence, empathy means the ability to sense other people's feelings and how they see the world, plus taking a genuine concern for their well-being.[4] It means you pick up unspoken emotions via nonverbal cues to what they are feeling and thinking, which in turn requires that you listen and observe them attentively.

The world champion of such attentive observation of nonverbal cues might be psychologist Paul Ekman. It took a year, staring at himself in the mirror, for Ekman to master how to voluntarily control all two-hundred-plus muscles in his face, from chin to forehead and ear to ear. But once he had attained that feat of self-control, he was able to map the patterns of facial muscle movement underlying each of six major emotions: fear, surprise, anger, sadness, joy, and disgust.

That mapping became the basis for the Facial Action Coding System (FACS), a method for researchers to read the emotions being expressed at a given moment on a person's face (the same system has also found use in animated cartoons, giving emotional expression to the faces of cartoon characters). For example, when we are stressed or worried, the muscle contracts between our eyebrows; when we give a genuine smile the muscles that give us crow's-feet by each eye tighten.

During the pandemic, when most of us masked our faces to avoid getting the coronavirus, researchers at McGill University's Laboratory for Attention and Social Cognition were able to use this mapping to assess the cost to empathic accuracy of mask-wearing.[5] The masks so widely used to protect wearers from the Covid virus hide the lower part of the face, and so block from view the lower facial muscles that are most active in specific emotions. In contrast, fear and sadness mainly change muscles around the eyes, which are more visible. Anger and surprise alter musculature both in the top and bottom part of the face.

We read these shifts in patterns of facial muscle tension in terms of the emotions that move them—and our ability to recognize what someone feels depends to a large extent on our accuracy in this. But that changes, understandably, if the other person's face hides in part behind a mask. The McGill study found that overall a mask reduced empathic accuracy for emotions by about one-quarter. Recognizing disgust was reduced by 46 percent; anger by 30 percent; and sadness by 23 percent. On the other hand, recognizing another person's fear, surprise, and happiness suffered the least.

Empathy at Work

When neurosurgeon Patrick Codd did his emergency room residency he was unprepared for the parade of patients with devastating brain injuries he had to treat—person after person who would never recover, all too many of whom would die. And he was not alone: he would find other residents in the hospital stairwell, in tears.

But there was a built-in escape: "Turning away from pain," Dr. Codd says, "is a self-defense mechanism that's been woven into the fabric of neurosurgery."[6] It's not just neurosurgery: research has found that physicians, uniquely, are able to practice a detached variety of compassion by activating a node in the brain that dulls empathy for another person's pain. This mechanism allows physicians to treat unflinchingly the huge range of physical suffering they attend to, whether, for example, in the ER or while doing surgery.[7]

Stifling your reaction to another person's pain and suffering has its pragmatic uses, as medicine has found—this ability to tune out the other person's suffering and stay focused on helping them seems essential in both the emergency room and the surgical theater. But if that indifference to the suffering of other people stays with you beyond work, you lose the capacity for empathic concern. You become unfeeling, aloof from the angst of everyone around you, including the people you love the most.

Dr. Codd, who became a neurosurgeon at Duke University Medical Center, felt one antidote to this uncaring attitude might be helping medical residents face their own emotional pain, such as from having to declare a patient dead or a bad medical decision they made. He created a monthly meeting for medical residents to talk to each other about their own roiling feelings.

As the first meeting began, Dr. Codd expected to be alone in the room. But the entire class of residents showed up.

A friend who had just seen a doctor at a new clinic was told by this physician: "I'll tell you everything I find. If I were sitting in your chair I'd want to know."

"When you feel they care about you," this friend said, it makes all the difference. And, he added with a tone of satisfaction, "they have empathy."

Empathy pays off in medicine in improved compliance by patients with what the doctor tells them to do, and in enhanced patient satisfaction. For instance, when medical residents got training in empathy—an unusual addition to the standard med school curriculum—their patients rated them as more caring.[8]

That empathy training for medical residents was developed by Dr. Helen Reiss, a Consortium member and psychiatrist at Harvard Medical School. Residents are urged to make eye contact with their patients, recognize the patient's feelings by reading their facial expression (and be more likely to mirror that expression on their own face), and listen attentively and without judgment. Even better: name what the patient feels, and respond in a way that shows understanding, in a soothing tone.

That's good advice for any parent or leader. Empathy represents a quality we all want in our loved ones—our spouses, our friends, our family—and in anyone we regularly spend time with. Take the world of work.

Why Empathy Matters

The consulting division of a tech company had a brilliant employee, but one whom they never would allow to interact with their clients. The reason was simple: though he could analyze their troubles, he could not connect. Small talk eluded him; in fact, he just could not relate to clients at all—never asked about them, what they thought the problem was, nothing of the sort. He'd just launch into what he saw as the solution— and turn off the client. That consultant lacked empathy, the ability to tune in to how others feel, to see their world and their concerns.

"People will try to convince you," Apple's CEO Tim Cook said at a Massachusetts Institute of Technology commencement, "that you should keep empathy out of your career. Don't accept this false premise." Cook is not alone in valuing empathy in a business; more than 80 percent of CEOs in one survey agree that empathy matters immensely for collaboration, resilience, and morale.[9]

While a viciously competitive business culture offers a recipe for failure, one that encourages empathy will be more likely to thrive, argues Stanford's Jamil Zaki.[10] He emphasizes to his students that empathy is more like a skill that can be enhanced rather than a fixed trait, and offers ways to develop this attunement to others. One of the most powerful ways to do so, researchers at Stanford and Harvard found, was to set an example; generosity and kindness, they found, can become contagious, setting a social norm that others follow.[11] And when leaders spotlight such exemplars, the norm spreads more quickly and takes hold more deeply in the organization's culture.

As *Forbes* magazine proclaimed, "Empathy is *the* most important leadership skill according to research."[12] The advantages of an empathic culture range widely, from increased innovation, greater engagement, and talent retention to feelings of inclusivity and even a better work/life balance.

Consortium member Ruth Malloy, who assesses C-suite executives of global firms for the Spencer Stuart consultancy, says she finds every successful executive needs strength in the Achieve competence to get where they are. But when they lead others, they need to temper their achievement drive with another leadership ability: the caring side of empathy.

Without caring, such high-achieving leaders may get short-term results, but in the long term they hollow out the organization's human capital.[13] "Talented, high-performing people get frustrated," Malloy says. "They look for other opportunities, while the mediocre stay."

Feeling that someone encourages, comforts, or otherwise validates how you feel has a positive impact on your mood. This can be about some trouble you are having in your personal life, or just being with someone and having fun, a Harvard study found.[14] Days when people collaborate in some way tend to make them feel good. Indeed, there's something about just being with someone you like that feels uplifting, the research discovered.

The first person to benefit from compassion is the one who feels compassionate. That principle was underscored in a diary study of how people felt over a series of many days. Being a nourishing person not only energized those receiving the nourishment—words of encouragement, praise, and the like—but those giving this got better performance ratings and quicker advancement compared to those who failed to nourish.[15] In contrast, rudeness and incivility at work result in—no surprise—poorer performance, less collaboration, a deterioration in customers' experience, and more people quitting.

Service Without Empathy

The other day Dan left his car to be serviced at a local auto dealer. He was directed to the desk of a "service advisor," who actually gave him no advice—in fact, the advisor barely glanced at Dan before he walked off on a mysterious errand, without explaining what called him away, or how long he would be.

After a very long stint of Dan sitting there waiting, the advisor returned, and promptly got lost in his computer screen, still without saying a thing to Dan, or acknowledging his presence. Plus this was during a Covid surge, and a sign on the door to his department said that wearing masks was mandatory to come in the room. The advisor's own mask was down around his mouth, leaving his nose exposed.

All of this equated to a miserable experience. If Dan were someone who rates businesses on Yelp or a similar app, this dealership would get the lowest rating he could give. And in a competitive world, those ratings matter. In a time when people are constantly rating other people, there's a pragmatic reason for being more empathic. As one world-famous executive coach explained to a client—a CEO—"You'll get better ratings" if you're empathic. Even so, collecting digital data about how customers react, though a popular approach, leaves out the personal experience a customer has, and so lacks an empathic understanding.

Norms are changing. Not so long ago a top executive (or teacher, sports coach, or clergy—or anyone in power) might get away with actions that today will bring public condemnation, if not jail time. The spread of social media ratings "upward," whereby a less powerful person can give a public opinion of someone more powerful, has changed social standards.

All of this creates a pragmatic argument for having more empathy—that is, the ability to tune in to the other person's way of seeing, feelings, and what's best for them. Besides, developing strengths only for ourselves can open the door to narcissistic self-absorption, while empathy and concern for others offers an antidote. Our empathy encourages us to use our emotional intelligence for a wider benefit.

Norms for Caring

A home goods company had recently had a change in top management, and the new bosses pushed for cost reductions across the board. At a meeting of one unit the division head turned down the idea that the team should brainstorm ways to reduce cost; instead he pressured his group to find ways to present their results in the best light, even if it meant inflating their performance numbers.

Though no one resisted him aloud, everyone there felt betrayed—that not only did their ideas not count, but that their boss was unworthy of their respect. They felt he could no longer be trusted, and the general mood was frustration, even despair.

The impact of bosses' actions on their direct reports can be devastating, as with this home goods team. Empathy has a direct effect on the relationship of those involved, for better or for worse.[16] One powerful reason: our emotional circuitry attunes us to the mood of those around us, particularly anyone more powerful than we are. That interpersonal link, brain to brain, can either help us or hurt us. Emotions, years of research shows, are contagious.[17]

Words of advice or encouragement might help us get or stay in our optimal state, while thoughtless criticism can devastate us. Being fully present to the other person is the first step in rapport—and essential if that other person is to feel seen and cared about.

For instance, the last straw for Doris, an intensive care nurse, came the day she kept a patient alive for forty minutes with the last-ditch device that had her hand-pumping a bellows every two seconds to rush air into failing lungs. Those precious minutes gave the patient's family time to say their last goodbyes. During those forty minutes her hands blistered from her struggle with the bellows. But the family, rather than being grateful, doubted the hospital had done everything possible.[18]

On the other hand, boosting a person's empathic concern, research shows, increases the odds that person will go out of their way to help someone in need—donate money, give someone on crutches a seat in a crowded room, and so on. Taking compassionate concern that final step—actually acting to help the person—requires the activation of brain circuitry beyond that involved in simply caring. This added effort over and above that made just to help oneself registers as a boost of activity that can be seen in the person's brain.[19] This extra neural effort may make the difference, for example, between a person acting to save the environment or not, or doing what helps another person in need, whether just holding a door open for them or offering a blanket to a homeless person.

Boosting Empathy

Practice a Caring Mindset

One method for upping the likelihood a person will feel empathic concern involves expanding the "circle of caring." This mental exercise begins by having a person recall someone in their life who has been kind to them, perhaps a mentor or caretaker, and wishing that person to be safe, happy, healthy, and thrive in their life. Then make those same wishes toward oneself, then to those the person loves, followed by wishing the same for mere acquaintances—and finally for everyone everywhere. This simple inner workout, if repeated daily, has been found to increase the likelihood someone will go out of their way to help others in need.[20]

Find a Sympathetic Ear

The CEO of a large residential facility for people with disabilities was overwhelmed by land use hearings for a planned new building. He had to testify in thirty such hearings, and endure brutal cross-examinations by lawyers. But he managed the stress well—mainly because of his friendship with the director of social services. They would talk over what had happened, and the CEO feels his friend—who was trained in a seminary—really listens. That CEO ends up feeling a lot better.

Empathy matters. How well people listen—whether they are not really hearing on the one hand, or wanting to understand you on the other—makes you feel either valued or ignored. Being treated with civility matters. Other people's politeness and respect, one study found, lower a person's level of emotional exhaustion.[21] Of course, the opposite—rudeness and disrespect—raises it.

Practice Kindness

Another way to promote compassion: model it. Some years ago Dan was going down the stairs to a subway station on New York's Forty-Second Street when he came upon a man sprawled on the steps, unconscious. People were simply stepping over or around him.

In the weeks before the subway incident, as a journalist for the *New York Times*, Dan had been traversing the streets of Manhattan in a van equipped with sandwiches, riding along with folks from a nonprofit that helped the homeless. They would spot someone living on the street and bring him or her a sandwich and tell them about a shelter and social services they could get. This broke the spell of invisibility of the homeless for Dan.

So on those subway steps he stopped to see what was wrong with the guy sprawled there. The moment Dan did so, a circle of people gathered to see if they could help. It turned out the man slumped on the stairs spoke no English, had been wandering penniless, and had not eaten for days. He had fainted from hunger on the steps. Someone went to get a subway guard; others went to get orange juice, a hot dog. In a matter of minutes he was revived, fed, taken care of.

But remember, dozens, maybe hundreds, of people just stepped over him, as though he did not exist. That was the implicit norm the helpers all broke. People who have become homeless will say one of the worst parts of their lowered status is becoming invisible. We all have a spectrum of attention, ranging from utter self-absorption to mindful awareness of our surroundings and the people there. The latter form of attention allows for empathy, and, if need be, compassionate action.

Showing compassion remedies cynical thinking, a mental virus that can easily lead to burnout. By wishing the best for someone we implicitly recognize their better side rather than their worst. And feeling compassion for ourselves offers an antidote to emotional exhaustion.[22]

A WORD OF CAUTION HERE. IT CAN BE ALL TOO EASY TO "BLAME the victim," the person burning out. But organizations themselves may be to blame for the burnout—not some lapse in the person's emotional intelligence. When workers on oncology units were surveyed, it turned out their stress was not so much due to their daily encounters with the pain and suffering of their patients. It had more to do with work overload, time pressures, interpersonal conflicts, and feeling a lack of support from management—sources of stress that might be found in any workplace.

That resulted in an intervention targeting these sources of their stress, seeking to lessen work overloads, time pressures, and the like. Results: after six months the group's burnout scores were significantly lower than a comparison group's, as were their emotional exhaustion scores.[23] They could approach their optimal zone again.

Organizational Awareness

Rachel, a seven-year-old, had a remarkable sensitivity to the social world of her classroom. She could tell you quite accurately which second graders were friends, who played with whom, and which bully nobody liked.

Her awareness of this social web attests to her high social intelligence—in particular, what we'd call "organizational awareness." While Rachel's astuteness was displayed in the small world of her second-grade classroom, this awareness can apply to any network of people, from your family of origin to a huge corporation. It helps you sense how emotions play out as they weave through a given social web, and gives you a rough map of the particular connections between people.

In your own extended family, for instance, can you say who influences whom—who does Uncle Joe listen to and who does he ignore? Or in a meeting, can you sense whose opinions matter to most of those involved? Can you step back and track the emotional tone of a conversation? Or at work are you aware of the unspoken rules that govern who says what to whom, or who has the most clout in making decisions?

Our colleague Richard Boyatzis makes this recommendation to enhance your organizational awareness: "Reflect in your next meeting on who in the room has the most power and next most and so on until you notice the person with the least. Who is listening to others? To whom are they listening? Who are the leaders? Who are the helpers or coaches?"[24]

This variety of empathic awareness was likely stark during your high school years, where it may have taken the form of recognizing who was in the "cool" group, who was in the athletes' clique, who were the "bad kids." Such an understanding of social networks tends to mature, for instance, into a sense of organizational awareness in your workplace. This competence lets you apply your empathy to a larger realm, being sensitive to the system of which you are part—whether an informal social network, your extended family, or your organization at work. As we'll see in Part IV, organizational awareness builds the rudiments of systems thinking, the ability to read the dynamics of large networks. Take how this applies to reading social hierarchies.

What Impairs Empathy

Every society, culture, or nation has what Vincent Cunningham calls a "murderous hierarchy," a group that's on top and one that's an underclass. A Black journalist at *The New Yorker*, Cunningham notes that "it's possible to be Black and degraded in America while also profiting from wanton extraction of resources overseas, oppressing millions of non-Black others, and living on land stolen from indigenous people. We are always joined in our sufferings, often by somebody we can't see through the darkness."[25]

Any way of thinking that fails to "imagine kinship with the stranded Guatemalan kid detained at the U.S. border or with the functionally enslaved Uyghur in China," he adds, "is lost in its own fog."

In a poem titled "The Curse of a Charmed Life," the poet Kim Stafford says that even those who seem to have great good fortune will, one day, die. But that's not the "curse." It's that having great success—whether material or in status—can blunt empathy.

As he puts it in his poem on the limits of success, Stafford worries that a charmed life course can leave someone deaf and blind to the needs of the homeless and mentally ill.

Empathic concern lets us feel across divides with empathy for the common humanity we share with everyone. Then there are no people left out, no "Others," people whom we dismiss out of hand. Yet many of the widespread ways of seeing our world do just that: exclude one or another group as "other," undeserving of help or caring, let alone of empathy. Take, for instance, a group that Stafford's poem speaks to, dubbed "Smart" by journalist George Packer.[26] "Smart" refers to the "caste" of academics, professionals, executives, and the like who have attended elite colleges or otherwise risen through the ranks of meritocracy to positions of social and economic comfort. But, as the poem about a charmed life spotlights, the danger of this worldview lies in ignoring those who do not make the cut, and whose status from birth may mean there are social and economic barriers to their ever attaining such lofty heights. The Smart group can be seen worldwide in the ranks, for example, of global corporations, governments, or universities. Their blind spot for those who have failed to succeed in the same way the Smart set did may mean such "failures" are not seen nor cared about—in other words making them into an Other.

So, for instance, someone who grew up in moneyed bastions of white privilege like, say, the Brentwood section of Los Angeles, or Greenwich, Connecticut, would likely attend an elite private school and then a highly selective college. Along the way they would be unlikely to have as a close friend someone from Watts in Los Angeles or Spanish Harlem in Manhattan. Instead they would mix with other Smart people. This social distance means the privileged can more easily "blame the victim," dismissing how childhood trauma, poor nutrition, and biases against a given group could handicap the poor.

The Smart group is one of four very different "self narratives" Packer names, each of which drives the actions of powerful divisions in the world's social and political fabric. Another of these, whom he dubs "Real," combines libertarian ideas with consumer capitalism and a distrust of government, touting the individual. This tight grasp on a black-or-white outlook casts those who do not hold to these beliefs as Other—the "Them" who cannot be tolerated by Us.

What Packer calls the "Free" group celebrates the rugged individual, the person who succeeds despite all odds, winner-take-all. This attitude, for instance, sees the sole purpose of a business as increasing the wealth of its investors, while ignoring its impacts on employees, customers, community, and nature. Worldwide this viewpoint justifies, for example, the devastation of rainforests to make room for cattle farms—profit now despite the planetary costs. The Free view has little or no compassion or even pity for those who form the oppressed or exploited—those whose toil supports the "Free"—seeing them as Other.

Finally, the "Just" group eagerly looks at the injustices that are built into social structures, and seeks to mend them. The Just outlook openly confronts what all those who benefit from an existing social order want to avoid. Worldwide the Just perspective takes the form of street demonstrations, investigative journalism, and movements seeking to right long-standing wrongs. But when those ends lead to an uncompromising stance, this outlook forgets reconciliation (and overlooks potential allies) and so dismisses out of hand those with positions of status in the existing order, seeing them as Other.

These narratives create compelling stories that bind each group together, but also divide us into warring tribes; each Us creates a Them. Of course these are stereotypes; not everyone who falls into these categories necessarily shares the us-them view Packer ascribes. And a wider empathy offers an alternative to these cramped camps: a more compassionate view with an overarching purpose, the *greater good* that, hopefully, might unite all groups in a larger mission. In this view there are no "Others," only Us.

This empathic vision embraces us all, seeking a universal betterment. Paved roads, clean water, and basic hygiene like brushing teeth help everyone regardless of their group, identity, or belief system. Human history marks a successive cascade of such innovations that raise all boats. In the last century incremental improvements, like wide access to healthy water, have doubled the human life span. Such improvements are "meta" to divides, upgrading lives without regard to where they stand in terms of these narratives.

A focus on what we agree on, rather than our divides, might bring a reframing of Us-and-Them thinking to make it less divisive.[27] But there is no sure cure here. We are at a loss to say exactly what reframing ideas might be most powerful for closing these divides.

As the future plunges us into a world of constant crisis, caring will have increasing value. As Mr. (Fred) Rogers, the host of the eponymous children's TV show, famously said, when there's trouble, "look for the helpers." Anyone in distress welcomes someone who offers succor in any form.

Sometimes there may be more to gain from giving emotional support than getting it. Being at the receiving end of support can make someone feel incompetent or otherwise defective, while *giving* support can enhance a sense of confidence and even meaning in life.

Scientists find that helping someone else activates the feel-good dopamine circuits in the brain of the person who helps. That may be the neural explanation for a bit of wisdom from the Danish philosopher Søren Kierkegaard: "The door to happiness always opens outward."

Compassion, many traditions hold, should be gathered for ourselves as well as for others. The self-awareness and self-management parts of EI are a form of caring for ourselves. The social awareness—particularly empathic concern—and relationship competencies are a means to spread that compassion to people we encounter.

For instance, an executive who lacks this outlook might well dismissively rationalize the stress employees are under and ignore their suffering. On the other hand, one who has compassion would do something to ease that stress—perhaps give practical support, change their circumstances, or help them develop more resilience.

Some key points to remember about empathy:

- There are three kinds, each based in different brain circuitry.
- Cognitive empathy lets us understand how a person thinks, the language they use, and their perspective. This lets us message them in ways they will best comprehend.
- Emotional empathy means we sense how the person feels. Having this kind of empathy means we can make our messages to that person land with impact.

- Empathic concern means we also care about that person. Showing this kind of empathy enhances the person's trust and respect for us, and strengthens our relationship.
- Organizational awareness takes empathy to a larger arena, applying social intelligence to read the networks of friendship and influence behind the formalities, whether in a family or a business.
- Seeing a given group as "other"—creating a divide—inhibits empathy. When empathy withers, so does the relationship.

Effectiveness in relationships depends on our empathy. From empathy springs an interpersonal deftness that lets us more readily influence, guide, and even inspire those around us—and lets us connect for optimal impact.

8

Manage Your Relationships

The president of a startup got upset when a client complained. So in the next meeting with his direct reports he bitterly attacked the executive who handles that client, yelling and even insulting him. That fiery criticism was done in front of the whole group, leaving the hapless executive demoralized.

Giving performance feedback, of course, is necessary. The president's feedback could have been done differently, in a way that would help the executive do a better job. But artful feedback takes both self-control and empathy, and the president of that startup had neither at that moment. He had no idea how devastating that public critique would be.

Our effectiveness in relationships stems from empathy; lacking this human glue, like the president of that startup, we fail to connect in a way that strengthens our relationships.

The drop in trust of public figures—those in politics and heads of major corporations—has been dramatic. The Great Place to Work Institute, for instance, finds that trust plays a large role in a company being nominated as a top-tier workplace. Companies where trust is high outperform the S&P 500 by a factor of three.[1] Empathic concern—a company showing that it cares about employees and customers—ranks among the main builders of trust.

Many businesses are seeing that empathy lies at the heart of employee and customer trust and satisfaction. But this essential skill makes or breaks *any* relationship. Friendships, romance, family life, parenting—

most all of our personal life—offers a ripe arena for empathy. If we have it, those relationships are more likely to flourish. If we lack it, they might well fail.

From empathy springs interpersonal deftness that lets us more readily influence, guide, and even inspire those around us—and lets us connect for maximal impact. Empathy also acts as a key ability in handling relationships well, from resolving differences, to being a productive community member, to coaching everyone from our children, our students, a youth sports team, or those who work with us.

Developing strengths only for ourselves can open the door to narcissistic self-absorption, but empathy and concern for others offer an antidote. Relationship abilities like empathy encourage us to use our emotional intelligence for a wider benefit. Let's see, for instance, how empathy-based relationship competencies matter in the workplace.

Coach and Mentor

The CEO of a medical technology company asked Jonathan, a senior executive, to help another senior executive, Manny, who had recently joined the company. Manny was a brilliant, hard-driving manager. Jonathan described him as "highly reactive emotionally . . . loud . . . highly opinionated . . . rough around the edges."

That style had been rewarded in his previous company, but it didn't fit the new one. If Manny didn't change, the company would fire him, despite his success in meeting his performance goals.

Coaching a peer can be a tricky assignment. In this case, it was especially so. After Jonathan tried to talk with Manny about his reactivity two or three times, Manny exploded. According to Jonathan, "He told me I was out of bounds and that I had no right to question his approach or behavior. And then he gave me the finger and told me to leave his office!"

But Jonathan persisted. He would take Manny aside as soon after a misstep as he could and in a one-to-one say, "Look, Manny, here's what I saw you do, and here's what I'm hearing from other people about how they felt. Do you realize what you're doing and how you're being seen?"

Jonathan also looked for ways to help Manny—which of course strengthened their link. For example, Manny had moved cities to take this job, and was having trouble finding housing he could afford. So Jonathan arranged for the company to give Manny additional funds to cover the costs. The help meant a lot to Manny, deepening their relationship.

It finally paid off. Manny began to accept Jonathan's help. According to Jonathan, "He no longer saw me as the enemy. Now when I gave him feedback, he really listened. He would even stop in my office and ask me for advice."

Manny began to change, and he gave Jonathan "all the credit for it."

Jonathan needed a high degree of emotional intelligence to succeed in coaching with someone like Manny. The Coaching and Conflict Management competencies were especially important. But it also required a high degree of emotional self-awareness, self-management, and empathy.

Being effective as a coach or mentor stands as one of the key relationship competencies, all of which build on empathy. Each of them, of course, requires additional skill sets: coaching and mentoring means helping another connect with their ideal self and what the concrete steps might be toward realizing that ideal.

The Influence competence requires that we be seen as trustworthy; competence in managing conflicts goes best with a talent for helping all parties recognize their shared values and human needs. But each of these relationship abilities requires that we be empathic in the first place; lacking that attunement, we will flounder in attempting any of these.

The EI competence of being an effective Coach or Mentor, which Jonathan deployed to good effect, stems from the ability to foster long-term development in someone else by offering timely and constructive feedback and support.[2] It builds on the positivity, or "growth," mindset where you see that other person as able to learn and improve, and adds empathic concern: you are genuinely interested in helping them grow new strengths. For instance, because you understand their own goals for improvement you might try to arrange "stretch" opportunities, challenges that will help them attain those goals.

Ask any highly successful businessperson if they're grateful to someone who helped them along at some point in their career, and the answer is most always, Yes! Even so, this essential task of leadership often gets skipped. All too many leaders have reduced this function to the yearly or semiannual performance review. But helping a direct report become better at what they do requires ongoing involvement, feedback, and suggestions on how to improve. A survey among companies showed that most coaching in the workplace is for emotional intelligence—either the self-management competencies or those relationship skills based on empathy. That survey was done just before the Covid pandemic; we can surmise that the demand for the skills of emotional intelligence among leaders has only increased.[3]

Consider how a manager gives performance feedback, one of the routine ways this competence can be displayed—or not. Consortium member Richard Boyatzis, with colleagues at Case Western Reserve University, scanned the brains of volunteers who were being given feedback on their performance.[4] If feedback focused on what the person had done wrong—in other words, was stressful—their brain circuits for handling threats and being defensive activated. This closes the person down, narrows what he or she can perceive, and so limits the options they entertain—this circuitry impairs thinking.

On the other hand, a focus on the person's strengths and potential for growth has the opposite effect: it energizes and motivates the person, leading to better learning. It's not that a manager needs to ignore a lapse in performance, but that there be more positives than negatives in the feedback.

Boyatzis calls this "coaching with compassion." He argues that people can develop more strengths if they are encouraged to reach for their dreams and values.[5] But all too often performance feedback becomes coaching for compliance, which has a negative impact. It's a missed opportunity to help that person develop further.

In short, the best coaching helps the person being coached pursue their own life goals and develop more strengths, rather than just evaluating them as they are now.

Unfortunately, many leaders are not aware of how they are giving feedback—or even if they are giving it at all. In one study, supervisors were observed interacting with their staff during the day, including how often they gave feedback to their staff. There was feedback in only about 2 percent of their interactions. But when the supervisors were asked how often they thought they had given feedback, they said on average about 10 percent of the time—and they all felt that they should be giving feedback even more. Needless to say, the supervisors were dumbfounded when they learned how little feedback they were actually giving.[6]

The power of such feedback was clear when some of these supervisors were given this data on how often they gave feedback, and then were again observed. The second time around they were now giving more feedback to staff than before. This simple data was taken as constructive feedback, showing the sheer power of helping someone become more self-aware of how they act.

Influence

At Nike, the giant shoe company, Darcy Winslow, then head of advanced research, saw data from a toxicological study about the materials used in their shoes. She was alarmed that the analysis revealed there were poisonous parts in their shoes, and resolved to find ways that Nike shoes could become less toxic.

But though the data were clear, no one at the company seemed to care enough to change. People there would agree with her that they needed to improve, but there was no movement in that direction.

As Darcy thought about who at Nike was most influential in this regard, she realized it was the people who designed their shoes. So she asked for a few minutes of time from a range of in-house designers, sharing the toxicity data with them. After many such conversations, Darcy had about twenty designers who seemed to really care.

Some of the most toxic materials, it turned out, were in the glue that held the top of a running shoe to the bottom. This was where designers got most excited: the challenge was to reinvent how uppers and lowers were fastened together. No one had ever done this before, and that captured the imaginations of the designers.

So the designer group reinvented shoe glue in a way that was nontoxic. And today the Nike corporation has embraced goals of zero toxicity across their entire product line.

Peter Senge, the MIT systems thinker who tells this story, points out that having such influence "happens informally, with people who are good listeners, respectful of their culture, and who look for windows of opportunity."[7] They don't engage in reactive problem-solving, but rather in creative thinking, and they "build a critical mass of people" who "support them in spreading their influence."

Also, he notes, such changemakers do not have to hold some high-ranking role in the company—they can start from wherever they are, like Darcy Winslow did.

It's the Relationship

It was one of the low points of the American War of Independence. The colonies would lose unless they could secure the active support of France. But the French were reluctant to get into another war with Britain. So the Continental Congress sent Benjamin Franklin, the polymath from Philadelphia, to win them over.

But when Franklin arrived in France, he spent most of his time in salons chatting with beautiful ladies and at parties where he enchanted both the ladies and their escorts. He seemed to spend very little time doing much of what his colleague John Adams considered real diplomacy.

But Franklin knew what he was doing. He realized that to win over the French, he needed to develop warm relationships with all kinds of people. He also learned who were the most important people to befriend and how to use those relationships to further the cause of independence.

The network that Franklin had cultivated included a number of those who had direct input into whether or not France should enter the war on the American side. For example, at one point the Congress ordered him to exclude France from the treaty discussions with Britain to end the war. Vergennes, the French foreign minister, was incensed. But Franklin wrote a remarkable letter apologizing to him. Then, in the same letter, Franklin asked for more money! Vergennes provided it, a sign of the strength of their relationship.

Franklin's approach worked. The French, of course, eventually entered the war, and their participation was crucial to American victory.[8] Franklin knew influence relies on strong relationships.

People adept in the Influence competence build trust in relationships and have a positive impact on others, persuading them and engaging them to build buy-in from key people.[9] To change someone's mind you first need to build a strong connection to them, so they are more open to what you have to say. And since leadership entails getting work done well through other people, managers and executives skilled at influence get better results.

While a keen organizational awareness lets you know who makes key decisions, it's the Influence competence that tells you how best to sway that person's thinking. Darcy's actions at Nike displayed both these abilities.

One winning approach to influencing another person comes down to appealing to their deepest motivations. David McClelland, Dan's grad school mentor, classed motives in these categories: the need to achieve, the need to affiliate, and the need for power. Sensing what compels a person the most—accomplishments, relationships, or impact—means you can appeal to that motive in persuading them. More generally, the method called "motivational interviewing" helps you draw out a person's main drivers in their own language.[10]

Another way to think about influence goes back to the idea that the ultimate purpose of emotional intelligence is to help yourself and others get and stay in an optimal state. This—perhaps the highest form of influence—means you use your ability to impact what someone else does in their best interest. In a leader this can mean, for instance, giving someone an assignment so they can learn new skills that will help them advance in their career.

This stands in contrast to another spin on influence, a more Machiavellian application where someone uses their sway over others solely for their own aims. This more self-focused use of influence can boomerang as those who are so manipulated lose trust in the influencer, distance themselves, or even burn out.

A lesson in the better sort of influence points out the shadow side, and urges a genuine concern for the other person's well-being.[11] Since influence builds on strong relationships, reflections include, for example, whether you find yourself consistently following through on your commitments and promises, and so build trust. People learn to use "We" language—for instance, "What can we come up with?" rather than "Give me some options." Also, rather than prescribing formulaic ways to demonstrate caring and commitment, people are urged to come up with their own specific ways to show others they care.

At its best, influence can be used to advance shared interests. Here the emphasis is on common goals. In this case a leader's influence shades into the next emotional intelligence competence, Inspiration.

Inspire

There is no "Tom" at the head of TOMS, the legendary shoe company. Founded by Blake Mycoskie, the longtime CEO, "TOMS" stands for "Tomorrow's Shoes," a reference to the company's famed "buy one, gift one" philosophy: give a pair of shoes to a poor person for every pair sold.

But Mycoskie, who had great enthusiasm for his company's purpose at the outset, eventually found himself losing interest and energy.[12] Taking time off to reflect on why he was feeling this way, Mycoskie realized it was because his company was pursuing growth and sales by offering discounts and other sales prods, like any other shoe company. In trying to meet aggressive sales goals, he felt, the company had lost its soul.

So Mycoskie refocused on the organization's purpose. The company diversified into coffee—for every bag of coffee TOMS sold, they gave a week's worth of drinkable water to people where that was scarce. Another example: TOMS started selling handbags to underwrite safe births in parts of the world where infant mortality is high; another effort sold backpacks to fund programs to lessen bullying.

In short, as Mycoskie put it, business can be used "to improve lives."

Leaders strong in the Inspire competence are able to guide people to get the job done by articulating a shared mission that motivates. They offer a sense of meaning and purpose over and above a person's day-to-day tasks and inspire people not just to get the job done, but to bring out their best.[13]

Workplace research finds that when a leader can articulate a shared mission or vision in ways that move those they lead—that is, they inspire—the resulting emotional climate becomes highly positive. People love what they are doing because it has meaning.[14] They feel deeply satisfied and proud, and give their best efforts.

When Covid-19 first emerged, Pfizer CEO Dr. Albert Bourla recognized the coming pandemic as an unprecedented threat to life. So he challenged his team to do the impossible: come up with billions of doses of a Covid-19 vaccine in the next nine months (as he later detailed).[15] At the time developing a new drug took an average eight years, and Pfizer's capacity for producing doses of such a drug was topped at 2 million. But in March of that year a spike in cases—and so in deaths—was predicted by winter, when people once again gathered indoors. So Dr. Bourla posed an impossible challenge: develop a vaccine for Covid-19 in nine months, and create billions of doses. That was the "moonshot."

In posing this challenge Dr. Bourla invoked the company's purpose, to discover biomedical breakthroughs that would improve people's lives. So inspired, the teams at Pfizer, in cooperation with Biogen, did the impossible: they found a new, quicker way to develop the vaccine, and met those unlikely time and number goals.

A leader can either squelch inspiring feelings or promote them, in many ways. Take an everyday event, meetings. "When executives open meetings with financials, they turn people off. Of course the numbers are important, but if that's what you do to set the mood for the meeting, that mood is now anxiety-driven," our Consortium colleague Richard Boyatzis points out.

On the other hand, he knows CEOs of health care companies who open meetings by having staff tell about patients they've helped. "That makes everyone feel, *My job isn't to make budget. It's to heal people.* And that makes them feel pride in what they do."

Likewise, at another health care association during the pandemic the top echelons were debating whether they should endorse Covid vaccinations for the general public. Their CEO reminded the group that "we are healers. Our duty is to the health of the public. The more vaccinations, the more healthy the community."

What does it take to inspire others? You don't need to rouse thousands to action; the scope of our impact may be more mundane, limited to family, friends, associates. But the path to being able to inspire—whether a few or multitudes—starts in the same place.

First you need to feel inspired yourself. Visionaries give voice to a mission they wholeheartedly believe in. This gives conviction to their words, so they naturally express that mission from the heart to the heart—that is, in a bull's-eye way that hits home with their audience. This, of course, draws on both self-awareness and empathy, tuning in to other people. When someone feels deeply moved and can articulate that feeling in ways that resonate with listeners they create a positive emotional field.

Inspiration can be indirect, rather than a pep talk. Aaron, the CEO of a construction company, had a town hall meeting with all of his employees each month. One month he began by telling them that he had met with a group of workers at their job site in lower Manhattan when their shift started at 6 a.m. He went on to tell the assembled group how proud and inspired he was. He said, "These people are out there at six in the morning every day. And they don't live in New York. And what really impressed me was, we were sitting around the table talking about what they were going to do for the day, sloshing around in the mud. And there was just so much enthusiasm!"[16]

Aaron later reported he got "tremendous feedback" the next day from several of the employees who heard him tell that story.

Conflict Management

Delores had just become the new director of training for a large, international hotel chain. It didn't take her long to discover that the training program needed to be updated so that the offerings were linked to the company's business strategy. Her biggest challenge was influencing Paul, the head of commercial business, who was second only to the CEO.

The complication: Paul was also competitive with Delores's boss, who told her to ignore Paul, work around him, and go ahead with her plans. But Delores believed that without Paul's support, she would not succeed.

So Delores put the time and effort into developing a strong working relationship with Paul to find out where his resistance and passions were. She discovered Paul was revenue-focused, very driven by the numbers. So initially she tried to show him that she understood what was important to him, to get him to see she understood the importance of numbers, too.

Once Delores had developed a good relationship with Paul, she began to propose some of the changes she had in mind. As she listened carefully to his reactions, Delores also was careful to give him the right to opt out of any option they might try. That made Paul feel more comfortable about trying something new. Just to be sure Paul was on board, Delores waited to change the training in Paul's area until she and her team had shown its soundness with most of the other areas in the company.

The plan worked; Paul became a strong supporter of the new training. Delores's approach to Paul illustrates the very best kind of conflict management: form a strong relationship, empathize with anyone who poses a potential challenge, and avoid the conflict in the first place.

"If you're a leader or a manager," a CEO tells us, "it's crucial to identify conflicts early on, before they explode and make the emotional environment more toxic." The same holds, of course, for husbands and wives, parents, friends—any relationship.

One of the first moves to heal conflicts, that CEO adds, comes when you help both sides see what they agree on before you explore their differences. For instance, his chief information officer liked an "agile" budget style, which means flexibility in solving challenges as they emerge and using feedback to reallocate resources on the spot so as to improve performance.

His chief financial officer, in contrast, strongly favored a more traditional, fixed fiscal planning method where the board settles on a budget and the CFO manages spending accordingly. The two were at loggerheads. But the CEO valued each of them and wanted to make peace.

He started by reminding them both why their organization existed—as a health care system, the fundamental mission was to heal. Each of them, in their own way, was aiding that mission. The CEO pointed out that having budgetary discipline helped ensure they could accomplish that mission while agility was called for at times—and from this perspective their differences were minor.

"I wanted them to see they have much more in common instead of wasting time attacking each other," the CEO explained. He saw their shared sense of mission as a road to resolving the conflict.

In the end the CFO came around to agreeing with the usefulness for mission effectiveness of agility in budgeting, and adopted that method.

Conflicts are inevitable in any group, from a couple or family, to neighborhoods and communities, to a mom-and-pop business on up to the largest corporation. How we handle those disagreements begins with how well we manage ourselves.

At a town meeting on Martha's Vineyard a group of fifth graders were urging a ban on single-use plastic bottles—this on a summer resort island where one of the biggest-selling items on those hot days happens to be water bottled in single-use plastic. So there was heated opposition to the young people urging a bylaw that would ban plastic water bottles, particularly from business owners, for whom selling bottled water represented a healthy profit margin. One store owner was adamant, insisting that water in plastic bottles was a major source of income for him. He was yelling at the kids.

One of them recalled, "I kept reminding myself that he wants me to get mad and yell back at him. But I stayed calm, and listened to find points we agreed on. Then I kept presenting him with new facts."

Those facts included that the store's distributor offered alternative products, like water in more easily recycled milk-carton-style packaging. The store owner changed his mind and ended up supporting the ban on plastic water bottles.

That fifth grader displayed remarkable conflict management skills, which in turn require a host of emotional intelligence abilities: self-awareness, to monitor your own emotions; emotional balance, to let you stay calm and manage your own reactivity; empathy, to listen well to the other person and find points of agreement.

These EI skills allow for *presence*: those fifth graders did not get angry but rather absorbed the energy of being yelled at without getting triggered themselves. They could listen carefully to find points of agreement, and so stay clear enough to marshal the facts that might sway their opponents.

Emotional balance—that ability to manage your own emotions—offers an essential step in managing conflict. In a difficult conversation you may find yourself talking with someone in tears, or may find yourself consumed by anger. In either case, keeping your cool so you can listen, think, and respond well requires you handle your own emotional reactivity.

Staying calm in conflict—a fruit of strong cognitive control—lets you remain clearheaded so you can recall key facts and counterpoints. Also, as the Harvard Negotiation Project famously urges, the smoothest pathway to resolution lies in finding a "win-win" compromise, one that lets both parties feel well enough about the agreement that they can go along with it. This might mean, for instance, drawing on the Inspire competence to articulate a higher principle that you can both agree on.

A more strategic look at handling differences of opinion in the workplace encourages a mindset that sees disagreements—for example, over budget priorities, marketing plans, allotting credit—as both inevitable from time to time and an opportunity rather than a setback.[17] This mindset sees such disagreements as chances to get better at our work.

For instance, in arguing with a workmate about a decision, both of you will need to explain why your approach makes sense, assess pros and cons—and perhaps arrive at a creative solution.

There's another benefit, if you apply self-awareness during this encounter: you will learn about yourself—what matters to you, your preferences about how to work, what some of your triggers might be. Then there are the benefits for your relationship with the person you disagree with. You can learn similar insights about that person from your conflict—what matters to them, how they like to work, what *their* triggers might be. If you can resolve your differences in a positive way, going through that process can actually bring you closer to the other person.

Cary met with surgery residents who complained that post-Covid their hospital had combined two units, firing some of the staff. This money-saving reorganization—so common in business—upped the burdens on the remaining staff, who now had to handle the same number of patients with fewer people, plus two groups were thrown together who had their own way of working. They wondered what they could say or do to remedy the situation.

Cary suggested that first they be open about their feelings with each other, and then meet with their teams about the dilemma, starting with their own feelings, and listening to how their team members feel while restraining their surgeons' "fix-it" impulse to impose a solution. Only then would they talk about their thoughts on how to solve the problem.

This called on two key EI abilities: managing one's own feelings, and empathizing with the feelings of others. Inner preparation for an anticipated bout of difference can help greatly. You can reframe what's about to happen from nervously seeing your encounter as a he said/she said match, to instead thinking about how you might be able to help the other person—or yourself—do a better job. This might mean, too, seeing the other person's point of view as something you might learn from—why, for instance, is that person arguing for this position?

Then there's the preparation for the actual encounter: considering what you want to achieve, thinking about the difference between what you say and what the other person hears, considering how you might respond to different ways that person might react. In short, conflicts can be opportunities to learn, to strengthen a relationship, and a leadership skill that can be honed.

Empathy always helps. Take a group of administrators in a school for children with special needs who had been having problems working together. With Cary's help, they set aside a day for a retreat. During the retreat, several members complained that Dick, the school's misbehavior management expert, was "never available" when the teachers needed his help with a child who was having a "meltdown." Dick was defensive, and the discussion became increasingly heated.

Cary then suggested the group brainstorm all the things they could think of that might prevent Dick from coming to help when there was a crisis in the classroom. That helped the group *join* with Dick rather than argue with him. The group and Dick together identified all of the teachers' needs and concerns in those situations. The group then worked together to identify ways in which they could deal with those problems when Dick wasn't around, and Dick could arrange his activities so that he would be more available when needed. The exercise helped the team avoid open conflict and confront the problem in a constructive way: supporting one of their members rather than attacking him.

Each of the EI relationship competencies offers ways to reinforce and strengthen our connections to those who matter most to us, whether in our private life or at work. Influence itself demands a strong relationship, one with high trust. Inspiring others means first attuning to what we find most meaningful, and using empathy to best articulate that moving purpose in ways that will resonate. Both coaching and resolving conflicts depend on an underlying connection that's strong enough to manage bobbles. Having relationships that flourish is a sign that you are in the optimal zone.

WHEN WE FOUNDED THE CONSORTIUM FOR RESEARCH ON EMO-tional Intelligence in Organizations decades ago, there was little or no hard data to show that EI mattered for success. The crucial role of EI in workplace performance was just a strong hunch when Dan wrote his book *Emotional Intelligence*. Now, decades later, that data is convincing: These EI strengths matter greatly for personal success and for the effectiveness of organizations of all kinds, from churches and schools, to nonprofits and governments, to businesses and corporations of every size. The EI advantage, the findings confirm, matters for leaders, for teams, and for business units as a whole—as we'll see in Part III.

PART III

Emotional Intelligence at Work

9

The Many Names for Emotional Intelligence

Mel supervised apartment complexes, a job he loved—although it could be very stressful. One day a fire broke out in one of them, a crazed renter took a baseball bat to the sprinklers of another, and at still another building a drive-by shooting left a resident paralyzed.

Mel did the best he could, personally visiting each of the buildings to help folks recover from the various crises. Addressing each issue required the timely filing of insurance claims, contracting for repairs, and dozens of other steps. But Mel figured out that something else was needed. His site people were traumatized; in addition to focusing on getting an enormous amount of work done, he had to attend to their emotional needs.

And so, despite the pressure to get a great deal done, he gave his teams extra time off. In the end, it led to better performance.

Mel's empathic concern was an expression of the firm's core operating principle, "Excellence with kindness."

The competencies of emotional intelligence—and so the active ingredients in optimal performance—go under differing names from place to place. Nevertheless, the fundamentals of EI matter everywhere.

Self-awareness, for example, helps us attune to our sense of purpose and makes possible managing our emotions; emotional balance and the other self-management strengths let us stay agile in response to changing challenges, be upbeat and resilient despite setbacks, and keep our goals in mind despite the daily distracting wildfires.

By the same token, empathy offers a foundation for must-haves, like the abilities to influence and inspire, to coach people so they enhance their own skill set, to surface and resolve differences, and to be a great team member. But as we'll see, the labels used for these abilities vary greatly from organization to organization. Every company (and every family, for that matter) represents a unique culture, which includes its particular ways of referring to the EI skill set. But there's surprisingly wide agreement that everyone needs emotional intelligence.

While there are countless models and names for different aspects of the emotional intelligence universe, you can think of all of these as loosely looking through different lenses at "soft skills," a vague term that contrasts this area of abilities with "hard skills" like computer coding, which draw on our cognitive abilities but are indifferent to emotions. But soft skills are in increasing demand as companies look to their future and the strengths they will need in their people.

For instance, research on nearly 5,000 job descriptions for C suite executives tracked these "help wanted" postings over almost two decades since the turn of the century.[1] The trend was strong: soft skills—emotional intelligence being the core—are steadily increasing as what companies want in their top leaders. In contrast, hard skills are on the decline in what companies seek in their top-level hires.

Job descriptions for high-level leaders naming strengths in soft skills increased almost 30 percent, while those specifying hard skills like financial and logistic expertise dropped by 40 percent. The trend continues. Top leaders, the report in the *Harvard Business Review* concludes, need to be "good with people," not just with numbers.

While hard skills like finance and operations matter, too, the new markers of outstanding performance for executives are mainly in the emotional intelligence domain: self-awareness, empathy (for example, sensing what others are thinking and feeling), social skills like listening deeply and communicating effectively, and working well with many different kinds of people.

These emotional intelligence abilities are sought in heads of HR, finance, marketing, and the chief information officer—and, of course, the CEO. As the *HBR* article explains: "Today firms need to hire executives who are able to motivate diverse, technologically savvy, and global workforces; who can play the role of corporate statesperson, dealing effectively with constituents ranging from sovereign governments to influential NGOs; and who can rapidly and effectively apply their skills in a new company."[2]

It's not just the C-suite—the competencies of emotional intelligence are becoming more vital for everyone, as that same article notes: more and more jobs at every level require "highly developed social skills." What's more, such jobs are growing at a rate faster than the labor market generally.

Emotional Intelligence by Other Names

When the Conference Board did a global survey among its many corporate members of what strengths executives were being coached to develop, the top five categories were all parts of emotional intelligence (way ahead, for example, of strategic thinking and business acumen).[3] But these aspects of emotional intelligence went under other rubrics, including "leading teams and people development," "executive presence and influencing skills," "relationship management," and "coping with and leading change." And, oh yes, "emotional intelligence" itself (though it's unclear what was meant by the term).

What's striking here: the naming of several emotional intelligence abilities as though they were unrelated to what the survey calls "emotional intelligence." This highlights the difficulty of pinpointing an organization's degree of interest in having its leaders cultivate this skill set. The idea that emotional intelligence is the heart of effective leadership has become so widespread that the term itself is both everywhere and nowhere—at least by that name.

The penetration of emotional intelligence into a company's culture can be subtle. Companies often use their own terms when they refer to emotional intelligence or its competencies, so it can take translation to spot EI. The elements of EI may have been baked into the culture at many organizations without their members noticing. We see this as a sign of the maturation of the emotional intelligence concept: that it has become so widely accepted that its value has become taken for granted (like, for example, the "balanced scorecard"). When executives hear the term "emotional intelligence" or its slang "EQ," the typical response is "Of course," not "What's that?"

When the term "emotional intelligence" gets absorbed into the language and DNA of the company, even disappearing in the terms used, the concept can still be powerful in people's behavior and as part of the culture.

At a construction firm, for instance, these norms have become deeply embedded though the term "emotional intelligence" is rarely used. But their CEO doesn't see this as a problem; as she told us, "Emotional intelligence is not a thing; it's a behavior that is used to achieve business goals."

Another example: a global organizational consulting firm with a large human resources consultancy uses the term "success factors" for its list of competencies, which overlaps greatly with emotional intelligence. The competencies in the success factors list have been dispersed widely to corporations around the world, with name changes to fit the particularities of company culture.

Or take another example, a description of what's essential for "productive human action" and "the underlying drivers of real productivity" both "within us and between us": "a calmer, more open and undistracted mind, greater self-awareness, and an enhanced capacity for self-transformation—not to mention disciplined passions and stronger human relationships."[4] It doesn't take much imagination to read that as emotional intelligence in disguise—self-awareness, self-management, empathy, and relationship skills.

Some other terms for emotional intelligence strengths can be found in the language of companies like Google, Merck, Citibank, and Cummins. These include "executive presence," which refers to empathy in the sense of paying full attention to the person you are with; "listen to customers," another application of empathy; and "leadership charisma," the ability to move people to give their best by reminding them of a shared mission or purpose. There's also "being a good coach" and "developing your people," helping others develop further strengths in emotional intelligence. "Being collaborative," or teamwork, means working with others toward a common goal. As we've seen, all of these are aspects of emotional intelligence.

That article in *Harvard Business Review* highlighted several examples of what's meant by "soft skills":

- "Social skills," a range of interpersonal abilities
- "Theory of mind," the ability to infer how other people think—a variety of cognitive empathy
- Listening and communicating well—also aspects of empathy
- The ability to work well with a diverse range of people—again, a function of empathy
- Self-awareness, which research has found offers a foundation for developing other emotional intelligence strengths, like self-management
- Managing conflict, itself an EI competence
- Effective response to unexpected events, or adaptability

Again, all of these skills fall within the EI map.

Emotional intelligence will matter more for a company's success, some argue, even in businesses where information-processing technologies are spreading automation. The reason: "When every major competitor in a market leverages the same suite of tools, leaders need to distinguish themselves through superior management of the people who use those tools. That requires top-notch communicators in every regard, able both to devise the right messages and to deliver them with empathy."[5]

Add to that trends toward diversity and inclusion and the way social media have spotlighted high-level executives, making them public figures, and the argument for better EI becomes even more persuasive. The hybrid workplace weakens interpersonal ties. Consider, too, how an increasing number of extreme weather events due to climate change will not only hamper our cognitive abilities but also add to the stresses on all of us. Then there's the intensifying velocity of change. These trends alone argue for the need to better manage our turbulent feelings with emotional intelligence.

How EI Matters for Each of Us

Yolanda was devastated. Her boss had told her point-blank, "Look! I'm your boss. You better get it. And if you can't, maybe you don't really belong here. Are you sure you want to be here?"

Yolanda and her boss could not get along, but this was the climax of their bad chemistry. The rupture had hurt Yolanda's work performance and even her sense of well-being: she spent too much time trying to read her boss, let alone take care of her own needs. Yolanda, desperate, tried to figure out how to improve their relationship, but, as she put it, her boss was "very hard to read."

But Yolanda persisted. Her first challenge was managing her own emotions—particularly the panic she felt. Her boss's condemnation sent her into a spiral of catastrophizing: her mind readily went from "she disapproves" to "I'm going to lose my job." So her first challenge was spotting those dire thoughts and finding a way to calm down.

Somehow she managed to find a calm and clear perspective on what had seemed a catastrophe. She then turned her focus from her own panicked reaction to trying to understand her boss—from a self-focus to empathy. Gradually she got better at figuring out how her boss was feeling and what her boss wanted. "What I learned to do was to ask more questions in a really respectful way and try to get what her thinking was."

Yolanda's concerted effort at empathy worked. The relationship improved. Once Yolanda was able to better manage her relationship with her boss, she stopped worrying so much and instead found ways to anticipate what her boss was wanting from her. They ended up getting along extremely well; Yolanda flourished in her role. Her performance was noted at higher levels in the company—and Yolanda eventually rose to become a senior executive.

The challenge of working day in and day out with someone we find difficult represents but one of myriad troubles we might encounter at work. So many of these problems can be resolved by better handling ourselves and those we work with. That's a major reason our emotional intelligence—the ability to accurately perceive, understand, and manage our own emotions and those of others—can help us to become better performers at work, as well as getting into our optimal state.

One of the widespread confusions about just what the ingredients of an optimal state might be comes down to putting too much emphasis on cognitive strengths and too little on emotional savvy. As we've shown, it's getting in a better emotional state that maximizes our cognitive ability. But that's not always apparent.

The Big Mistake About IQ

A Silicon Valley biotech outfit had a problem that paradoxically stemmed from what they called their "culture of genius," where winning the game at work meant the smarter you are the better you'll do. But the company found that this I'm-the-smartest game was breeding a decidedly unhelpful sea of jealousy and competitiveness rather than trust and cooperation. So they invited Dan to tell their very top executives that emotional intelligence matters, too, not just having a high IQ.

Dan told them of course it's an advantage to be smart—but you also need to be motivated, empathize, work on a team well, inspire those you lead, and help them develop further strengths in leadership. All of those abilities reflect your emotional intelligence.

That's a message Dan has often brought into a company to deliver, particularly in sectors like tech itself, engineering, biotech, finance, and the like where being the smartest person in the room matters greatly—at least in the operative belief systems of folks in those sectors. So, for example, a global cell phone maker asked Dan to talk to several hundred of their engineers who believed that all that mattered is their IQ.

The standard view of how IQ matters assumes that what makes you successful in school and academics is all you need for success in your career. A more nuanced understanding recognizes that over the total course of your career *both* IQ (and other cognitive abilities) and emotional intelligence and other such "noncognitive" abilities will matter, though in disparate ways at various points over a career.

Of course, excellence takes a requisite degree of cognitive smarts, whether particular tech adeptness, business expertise, or sheer IQ. But emotional intelligence adds power to each of these—for instance, in being able to sway people to your point of view, or, even better, inspire them to give greater effort for a purpose that has meaning for them.

While both IQ and emotional intelligence matter in your career, they matter differently. IQ has its strongest benefit during our school years, but over the course of a career IQ's predictive power for success wanes as emotional intelligence matters more.

Doing well in school is no guarantee you will excel in your career.[6] The correlation between your college grades, for example, and how you perform on the job is quite modest in someone's first year at work, and dwindles to become trivial as you progress.[7] When high school seniors were interviewed—and tested for IQ—then followed up when they were thirty-five and again at fifty-three, economists at Harvard and MIT found that IQ had been overrated as a force in achievement later in life.[8]

Of course, your cognitive abilities matter—to a point. An IQ of 100 is, by definition, average. It takes an IQ about one standard deviation above the norm—around an IQ of 114 or 115—to get a graduate degree like an MBA. And in general there's no doubt that your IQ largely determines how well you can do in school, what colleges and graduate programs you might get into, and the level of cognitive complexity you can handle, which in turn can help you get into a given job/role.

But once you are in that job, there's a floor effect: everyone else is about as smart as you are. EI makes the larger difference. The interplay between cognitive talents and emotional intelligence can be thought of this way: writing software code represents a purely cognitive ability, while being a successful member of a team writing code means your success depends on your self-management and relationship strengths; being an effective accountant demands cognitive strengths, while handling your clients effectively demands empathy; being a competent physician, dentist, nurse, or other health care professional depends on your cognitive smarts—but connecting well with your patients so that they will comply with what you need them to do requires additional emotional intelligence.

Textbooks in management education typically devote about twice as much space to emotional intelligence as they do to IQ, one perplexed—actually, indignant—group of academic authors noted. They protested that IQ's ability to predict outstanding performance has been well established by countless studies, while that is far less true for emotional intelligence. So, they imply, shouldn't the reverse proportion of IQ versus EQ coverage be better?

A widely cited finding suggests that a high IQ predicts that you will perform well on your job. But a careful look at that data suggests this may not really be true—that there is much room for other factors (including emotional intelligence) to be at play.[9]

Both IQ and emotional intelligence matter in your career, but each makes more difference at certain points. IQ has its strongest benefit during our school years, and your IQ will be far and away the best predictor of how well you do in school. But over the course of your career IQ's predictive power for success wanes.

Why? Because the smartest person in the room can be an interpersonal idiot. Star performers in the workplace have particular strengths in emotional intelligence. While our cognitive abilities matter to a great extent, whatever such talent we may have gets amplified by our EI. So where emotional intelligence might have once been seen as "nice to have," now this skill set has emerged as an essential booster of any expertise we might bring to the table.

The state-of-the-art measure of the emotional intelligence competencies is the Emotional and Social Competence Inventory, or ESCI, a 360-degree assessment of a person's personal and interpersonal skills. The ESCI measures a dozen of the specific EI competencies that typify high-performing leaders (we unpacked each of these competencies in Part II).

It's a "360-degree" measure, meaning each person chooses ten or so raters who know them well, and whose opinions they respect; the raters are anonymous, and so can be frank in their assessment. This view through others' eyes overcomes a bias in self-awareness: people can be poor at judging themselves where they have blind spots in their own skill set. The "360" means you are seen from many angles. The averages of all these ratings give the target person a profile of their strengths and limitations on the key EI competencies—a baseline that ideally they can use to track their progress by taking the ESCI again after they have gone through an EI training or coaching.

By now the ESCI has had extensive use, with more than 1.3 million independent raters of the target person, in almost ten thousand different organizations worldwide. In one analysis of all that data, of 155,000 leaders who had gone through the ESCI evaluations only 22 percent showed strengths in EI—that is, in 9 or more of 12 competencies—as rated by those who work with them. About 4 in 10 leaders had paltry strengths in the EI competencies.[10]

This EI gap matters more than ever. These times are creating a new array of challenges for business, where realities and demands change constantly, placing an ever-greater value on adaptability. The need to communicate effectively within an organization and to its stakeholders means a greater importance on reading emotions in the room and in the world at large. Crises seem never-ending, and so people are placing ever more value on steadiness and resilience in leaders—that is, on emotional balance—as well as empathy and heart. These, as we've seen, are signs of emotional intelligence.

Some key points: the competencies of emotional intelligence are widespread in companies but can be hard to spot because they have been renamed in keeping with the organization's culture. Such "soft skills" are in increasing demand, as seen in the specific talents companies are seeking in their new hires. Emotional intelligence differs from IQ and other such cognitive skills. But those abilities become more effective if a person adds emotional intelligence, and data suggest many executives may have a gap when it comes to their EI.

Yet as we'll see, the EI advantage marks outstanding leaders, star teams, and even entire business units.

10

Leading with Emotional Intelligence

The company, an engineering firm, had once thrived but it had fallen on hard times, leading to layoffs and all the anxieties those bring. The CEO had weekly meetings with her top leadership team and each week the financial reports were bleak. Then one week the CFO gave a more positive report, one that showed things were looking up. Yet the C-suite group barely noticed—when that report ended, they were ready to move on to the next item on the agenda.

But the CEO noticed she now felt less anxious—she was even more optimistic after hearing that more upbeat report. Sharing her better mood with her leadership team, she said, "Wait a second. This was a great report! Things are looking up. Let's stop for a couple of minutes and talk about all the good things we've been doing to help things turn around."

So they did. As they talked about the ways they might have contributed to the improvements these top executives began to feel good again; some even smiled. The atmosphere in the room continued to be upbeat during the rest of the meeting. When it ended and these executives left the conference room, their direct reports saw that their leaders looked happier and more relaxed. Those good feelings spread.

The CEO had tuned in to her own feelings and spotlighted what made her feel better to the whole group. Her use of emotional intelligence in that moment had a positive impact on the emotional atmosphere in the top management team, and those good feelings rippled through the company. Being open about one's feelings builds authenticity, which in turn strengthens trust in relationships.

When an organization's leaders are skilled at managing their own emotions and those in their relationships, the entire outfit and its people benefit, seeing better performance in every sense. When we began the Consortium more than twenty-five years ago there was sparse evidence for this, but by now there is substantial data, drawn from studies of hundreds of organizations, documenting a wide range of benefits, when leaders, teams, and employees embody the ingredients of high performance—a collective reflection of the optimal state. These benefits, as we saw in Chapter 2, include: higher job satisfaction and lower turnover, better engagement and morale, more "organizational good citizenship," and hard numbers for increased profit and growth.

All this starts at the top, with the leader. It feels liberating to work for an emotionally intelligent leader; our optimal zone seems more attainable. People have more good days.

EI: The Essential Leadership Skill

When Eric Adams was elected mayor of New York City in 2021, he repeatedly said that he wanted leaders in his administration to be "emotionally intelligent."

In fact, he said it was the "No. 1 criteria" for selecting his top officials. "Don't tell me about your Ivy League degrees. Don't tell me about where you went to school and how important you think you are. Don't tell me about what you are going to do because of your philosophical theories. . . . I don't want to hear about your academic intelligence. I want to know about your emotional intelligence."[1]

When the Walt Disney Company fired its CEO Bob Chapek in 2022 and replaced him with the previous CEO, Bob Iger, one reason given was a lapse in Chapek's people skills. According to a *New York Times* report, Chapek seems to have had a lack of empathy and emotional intelligence, "which resulted in an inability to communicate with or relate to Hollywood's creative community."[2]

The need for EI in leaders became glaringly clear several years ago when our Consortium colleague Claudio Fernández-Aráoz, then–head of research for a global executive research firm, asked a radical question: Why would executives who seemed so apt for a job fail once they got it? Though most of the candidates his firm found to fill C-suite jobs succeeded, a few were fired. When he analyzed these firings, it turned out that around the world—Japan, Germany, the Americas—the pattern was the same: the executive had been hired for hard skill credentials like business expertise—but fired for a soft skills lapse in emotional intelligence, like blowing up in anger at a direct report.

Claudio's hunch has morphed into standard operating procedure in organizations worldwide. As we note in Chapter 9, postings for C-suite positions increasingly list "soft skills" rather than hard ones as what they are looking for in new hires.

When we first created the website for the Consortium for Research on Emotional Intelligence in Organizations (CREIO), the topic that consistently attracted the most visits was "The Business Case for Emotional Intelligence." It's no wonder. Whether it's a small business, a large corporation, or a nonprofit that doesn't usually think in terms of a "bottom line," performance is the key. By now the hard evidence confirms that emotionally intelligent leaders are more effective: their employees perform better and feel better at work, and their organizations excel.

Take a study of executives in a large public service organization.[3] The executives completed an EI test, and their managers rated them on how well they "achieved business outputs during the financial year." The executives' bosses and subordinates also rated the executives on their leadership abilities. Result: the most emotionally intelligent leaders were also the most effective.

What's more, the EI advantage held over and above the executive's personality (for example, having an outgoing personal style did not matter as much). Even being smart—having a high IQ—did not make a leader as effective as having a higher EI.

Our colleague Richard Boyatzis and his team from Case Western Reserve University looked at senior executives in a financial management firm who oversaw financial advisors and their managers.[4] They asked each divisional executive's peers and subordinates to rate the executive on multiple dimensions of emotional intelligence. Then they looked at how many new financial advisors were recruited by each executive during the last three years—a key performance indicator of executive effectiveness used by the company.

Higher EI in a leader meant more financial advisors he or she recruited. Again a leader's general mental ability and profile on a personality test failed to predict their performance. Only emotional intelligence made a difference.

EI seems to matter for leaders everywhere—even parish priests.[5] The Boyatzis group note that "[p]astoral leaders of parishes have an effect on people's lives and communities. . . . From sermons and fund-raising to the confessional, they must use emotional intelligence to achieve both worldly and sacred goals. . . ."

The findings: the more highly parish priests were rated on their emotional and social competencies, the more satisfied their parishioners.

The edge gained by a high-EI leader seems to apply at every level, from senior executives to blue-collar workers. For instance, in a study of workers in a copper refinery, their supervisor's emotional intelligence accounted for the greater part of differences in how they performed.[6] Consider all of the many factors that might influence a worker's performance; they range from their years of experience on that job, to their age, education level, IQ, and personality traits like conscientiousness and agreeableness. Oh, and add sheer luck to the mix. But all these factors accounted for only about 30 percent of the difference in performance among these workers. Their boss's degree of emotional intelligence was linked to 70 percent of the workers' performance. It comes down to the importance for a worker of their relationship with his or her boss. If you hate your boss, your ability to do your job suffers; if you love your boss, it can soar.

Studies like these were included in a meta-analysis by a multi-university group, including our Consortium colleague Ronald Humphrey, that pooled results from a broad range of leaders in many different kinds of organizations.[7] Their analysis included twelve different studies with a total of 2,764 participants. Their results showed that the higher a leader's EI, the better their workers performed—it accounted for 25 percent of the advantage.

Think of all the factors that might affect someone's workplace performance: they range from on-the-job experience, to age, education, IQ, traits like persistence, and beyond. So statisticians would say that having EI account for 25 percent represents a surprisingly large impact. Data from regions as varied as Asia, South America, and Europe reveals this holds in cultures around the world.

Another meta-analysis focused on more than 65,000 entrepreneurs in all kinds of businesses. It looked at hard-nosed outcomes like financial success, firm growth, and firm size, as well as subjective success. But being a successful entrepreneur depends to a great extent on how that person manages their own emotions and leverages their relationships. Again entrepreneurs with higher EI had better outcomes. Even more striking: comparing the relative importance of emotional intelligence and cognitive intelligence, they found that EI's impact was more than twice as high as IQ.[8]

Beyond the Bottom Line

Jessica Andrews, a nursing administrator in a county health department, got into a bitter conflict with the local sheriff over the way her nurses who worked at the jail were treated. Without hesitation, her boss defended her, confronting the sheriff directly and getting him to admit that he was in the wrong.[9] Jessica was one of those in Cary's study who did not burn out on her job; she remained satisfied and committed for her next decade in the same position—in large part due to the support that she had from her boss.

Contrast Jessica with another nurse administrator who said that she had never had her boss's support: "I felt after a while that I lost a lot of initiative and creativity, and I started feeling not very good about myself, which I think probably carried over into my work." Unfortunately, the second nurse's experience is more typical. A survey found that 75 percent of employees say the most stressful part of their job was pressure from their immediate boss.[10]

There's a powerful reason emotional intelligence in a leader matters for how well their workers perform: an employee's relationship with his or her boss is the best predictor of job satisfaction, which in turn is a strong predictor of overall life satisfaction.[11] Again a meta-analysis makes the case: lumping twenty studies with a total of 4,665 employees, a meta-analysis found those with more emotionally intelligent leaders were more satisfied with their jobs.[12]

But it goes beyond your relationship with just your boss—your workmates matter, too. Employees are more likely to go out of their way to help a colleague—that good organizational citizenship—when their bosses are more emotionally intelligent.[13]

Another indicator comes from turnover, particularly whether the best people quit. One study, which involved 260 workers at major companies such as Dell, Electronic Data Systems, Microsoft, and IBM, found that when the employees worked for an emotionally intelligent boss, they were less likely to look for a job elsewhere.[14] When the researchers looked more closely at what was going on, they found that the leaders created more challenging work tasks, more trust, better communication, and a greater feeling of belonging for their workers. All these improvements of the emotional climate made workers less likely to quit.

The notion that worker well-being was irrelevant—that employers' responsibility ended with a paycheck and safe working conditions— began to change decades ago. Today we know that how people feel at work is more important than ever. For instance, Microsoft's *Work Trends Index 2022 Report* found that workers are more likely than before the pandemic to view their health and well-being as more important than their work.[15]

At first researchers thought that employee burnout was due to per- sonality styles like perfectionism. Now it's clear that your relationship with your boss matters more. When leaders managed their own emotions and provided empathic support to others—like Jessica Andrews's boss pushing back with the sheriff—employees can withstand high levels of stress without burning out. As one executive told us, "Part of my job is to protect my people from the craziness higher up in the organization."

When employees in the tech division of a large medical facility completed a daily survey for two weeks asking about their current well-being, results showed that groups of employees with empathic managers experienced lower average levels of somatic complaints like headaches and upset stomachs. The employees with such physical complaints suffered more, as did their progress at work.[16]

When European researchers reviewed research on the impact of leadership style on employee well-being, they found that the stress on a leader lessened the support, consideration, and empowerment they showed those they led. Leadership styles reflecting emotional intelligence, in contrast, had a positive impact on the stress levels employees felt and on their emotional state.[17] For instance, a study of athletes and their coaches found that when emotional exhaustion was high in the coaches, it also was high in their athletes; such burned-out coaches tended to use a dictatorial style and so were less likely to use praise, empathy, and effective communication.[18] In a group of managers working for a food retailer during a period of organizational restructuring, the employees of managers who used a more supportive leadership style reported feeling less stress and being more satisfied with their job.[19]

Leaders and Emotional Labor

The head of a child protective services office woke up one morning to learn that a mother who had been one of their clients had murdered her child during the night and then killed herself. It was the most horrendous incident that he or any of his staff had ever encountered. As he was dressing to go into work, he focused on the most important task on hand, which was to set aside his own feelings for the next few hours and focus on helping the staff process their own.

This incident maps directly on one of the more onerous tasks of leadership. All too often a leader's duties involve projecting a hopeful outlook during discouraging times for a business, or carrying on with optimism even when he or she harbors doubts about a company's strategic course.

This inevitably requires a bit of acting, suppressing some feelings while projecting others to the world. Sociologists have long studied such workplace performance as "emotional labor": managing your own feelings to fulfill the expectations of a role at work. While this research has often focused on the emotional challenges facing frontline workers—for example, "service with a smile" even with rude customers—leadership, too, demands such managed feelings.

One reason leaders engage in emotional labor: feelings are contagious in a group, and all the more so from the leader to group members.[20] As the leader's mood grows more positive, so do the moods of members—and their performance improves. If the leader is in a foul mood, that negativity spreads through the team and their performance suffers. Behind this emotional spreading: it's only natural for people to place more importance on and pay more attention to the most powerful person in that group. This rule of thumb applies from the CEO and those in the C-suite down through any organization to teams and their leaders at the front lines.

These days, more than in the past, leaders are called on to perform emotional tasks like being sensitive to how work demands are impacting employees' mental and physical health, while keeping an eye on the bottom line. This demand for compassion and sensitivity applies not just to how they relate to those on their team, but also to how they relate to themselves. This emotional burden for leaders comes at a cost—their own increased risk of burnout or suffering poor health, let alone a hit to their own productivity. The demands of emotional labor may well play a hidden role in high turnover among leadership positions.

Leaders can be victims of a stereotype that they must be "strong," and so might be reluctant to reveal the side of themselves that harbors doubts, anxieties, or frustrations—any of which might make them look "weak." This may be all the truer for leaders who are women or people of color, who may be conscious of having to work harder than peers to get the same recognition, while also being role models for those in their own group.[21] Research finds that in some situations women and people of color are punished for expressing emotions while white males are not.[22]

But here's a complication: research finds that a leader willing to admit human foibles will also be more likely to notice and attend to the emotional needs of those they follow.[23] Being able to admit to one's own emotional limits makes others feel safe in surfacing their own.

The leadership requirement of emotional labor means being aware of your own emotions so as to be better able to manage them, as well as tuning in to the emotions of those around you and handling those relationships well. In short, this adds another argument for boosting emotional intelligence in leaders. This boost could well buffer leaders from the costs of emotional labor, which range from loneliness and cynicism to drops in their own performance—let alone health and emotional problems.

Take, for example, the burdens from suppressing leaders' own feelings and faking a brighter outlook that they may not feel themselves. Such internal suppression, psychology now recognizes, lessens a leader's ability for self-control, which can show up in lashing out at employees or rude comments. To handle the inner turmoil, some will turn to heavy drinking, or otherwise express their negativity at home when it actually originated at work.

Business schools do little or nothing to prepare MBAs for handling this emotional burden. Organizations, on the other hand, can intervene by creating a safe space for leaders where they can freely express their emotions—where it's "okay to be not okay." One experiment found that meeting regularly with leadership peers to air personal and professional troubles in a confidential setting not only relieved this emotional pressure, but increased the participants' emotional intelligence.[24] In general, helping leaders make gains in their emotional intelligence gives them a skill set to better deal with the challenge of emotional labor. Emotional intelligence matters the most among leaders whose positions require they handle well their own emotions and those of the people they work with.[25]

A *Harvard Business Review* article noting the increased demand on leaders for this kind of emotional labor urges organizations to help executives and managers handle their emotional world better.[26] We can only applaud the notion.

Leading During a Crisis

James was a senior vice president in a large health care insurance firm. At one point, one of the groups in his organization faced a particularly challenging time. The regular group leader had to take a medical leave while their business was undergoing intense regulatory scrutiny. James realized that "people were pretty well panicked" and that he had to be both "comforting and inspirational" to help them get through it.

James wanted to be close by to reassure and guide them through the crisis, but his regular office was located a mile or so away from where the group was based. So he temporarily moved his base of operation to a conference room at the group's location.

Beyond his reassuring physical presence, James also helped the group by managing his *own* feelings. He said, "I knew if I went in there panicked and overwhelmed, people would have been more panicked and feeling like, 'Oh my god, this guy's the boss's boss, and if he comes in and he can't help us, we're in a lot of trouble!' So I felt I had to demonstrate to them that it's not an ideal situation, but sometimes these things happen. And I think we're up to it."

He was right. The group managed to get through those difficult few weeks and successfully deal with the regulatory challenge.

The impact of a leader on his or her employees may matter most in a crisis. That's when a leader's emotional intelligence is really tested, as with James.[27]

Consider, for example, people's feelings during a major hospital restructuring in the Canadian province of Alberta that created massive disruptions.[28] The nurses, along with patients, bore the brunt. Researchers at the University of Alberta surveyed more than 6,000 registered nurses in acute care hospitals in the province.[29] Nurses working for leaders who used an emotionally intelligent style reported significantly less emotional exhaustion and psychosomatic symptoms and better emotional health.

In fact, those with emotionally intelligent leaders actually reported that their emotional health had *improved* during the past year, while nurses with more dissonant leadership reported their emotional health worsened during that same period. The nurses with more emotionally intelligent leaders also reported greater workgroup collaboration and teamwork with physicians, and more satisfaction with supervision and their jobs. Nurses with leaders who did not use emotional intelligence reported three times as many incidents of unmet patient care needs.

Then there are occupations where handling crises is the whole job. Take "incident team commanders," who head firefighter teams that fight the toughest wildfires in the United States. When Richard Boyatzis and his group compared outstanding commanders with average ones, they found that seven emotional and social competencies differentiated the two groups. The most significant ones were emotional balance and resilience, being able to adapt to difficult circumstances, to empathize with others, to serve as an effective coach/mentor, and to provide inspiring leadership.[30]

Leadership: It's All About Influence

Dorothy, the president of a small, nonprofit social services agency, was slated to speak at a meeting with potential volunteers that went on the day before she was to have surgery for breast cancer.

"It was the last thing I wanted to do, especially because I'm not that outgoing a person," she said later. "Yet as I spoke with them and began to talk about the families we serve and the needs of the clients we have, I could just see them nodding and saying things under their breath like,

'That's what it's all about' or 'That sounds great.' The same thing happens when I talk to the board."

Dorothy saw that such person-to-person meetings, especially with a moving story, got people more engaged. As she put it, "It's really important to share my enthusiasm, excitement, and sense of urgency with others. My energy and excitement perk up other people."

Such person-to-person influence is at the heart of strong leadership. This takes skill at using your own emotions to impact others. So, for example, feeling sad and expressing it can help leaders comfort those who have experienced a loss.[31]

As Carole Robin, who taught a popular course on interpersonal dynamics at the Stanford Business School noted, "There's a generation of leaders now—the ones that might be the really up-and-coming leaders of the future—who have discovered that actually it's almost impossible to really inspire people in the absence of feelings."[32]

While it can be helpful for leaders to express their feelings openly, they need to do so artfully. Norms in any workplace determine which emotions are "expressible," how strongly they should be expressed, and when. When leaders violate those norms, it can have adverse effects on their employees as well as on the leaders' effectiveness. Norms also affect *who* can express which emotions—for example, men who are leaders can "get away with" expressing their anger openly, while women may be adversely judged for the same thing.

Still, leaders feel their emotions whether they want to or not. Trying to suppress those emotions or avoid expressing them can harm a leader's credibility and influence. So, too, can a clumsy attempt to express an "appropriate" emotion that the leader does not actually feel. This is where EI is especially important, helping leaders express their feelings in a way that fits the setting's norms, and to do so naturally.

Take, for example, Aaron, the CEO of a large construction firm. He was the second in command when his predecessor suddenly collapsed and died from a heart attack during a major meeting. Aaron had been close to his boss, and he felt the loss keenly.

That night, he let the employees know that it was okay for them to feel as he did. He went to the hotel where the meeting had been and talked to the people there. Then he addressed the whole company: "My message was 'Forget about work today; this was our family who we lost, our friend. . . . If you truly love anyone in your family, I suggest you tell them today because none of us knows when our time will come.'" Those words, and the way Aaron expressed them, helped everyone.

Aaron was able to express his feelings very soon after the event. But some leaders may need to wait until they are more composed before they say what they feel. It's only human.

The Toxic Boss

The CEO of a large hospital that had a big staff burnout problem, and the hospital's HR department, had asked Cary to deliver a training program to help their managers.

When the CEO asked him what they had done in the last session, Cary said they talked about the importance of letting staff know how valued they were and how important their contributions were.

The CEO, appalled, replied, "I don't believe in that. Adults should work hard without being praised for it. They're getting paid to do that work. That should be all the reward they need."

After hearing the CEO say that, Cary better understood why the hospital had a big problem with staff burnout.

The negative impact of a toxic boss operates everywhere. A study of 693 players and 57 coaches in the National Basketball Association looked at coach style and player performance for two seasons. Coaches were rated on "abusive leadership" and aggression, and how well players performed was taken from hard measures like numbers of fouls and baskets scored. Having an abusive coach upped fouls and lowered scoring—even in later seasons.[33]

Employees recall more readily those times when a boss was rude or angry with them than when he was agreeable. That negativity bias in memory may be one reason the Harvard Business School study of good days found that negative events had a stronger impact than positive ones on how someone felt (and so, as we've seen, how well they can do their work). That argues for managers to lessen hassles for the people they manage, whenever they can.

Our brain seems wired to remember more strongly the things that go wrong in our life than the events that make us feel good—perhaps because of the evolutionary premium for survival in thinking over how to handle those emergencies or setbacks the next time they come our way.[34] As a result a child might remember more strongly the times a parent yelled at her than the loving moments they had together. Consider how we talk to our loved ones. When the kids frustrate us—or our partner or spouse does—do we yell at them out of frustration? The feelings we telegraph with our tone of voice can help or hurt the other person, adding to their stress or lessening it.

Since we pay great attention to what our boss does and says, that person has a great impact on how we feel. Many studies have confirmed what each of us knows in our heart: a rude, thoughtless, uncivil interaction with our boss has disastrous ripples in our emotional field. Bad bosses lower how committed we feel to what we do, how satisfied we are while doing it, and our overall mental state.[35]

By the same token, a nourishing boss—one who treats us with civility, respect, and politeness, for instance—increases our satisfaction with our work as well as our commitment to the organization and boosts our performance.[36]

What all this means is that managers need to be careful when providing criticism, because it will be much more strongly felt than praise. When a boss gives feedback, he or she may not realize that what they think is a mild reprimand may be perceived by an employee as a shout.

How Leaders Can Boost Their Emotional Intelligence

Karen, the district manager for a large industrial food services company, was aghast when one of their servers complained to the Occupational Health and Safety Administration (OSHA) that her company's practices were unsafe. Karen's first impulse: "wring her neck."

But instead she adopted an open-minded, inquiring mindset. First she determined that their practices were okay. Then she began to explore what might have made this server angry enough to lash out against the company. She talked to the employee's supervisor, observed the server at work, and then sat down with her.

Rather than angrily confronting the employee, she approached the session as a way to learn more about what was going on in the server's life. Though at first resistant, with Karen's empathic listening and gentle questioning, the server began to talk about her husband's cancer and the problems they were having with the health care he was receiving.

Karen was more than sympathetic; she helped her employee navigate the health care system. The server's stress and anger dissolved, and OSHA found no evidence for unhealthy practices.

That story emerged when Cary and his colleague Cornelia Roche asked veteran executive coaches, senior HR executives, and organizational psychologists to identify outstanding leaders who were especially skilled in using emotional intelligence.[37] Many of the leaders deployed the emotional intelligence competencies in similar ways.

One common tactic was simply considering how their own actions impacted other people emotionally—an act of both self-awareness and empathy. Take how Rita, the senior vice president for human resources in a large medical technology company, reacted when it became clear that the company was not going to make performance targets that senior management had set. In the past the company's top ranks would give themselves bonuses in spite of the poor performance, while lower-level employees would see their bonuses disappear.

But Rita realized that this would have a terrible emotional impact on the employees. Fortunately, she was able to convince the other senior managers and the board to exclude the top management group from the bonus pool and instead provide discretionary bonuses to those employees who earned it.

Consider how Rita used EI. From the start she was empathic, sensing how a bad decision would spread ripples of bad feeling through the tissue of the organization. While it's sometimes hard to tell how a given decision or action will impact other people, we can always tune in to ourselves to see how what others do feels to us.

One tactic for developing a keener radar for this: Think of a time when what someone else did made you feel bad. Ask yourself, what was it that gave you those bad feelings? Tone of voice? Body language? Words spoken or unspoken? What feelings resulted in you or others present? What did you do in response? Finally, if you could switch places with that person, what could you have done differently?

Now go through the same scenario with a real moment where someone made you feel good. That's the way you want to be.

Another Approach: Think Differently

The COO of a large steel company, whom we'll call Stanley, said that whenever an employee brought a particularly challenging problem to him and he began to feel his stress level go up, he reminded himself, "The world is a messy place. . . . Nine out of ten people who walk through my door have a problem. . . . It's usually too simple to think that all the problems are due to one person screwing up or that his screwing up is simply caused by incompetence or negligence. The world is usually just more complicated than that."

Stanley was changing his own perspective, a tactic many high-functioning leaders find effective. This self-management competence helps you regain your own emotional balance, so you can think more clearly and act more calmly.

Another example: when Rodney, the head of a large construction company, made a costly mistake, he would say to himself, "Okay. Don't beat yourself up. You're not going to get everything right."

Rodney would then remind himself that in his job, making decisions is like a batting average in baseball. "You don't need to get a hit every day. You're not going to get every one of them right. We make mistakes. . . ."

Still another helpful EI tactic for emotional self-management, a study of high-performing leaders found, was adopting an "inquiring mindset."*38* You can sharpen your ability for this via a simple mental exercise. Bring to mind a real dilemma, from work or your personal life, that's emotionally charged for you. Without editing what you write, just jot down a stream of consciousness that comes to mind about what you think might be going on. Consider what might be making the other person (or people) involved act that way. Then ask yourself, "Could I somehow be triggering them? If so, what might I be doing?" And then, "What else might be going on?"

The goal here is not to "solve" the problem, but simply to widen your perspective on it—to broaden your emotional awareness and understanding of the situation by considering different vantage points.

Put Yourself in Others' Shows

We all have our own private narratives, the dramas and scenarios that affirm our identities. These personal "shows" define who we think we are and how we wish to be seen. So being able to sense someone else's self-view marks a leader as having powerful empathy.

Much of a leader's emotional intelligence comes down to empathy. Amy, the director of a nursery school, often had tough conversations with parents about their children's misbehavior. Amy tries to remain empathic and nonjudgmental by thinking about her own experiences as the parent of a young child.

"I'm a mom," she said. "I can recall times when the preschool teacher called me about *my* daughter and the feeling *I* got." Putting herself in the parents' position helps Amy to understand how difficult it is for them to hear, especially when their child is the problem.

"Active listening" can help in these difficult moments. You can practice this skill with a learning partner, someone you know well and with whom you feel comfortable. Ask them to tell you about something at work or home that made them happy, sad, anxious, or angry. As they tell you about it, focus on what they are telling you.

To help you better understand, you can use prompts like:

- What's that like for you—tell me more.
- What was going on for you when that happened?
- What did you feel or think about that?
- What might someone else not know about this situation?
- What's your perspective on that?
- What else can you tell me?

After hearing the other person out, repeat back to them in your own words what you heard, asking them to tell you if you got it right or something's wrong in what you heard. Let them explain what you misunderstood or got right. Then just let the conversation flow naturally.

Here are some key points about EI for leaders. Having strengths in emotional intelligence—particularly in self-awareness and in empathy—enhances a leader's positive impact. Leaders who can be more open about their feelings are seen as more authentic, which builds trust in their relationships. Research finds that high-EI leadership predicts those who work for them will have greater job satisfaction, better performance, and feel more engaged. All of those help profit and growth.

On the other hand, toxic leaders—those low in EI—have poorer outcomes on all these metrics. Leadership means emotional labor, which can be taxing. But there are many ways to boost a leader's emotional intelligence, including becoming more emotionally resilient.

Bottom line: Emotionally intelligent leaders can have a huge impact on the well-being and performance of others, lifting them into their optimal zone. Leaders can enhance their impact further if they develop and nurture the emotional intelligence of others. Consider what this might mean for a team.

11

Emotionally Intelligent Teams

The Consortium for Research on Emotional Intelligence in Organizations (CREIO) began in 1996 as a group of nine people who came together every few months to learn more about the then-new concept of EI. They all had relevant areas of expertise, but they did not agree on everything. There was tension in the air, and the group's members were careful not to upset the uneasy peace.

Then progress stalled. Since the group was not accomplishing much, one member suggested that we take some time out to explore what was wrong. It was not an easy discussion, but in the end the group developed a set of interaction patterns—norms—that were designed to make the meetings more productive.

One of the norms was "Everyone, not just the chairperson, should help keep us on track if we get off, facilitate group input, and raise questions about our procedure." This could mean, for example, asking the group to clarify where it is going, offering summaries of the issues being discussed to make sure we have a shared understanding of them, and identifying areas where there are differences in understanding. Another norm was "Use good listening skills." Perhaps the most important one was that the group would review all the norms at the start of each meeting to remind themselves of how they should act.

From that point on, the group thrived, completing several research projects, books, and articles. Despite high entry standards, the Consortium has evolved into a network with more than one hundred members from all over the world.

The CREIO example displays a telling truth about teams. Even though the members had studied emotional competence for many years and consulted and coached others in how to manage and use those competencies, they could not achieve optimal performance until they confronted how they were working *together as a group*. The problem ultimately was not any individual in the group; it was their patterns of interaction. Once the team members developed new group norms—agreed-on guidelines—for interacting, a significant change for the better occurred.

While it can take many months of ongoing training and practice to increase an individual's EI, a team can become noticeably more emotionally intelligent in just one meeting through a shared awareness of how the members interact with one another and then changing the norms that govern those interactions. Of course the shift won't happen in just one meeting; there also needs to be ongoing awareness, feedback, and practice. Some members of the team may need additional help with the way they manage their own emotions and relate to others. But the change process can often occur more quickly and more powerfully with a focus on the team.

Never has the need for collaboration and teamwork been more critical. An HBR Pulse Survey found that 89 percent of business leaders prioritize collaboration and teamwork as "critical to their strategy for productivity and innovation."[1] When teams are performing at peak levels, the impact on an organization's bottom line can be enormous. A Gallup workplace report found that engaged teams are 14 percent to 18 percent more productive than low-engagement teams. The Gallup study also found that low-engagement teams experience turnover rates that are 18 percent to 43 percent higher than highly engaged teams.[2] And remember, costs to replace an employee can be far greater than that person's salary.

Other research has found that when teams are dysfunctional, the impact can be crippling. When Nichelle Carpenter and her colleagues at

Rutgers University examined dozens of studies, they found that teams with higher levels of counterproductive workplace behavior—like loafing, bullying, and lateness—displayed lower customer satisfaction and profit.[3]

Then there's the impact of the team leader, for better or worse. Research has found a strong link between the self-awareness of a team's leader with the overall emotional climate of the group.[4] Using the ESCI to evaluate the leader, data revealed that low self-awareness in the leader predicted a poor climate in the group he or she led. If your manager has little emotional self-awareness, odds are high that your team will do little to support your performance. Conversely, having a manager with excellent self-awareness means you are more likely to be in your optimal state more of the time.

What Makes a Great Team?

The software engineers at Google thought they knew what made a team great. As a Japanese saying has it, "All of us are smarter than any one of us." So put a bunch of really smart people in a room and they will develop brilliant products, right?

Sorry. That wasn't the case. After all, Google has long made a practice of hiring only the brightest. So to find what made some teams there great and others not so much, people at Google collected data from close to two hundred teams there. Some teams came from engineering and others from sales, and there was a mix of both high- and low-performing teams.[5]

The Google researchers collected data on every aspect of a team they and other researchers had thought of: who was on the teams, characteristics like tenure, level, and location, as well as personality traits such as introversion and conscientiousness. They also looked at the teams' group dynamics by asking whether team members agreed with statements like "I feel safe expressing divergent opinions to the team."

In the end, the most important factors had more to do with how the team worked together than with who was on the team. The most important factor "by far" was *psychological safety*. In other words, people on such teams felt safe to take risks without being seen by their teammates as disruptive or, even worse at Google, as ignorant or incompetent.

In a team with high psychological safety, teammates feel confident that no one on the team will embarrass or punish anyone else for admitting a mistake, asking a question, or offering a new idea.[6] Individuals on teams with higher psychological safety were better able to take advantage of diverse ideas members proposed. These psychologically safe teams brought in more revenue and were rated as effective "twice as often by executives."[7]

Google also found that clarity, another strong predictor of group effectiveness, seems to be related to psychological safety. Clarity matters because when people in a group are unclear about what's expected of them and what the group's goals are, they are less likely to feel safe.

IQ did not matter much; the average cognitive intelligence of team members or their previous experience were among the weakest predictors (of course there may have been a "floor effect" for IQ: Google prides itself on hiring high-IQ people). Members' personality traits also mattered little. What mattered most was what the leader did to help create psychological safety in the group.

The Sense of Belonging

Do you feel you belong on your team? Is it like family for you? These are key questions that suggest another doorway to that sense of psychological safety.

"Safety is wonderful, but people might still hold back," says Vanessa Druskat, a Consortium member who has studied and consulted with teams for years. "They don't want to step on others' toes. But even more importantly, they don't want to give away their best secrets. The higher you get up in the hierarchy, the more you have people who are holding on to information. It might be what makes them stellar, right? So, they might think, 'If I share this with the team, it's no longer mine.' And knowledge is power in the knowledge economy."

So the challenge, as Druskat sees it, is to figure out how to build such safety in a team that members won't withhold crucial information. That's where a sense of belonging comes in, as a way to build a climate of psychological safety. As she puts it, "Belonging opens you up." As team members begin to share more about their needs and emotions, the feeling of psychological safety increases, which leads to an even greater sense of belonging.

When members of a group have a sense of belonging, Druskat finds, they are more confident in voicing their views; they share ideas more freely and contribute more fully. The sense of belonging on a team lubricates the effective collaboration that every organization sees as a hallmark of its top-performing teams. What's more, that feeling of "I belong" makes people feel good about being a team member; they are more helpful to each other.

There are subtle signs of belonging that team members can attend to, and which tell who belongs and who does not. These, Druskat finds, often are nonverbal—moves that are not necessarily put into words. For instance, one of the most powerful such nonverbals comes when someone looks askance or frowns at us. When we feel someone disapproves of us, we easily assume that disapproval might be widespread, that we are seen as not belonging.

As we operate in any group we are unconsciously—and likely constantly—scanning for signs of approval (or the opposite), which we take as a gauge of the extent to which we belong. No matter how secure we may feel in ourselves, in a group reassurance comes from periodic signals that you matter, that you have worth and are a valued member.

Those signals might be as simple as everyone paying attention or taking notes while you speak, or someone agreeing with what you say. Lacking such reassurance, we keep our guard up; we might censor what we say, and hold back on taking risky positions. While you might assume that when people feel excluded they would be ingratiating, Druskat finds this sense of being left out might make people try to fit in at first, but eventually it leads to bad behavior: emotional outbursts, anger, interrupting, speaking too loudly. These are all signs, she sees, of the person wanting to regain a sense of belonging.

The Covid-19 pandemic did not help when it comes to having a sense of belonging. Druskat finds that it's harder to develop psychological safety and a sense of belonging when many of the nonverbals are missing—when a meeting is digital rather than in person. A virtual meeting, she's found, is "not quite the same. You don't get the emotional resonance that you get when you're face-to-face. You don't feel like you're part of something." That may be one reason many people who worked from home have found it rewarding to go back to working in-person, at least part of the time.

Greater than the Sum of Its Parts

Long before Google studied their top teams, Vanessa Druskat did a similar study. She went into a large manufacturing plant with three hundred teams and, like the researchers at Google, she began by identifying which teams were the top ones. They looked at hard measures of performance, but they also asked the top brass and focus groups with team members, "Who are the best?" Then Druskat focused on the teams that were in the top 10 percent on all of their measures. According to Druskat, she interviewed the members of those teams exhaustively in order to identify what made them different from the other teams.

Druskat didn't stop with that first company. She and Steve Wolff studied several other companies, using the same method. For instance, they identified the top drug development teams at Johnson & Johnson as well as those on the floor of a polyester fiber factory, and studied what made them the best.[8] After repeating this process in several companies, a picture began to emerge.

Druskat and Wolff found that the top teams developed those agreed-on patterns of interaction—that is, norms—that create a positive emotional environment. One set of such norms, for example, creates a sense of psychological safety and trust among team members—but there are many others. Key to creating a high-performing team are norms for awareness and regulation of emotions within the group and beyond it. Such norms, they found, predicted up to 30 percent of the value added by these exceptional teams. This competitive edge, they concluded, is due to group-level emotional intelligence.

Druskat and Wolff identified several levels of such norms in a model of *team emotional intelligence.*[9] Their mapping of high-performance teams' collective EI names three essential "buckets of norms." Top teams have norms relating to all three of those buckets.

The first set of norms create the group's self-awareness, the basis for how the team members take care of each other. These norms help the group surface and understand "the needs, perspectives, skills, and emotions of its members." Druskat finds that for teams to operate at an optimal level, members need to talk about "their own needs, talk about themselves, and talk about the team. . . . You can't do it all the time. But you do need to do it periodically."

One way this gets done, for example, can be seen in many groups who routinely check in at the beginning of each meeting in order for everyone to have a sense of how others are feeling. This simple exercise can boost group-level self-awareness. Members might mention a concern they have or something they did that they're proud of—all of which gives others on the team a stronger sense of each person on the team.

Other EI norms at the team level relate to how the team operates— ways the team members learn about the team itself and build self-awareness around the team, including how the team manages itself. This group-level equivalent of self-awareness means the group "is aware of how it is performing, its collective moods, and seeks information to help it evaluate how well it is working."

For instance, a team at Hewlett-Packard applied the norm of "interpersonal understanding." They were cross-training its members so that anyone could fill in for a teammate who was absent. But one member was resisting because he was anxious about learning new skills. Fortunately, the team had come to the realization early on that it was important to understand a member's behavior when something wasn't quite right, rather than become annoyed. So they made a special effort to provide extra support to the anxious member. Becoming aware of each other's feelings had become a useful norm for this team.

The high-performance norms also include *group management of members*, the team-level equivalent of self-management for the individual. This set of norms includes members showing that they care about each other. Technically, this can be seen in "the degree to which a group treats its members with respect, supports them, seeks their perspective, and validates their efforts."

On the other hand, just as the individual's self-management includes handling their own disruptive emotions, for a group this can mean confronting a member who is violating the group's norms or undermining their effectiveness. This "confrontation" can be done in a light way, simply reminding the person of what norm they are violating.

For example, at Ideo, the innovations consultancy, if you interrupt someone else in a meeting among certain groups there you will be pelted by everyone with small stuffed animals. It's a fun way to reinforce an implicit ground rule that everyone must hear each other out, so people can finish what they have to say. Caring for each other and confronting members who break norms can work together.

Then there are norms that build *group self-management*, where a group "anticipates problems and takes action to prevent them as well as taking responsibility and working hard to address challenges." That early meeting of CREIO, which we described at the beginning of this chapter, is an example. When things were not going well, we stopped and spent some time talking about what was going on, which led to the creation of a set of norms that we have been following for more than twenty-five years.

Another set of norms among high-performing teams concerns how the group relates to other units in their organization—a group-level equivalent of relationship management. These norms help the group better understand the team's stakeholders and build positive relationships with them.

While the internal environment of a team is important, to be effective teams also need to have an external view. This third set of norms can be seen as group-level organizational awareness. The group tries to understand the concerns of other parts of their organization, how its own operation impacts them, and how it all contributes to the greater goals of the organization. One result of such understanding, for instance, might be doing another group a favor—like nominating them for an award—to further relationships with them.

A team at one manufacturing company decided they needed to make three months more of a certain product in order to get ahead. Unfortunately, this meant that another team working further down in the process was overwhelmed with excess inventory. When the beleaguered team tried to explain the problem to the first team, the members of the first team were annoyed. They believed that getting ahead of schedule made them look better, and they made no effort to understand and help the other team. In this case, the lack of a norm for reaching out and understanding how another part of the organization might be harmed hurt the productivity of an entire line in the factory.

Awareness of what other groups might need directly informs how a team manages its relationship with them. High-performing teams are proactive, building relationships with other groups who can in some way affect their performance—for instance by providing resources. As Druskat puts it, "It's about understanding our stakeholders and building relationships with them. Oftentimes, this is the job of just the team leader because we tend to think of the team leader as being the boundary manager who goes out and brings stuff back. But what we found is that in the top teams, the whole team does it."

One way high-performance teams demonstrated this was in assigning certain team members to become "ambassadors" who help build good relationships with important stakeholders in the organization. This builds stronger ties to groups that a team might have to rely on for help or resources at some point in the future. "You don't wait for them to come to you," Druskat observed. "You go out and build good relationships with them. So they'll bring the resources to you when you need them."

The group EI norms are more than an ideal type. Druskat and colleagues use them as a map in hands-on development of these strengths in teams of all kinds.[10]

Team EI

Vanessa Druskat finds that by helping teams become aware of group-level EI norms, members get a boost in their self-management, empathy, and relationship skills. Druskat calls this path to strengthening emotional intelligence skills "team EI," using the dynamics of the group to build the EI competencies of its members.[11]

In this method Druskat puts her research into a pragmatic form, helping teams create the collective habits that make their interactions more socially and emotionally intelligent—and so more productive. The first step is a methodical survey of team members (who answer anonymously) of the team's norms, asking questions like "Does everyone on the team try to understand each other?" This spots where a team needs to build better collective habits.

That data then gets shared with the whole team, and everyone on the team discusses the data and what to do to improve. The team decides where to start changing norms, typically picking three or four to work on first. And, importantly, the team members themselves decide how to make the better way of working together into a norm.

Given how time-pressed people are these days, and how little time they may spend as members of a given team, Druskat notes, it might take months to make the new habit a norm. It's largely up to the team leader, she finds, to value EI and so give enough time and effort to the change.

Druskat and colleagues have helped develop EI norms in teams from sectors as diverse as the military, energy companies, hospitals, banks and financial services, universities, tech companies, and retail operations. Many companies measure their team performance by the percentage of organizational goals the team meets. In one analogue of this, Druskat assessed MBA teams working on projects and found that higher group EI of those teams correlated with how well their faculty rated their project.[12]

A More Rigorous Test

Druskat and Wolff's model of group-level emotional intelligence in high-performing groups derived from their hands-on work with a wide variety of teams. But they did not go the next step in scientific methodology, an experiment. Such a more rigorous test of Druskat's view that group-level emotional intelligence leads to high performance can be found in research by Anita Woolley, a psychology professor from Carnegie Mellon University. With colleagues at MIT and Union College, she studied hundreds of people working in groups of two to five to find the strongest predictors of a group's effectiveness.[13]

As was true at Google, the researchers initially assumed that the average cognitive intelligence of a group's members would predict how effective they were. But Woolley's team found that the correlation between the average intelligence of a group and its effectiveness in solving puzzles was weak: a group of people with very high IQs did not necessarily perform better.

The best predictors of high performance were in the emotional intelligence domain: the social sensitivity of group members, the equality in distribution of conversational turn-taking, and (perhaps surprisingly) the proportion of females in the group. In other words, the best groups were those in which the members scored high in their sensitivity to the emotions and needs of others in the group and took turns when speaking so that all members contributed—perhaps in part due to having more females than males. (This gender ratio, if duplicated by further research, could be a powerful data point in organizations' finding better solutions for equity.)

Psychological safety was not measured in Woolley's study, but the results suggest that it was an important underlying factor. When group members are sensitive to the feelings and needs of others, it is likely that they will act in ways that make everyone feel safer. When everyone speaks up—even those who tend to hold back out of fear of being scorned—it signals a higher level of psychological safety in the group.

What seems to occur in these highly effective teams is a "virtuous cycle" in which group norms contribute to greater psychological safety, and the safety in turn reinforces those norms. For instance, dominant members are discouraged from cutting others off, which enables others who might hold back to be more likely to voice their views. Groups in which everyone feels free to contribute are those that are most likely to come up with the best solutions.

All of the factors that can contribute to psychological safety in groups, such as a sense of belonging, social sensitivity of group members, and the equality in distribution of conversational turn-taking, bring us back to a team's emotional intelligence. When a majority of team members experience a sense of belonging, they recognize when it's safe to share more about themselves. When they are skilled in doing it in ways that are constructive and encourage others to do the same, psychological safety and belonging thrive. Emotional intelligence also helps team members to be sensitive to how other members of the team are feeling and why they feel that way. EI means they exercise better self-management, creating the space that lets everyone contribute rather than just a few dominant ones.

Woolley and her team found some concrete support for this link to emotional intelligence. They had the participants in their study take the "Reading the Mind in the Eyes" test, in which they had to describe what the people in photographs of faces were thinking or feeling. People on the more successful teams scored higher on this empathy assessment, while those on the less effective teams scored lower.[14]

Many studies of the impact of a team's emotional intelligence are based either on the average EI of a team's members or on the leader's EI. But researchers have found that a team's *culture*—the sum total of its norms—is a stronger influence on behavior than individual attitudes or personality. Since team culture comes down to group norms, this again speaks to the crucial importance of a team's collective EI.

Several studies have identified the link between emotional intelligence and team effectiveness. For instance, a study of project teams working in large-scale hydropower plants found a positive association between a team's collective EI and team performance.[15] A similar study found that project managers' teams did better when they brought more EI to their work; EI led to more commitment as well.[16] In managing complex projects, leaders used their EI to boost the group's performance, drawing on relationship skills like managing conflict and influencing how members acted toward each other and in working toward common goals.

Group EI, research finds, has practical benefits. For instance, a study of teams in a military organization found that group EI was linked to less raw material waste, fewer accidents, and a higher percentage of flight objectives met.[17] There also seems to be an interaction between individual team members' level of EI and that group's performance, with emotionally intelligent team members enhancing effective cooperation, communication, and goal-setting.[18]

Diversity, Equity, and Inclusion

An engineering company had a good record when it came to diversity, equity, and inclusion—at least at first glance. They were hiring equal numbers of women and men engineers, no small feat given that there were many fewer women graduating with engineering degrees.[19] But a closer look revealed the women were not receiving promotions at the same rate, and they were leaving the firm in significantly higher numbers. African Americans were departing at triple the average rate. While the firm's hiring numbers looked good, these other measures told a story of failure.

The struggle to increase diversity, equity, and inclusion (DEI) in the workplace has gone on for many decades. The DEI movement is based on the premise that diversity in numbers is not sufficient for an optimal work setting. Hiring more women and people of color does not guarantee that they will be treated fairly or that they will become truly accepted members of their workgroups. Forced diversity, where a company hires members of minority groups to meet some quota, can easily backfire at the psychological level—those hired might fear they are not really qualified, while coworkers might resent their being hired in the first place.

On the other hand, a sense of belonging creates an atmosphere where there can be inclusion as well as diversity. The message is "You're welcome to be here, and we're *glad* you're here." That message communicates most powerfully among the coworkers you see the most, whether office mates or teammates.

Consider the opposite: what it would be like to have the sense you don't belong in the place you spend eight or so hours a day. You'd be defensive, pulled back, afraid to express your feelings freely. In short, work would not be a safe space. Far healthier would be a workplace where everyone felt they belonged.

Unfortunately, many attempts to promote greater inclusion and equality end in failure.[20] Diversity training has been especially problematic. Part of the problem is that participation is often mandatory, which makes for resentment and resistance from the very start. Training programs also sometimes put white males "on trial," leading to a backlash that can make the situation worse rather than better.

As one letter writer put it in the *New York Times*, "Guilt-tripping white people—or any historically privileged group—doesn't work to develop DEI outcomes."[21] He went on to write, "DEI training should help individuals authentically explore and understand personal and interpersonal attitudes and beliefs that in turn help to shift our engagement at the cultural and institutional levels." While diversity workshops vary greatly, our sense is that a DEI initiative would be best facilitated by emotional intelligence in action—particularly empathy and team skills.

Research also suggests that DEI training by itself has limited value. There also needs to be concrete action on inclusion and equality problems in the organization. Robert Livingston from Harvard's Kennedy School has found that the most successful organizations "diagnose their specific problems with DEI and come up with concrete strategies for solving them,"[22] such as mentoring programs for minorities.

Back to that engineering company. The CEO thought they could do better when it came to DEI, and so his vice president of diversity and inclusion invited a trusted external colleague to help develop a DEI program based on emotional intelligence.

The program started with a half day just for their seven senior vice presidents, focusing on an exercise that would show that each of them had been excluded at some point in their lives. The exercise began by asking a series of questions, such as "Have you experienced someone making assumptions about you because of the way you look or talk or something else?" One of the participants, a man from Texas, told the group that "the minute people heard my accent, they deducted twenty IQ points."

After seeing how all of them had experienced exclusion and bias and could remember how it felt, they were trained in a methodology developed by Consortium member Stephen Kelner, deliberately designed to enhance their empathy on issues of inclusion and exclusion, exploring each other's stories with neutral questions like "What were you feeling? What were you thinking?"[23]

They then were tasked to use this structured methodology in one-on-one discussions with direct reports, members of their team, and others. Following the neutral questions lowered the executives' own anxieties about probing sensitive issues. When they reported on how the interviews went, reactions included "This is life-changing for me," and "This was a lightbulb moment for both of us."

Crucially, these executives saw that showing their interest in sensitive issues had a positive impact on both them and the other person: exhibiting empathy brought them closer. As for DEI, the executives felt more prepared to face these questions openly.

For one, they had learned how to explore sensitive issues with emotional intelligence—demonstrating empathy while keeping their own reactions at bay and strengthening the human-to-human connections. This gave them confidence that they had a "soft skills" toolbox that they could use with otherwise too-risky areas like diversity and inclusion as they arose. Plus their own experience of bias created an implicit motivation to act when such issues were raised.

When the old CEO retired two years after the program began and the new CEO dismantled it, the committee members continued to advocate for inclusion and equity. One of the most dramatic moments occurred when one member of this C-suite team stood up in a meeting of the top twenty-five people in the company and said, "I had thought I knew enough on diversity and inclusion. But there are things I did not see. There are things I did not hear. And I was wrong. There are things you did not see, and you did not hear. We have to address this."

The Learning Circle

Bill was the problem. Everyone else on the team worked well together. They listened to each other, they made sure they didn't dominate the discussion, and they tried not to show off. But Bill was not a team player. He *did* show off, dominated the discussion, and was opinionated. Worse, he made derogatory comments about others. He was smart, he worked hard, he always met or exceeded his goals. But his disruptive and critical stance in team meetings was affecting the other members' performance, making them much less productive.

A Consortium member presented the "Bill Problem" in the hope that others at the meeting could come up with ideas for dealing with his disruptions. One idea used the format for norms that CREIO had found useful: as a group develop "rules of engagement" for how people should behave, and review them at the beginning of every meeting until they became very familiar to everyone.

Another useful suggestion: make sure that one of those rules of engagement addressed how people should respond whenever someone does or says something that is disruptive. A good way to do this might be to say, "This is what I see you doing, and this is the impact it has."

A third: help group members get to know each other at a deeper, more meaningful level. One of the participants at the CREIO meeting suggested a way to do this that had worked well in his own company: "We get to know each other's values by having each person identify their top five, and share them with the group. Once we know each other this way, we give each other more slack. We also are able to challenge each other in a helpful way—we can call people out if they're acting contrary to their own system of what matters to them."

That discussion in the CREIO meeting was a good example of a "learning circle," a group who meet regularly to learn from each other. This was similar to an experiment involving managers and executives from several companies in the Chicago area put in small groups who met monthly. Each group had nine managers or executives from different companies with a trained moderator and a manual that spelled out the rules of engagement—the norms for their meetings.

The rules were meant to create a safe environment and encourage habits of positive social interaction. Some of the rules: maintain confidentiality, listen attentively, don't give advice, never attack or make demeaning statements about others, and speak twice only after everyone has spoken once.

Each month, one member presented his or her "biggest problem or concern at the present time," along with background information about the setting and that member's history. The other group members were to listen attentively and not ask any questions until the presentation was completed. At that point members could ask clarifying questions, but not offer advice. Once the question phase ended, the members could share personal experiences of their own with similar issues.

The learning circle process would then end unless the presenter wanted advice. If the presenter did ask for advice, members were allowed one minute to say what they would do if they were in the presenter's situation, using only "I" statements and avoiding "you should" statements.

During the second year of the program, members were able to present personal concerns or issues as well as business-related ones. They also were given a list of "Seven EI Habits," with the instruction that they practice one habit each month. Examples were "Practice good listening" and "Make a daily effort to compliment someone sincerely."

The payoff from following these EI norms: after two years, business leaders who participated in a learning circle showed a significant increase in emotional intelligence as measured by a 360-degree measure, while a randomly assigned control group showed no change.[24]

Bottom line: members of a group that models EI in its norms can have their personal EI increased just by participating, without necessarily engaging in an explicit program to increase emotional intelligence.

Even virtual approaches can help teams function better. A group in Spain developed an online training program based on Druskat and

Wolff's team EI model. The groups that received the training did better on problem-solving tasks than a control group.[25]

Google has experimented with workshops for teams where the trainers present scenarios in which behaviors enhanced or reduced psychological safety. The scenarios are role-played to make them especially vivid. Even an imagined team with more psychological safety enhances its effect in real life.[26]

Sometimes just providing the team with one new norm can make a difference. In one instance, a consultant who had been working with a team offered the group a technique to help them give each other constructive feedback in a sensitive and caring way by having them begin by saying, "I have a gift I want to give you . . ." Vanessa Druskat helped another team to enhance a sense of belonging among all members by adopting this norm: "We will put down our phones whenever someone in the group speaks no matter who it is." Take an experiment on a hospital ward with very sick patients, many of whom die after a long spell of treatment. The medical staff become close with many of the patients during that time, which makes it especially painful when those patients die. When teams on such wards were taught how to talk about their problems and come up with their own solutions for them, they were better able to handle these stresses.[27]

SOME POINTS TO REMEMBER ABOUT TEAMS: A TEAM'S PERFORmance depends to a great extent on the ways in which group members interact—their norms. At Google top-performing teams were found to have a strong sense of "psychological safety," otherwise seen as members feeling they "belong." This sense of security reflects a norm of collective self-awareness without critical judgments, one of several EI norms found among the highest-performing teams. These team EI norms parallel those that typify high-EI individuals, but operate at the group level. There are many methods for helping a team upgrade its collective EI. One sign of this: a positive atmosphere for diversity and inclusion.

Just as the culture of a team depends on the sum of the norms that members follow, so with organizations as a whole. It all starts with training.

12

EI Training That Works

Everyone knew Jerry was a jerk. He'd been hired as an executive vice president because of his outstanding track record in upping the bottom line at the company where he worked before. But those who reported to him directly saw him as a monster: he blew up at people, shamed them publicly, was distant and aloof. Worse, he had no idea there was anything wrong with any of this.

Could his company have avoided ending up with a problem like Jerry? Finding a way to screen individuals for EI is becoming a holy grail because it would allow companies to hire only people who already have strong EI. So what about giving a potential hire or promotion an emotional intelligence test? Buyer beware: EI can't easily be self-assessed.

For one, Jerry doesn't recognize his own shortcomings. Such people will blithely rate themselves as high on EI even though those around them can see glaring faults. So truly gauging someone's EI depends on hearing from those who regularly interact with them, if only because of the danger of self-deception in a self-test. For example, research finds that those low in self-awareness do poorly on the range of EI competencies— but they don't know it!

Jamie Dimon, chairman and CEO of JPMorgan Chase, proposes a more intuitive approach. He says, ask yourself: "Would you want your kid to work for this person?"[1] When looking to promote someone from within or at a potential new hire, he says, of course the hard skills count. The financial sector demands everyone be disciplined in "facts, analysis, details." Those are the givens, the threshold abilities, that everyone needs to be highly effective in the industry.

But being a "real leader," Dimon says, requires a skill set over and above being a numbers person. It's not just balance sheets; it's also emotional intelligence. Dimon gives some examples of what emotional intelligence looks like in a leader: "Do you recognize body language? Do you understand when someone is hurting? When you're talking to a crowd, do you know what they're not relaying to you? Do you have empathy?"

To find out if a candidate meets the mark, Dimon recommends asking people who know him or her well, but are free to talk openly. Check legalities, but ideally you'd talk to that person's boss, peers, and subordinates, or former bosses, peers, and subordinates—even a spouse or ex-partner. While this does not mean asking them to do a formal 360 assessment, a systematic conversation might unearth much the same information.

This lets you learn about the person from multiple angles, with fewer biased inputs from the person, and without depending solely on how people present themselves in an interview or on a test.

A caveat: more explicit use of emotional intelligence to screen new hires could pose legal problems. According to the U.S. Equal Employment Opportunity Commission, "Use of cognitive tests, personality tests, and similar tools can violate the federal anti-discrimination laws . . . if they disproportionately exclude people in a particular group by race, sex, or another covered basis, unless the employer can justify the test or procedure under the law."[2]

What this means in practice is that employers should not use an EI test for selection unless they have research showing that the instrument is not biased in any way—and few employers have the resources needed for this kind of research before using a test to select job candidates.

In addition, trying to pick job applicants for their EI may reflect a basic misunderstanding of the nature of this skill set. Emotional intelligence—seemingly unlike IQ—can improve over the course of life. So how someone looks at a given point offers a one-time snapshot rather than a video of how the person grows and develops as time goes on. A person's EI is fluid, not frozen in one moment.

Bottom line: We recommend using EI evaluations mainly for development purposes, not for hiring decisions. Using them to choose one candidate over another is risky business. Instead of using EI tests during the hiring or promotion process, recruiters and hiring managers can employ two methods to improve an organization's overall EI:

First, stating the company's commitment to EI in recruiting materials such as the job description, company career site, and LinkedIn page can help candidates self-select. MD Anderson Cancer Center cites "teaming" and "active listening" from their leadership model in their job postings, and they give candidates an EI self-test—not to make hiring decisions, but rather to communicate how much EI is valued there.

Second, a well-trained hiring manager or recruiting manager can ask in the job interview about "critical incidents" (like, "Tell me about a time you failed and what you learned from it"). During the job interview, asking for real stories from the candidate's past offers some sense of the candidate's EI skills firsthand.

For example, MD Anderson designed its interview guide to consider specific aspects of EI; the center assesses a candidate's relationship management skills by asking them, "Describe a situation, either at work or elsewhere, in which you feel you helped resolve a disagreement or conflict. What actions did you take to resolve the problem?" and "Have you been involved in a team where some of the members were not included in the decisions and actions of the project? What was the situation? What was your involvement?"

In short, while many organizations try to recruit for emotional intelligence, we favor a different strategy: hire for the skill set relevant to a particular job, and then train and develop people so hired for the emotional intelligence competencies that mark leaders as high performers. In an emotionally intelligent organization, EI can be used judiciously in recruitment and selection, but training and development for EI are most important.

Start with Training

Training in EI, we feel, holds the key—but seems to work best if promoted in a particular way. Developing "soft skills" like better listening has long been a staple of HR training departments—but now top leaders increasingly recognize its importance. In a survey of almost 1,000 CEOs, about 90 percent agreed that key executives need a personal transformation to succeed in improving their organization. That 90 percent agreement contrasts with just 30 percent of CEOs who said the same three years earlier.[3] Times are changing.

At the same time, there's strong evidence for the effectiveness of emotional intelligence lessons for kids. Children and youth from kindergarten through twelfth grade now are learning EI skills in schools throughout the United States and around the globe, and several studies have shown that these programs, when designed and implemented skillfully, add to improved academic performance as well as emotional and social well-being. A meta-analysis that looked across 213 studies involving more than 270,000 students found that social and emotional learning programs boosted students' academic performance by 11 percentage points. Students in those programs also showed improvements in classroom behavior (they were less unruly and disruptive), along with an increased ability to manage stress and depression, and had more positive attitudes about themselves, others, and school. These findings have been replicated several times since the initial study.[4]

But what about adults? Can grown-ups also increase their EI through training? For many years there was little research on the success of EI training for managers and executives, but eventually a host of strong studies were done—and the evidence is compelling.[5] If the training program is well designed and implemented effectively (a big "if," to be sure), adults can increase their EI and maintain those increases as time goes on.

A study at Progressive Insurance of the impact of EI training is still in progress as we write this book.[6] Early analyses from the Progressive study show that leaders who are perceived by their employees as being more emotionally intelligent have teams whose members have a greater sense of belonging. Given the crucial role belonging plays in team performance, as well as in initiatives on inclusion, this finding suggests that training in emotional intelligence can have direct benefits for team members and overall group performance.

The Progressive study compares individual coaching with an online EI training. When the legendary executive coach Marshall Goldsmith heard about the Progressive study, he was enthusiastic—such hard-nosed evaluations of the impact of coaching are rare but needed, he pointed out.[7]

There are many ways to deliver EI training, but far too few actual experiments on how to design such training. We described one such study in Chapter 11, where leaders were randomly assigned to a comparison group or to one where they met regularly to talk over personal troubles as well as challenges in their business. They felt safe enough to voice difficulties that they had no one else to talk to about. As we reported, at the end of two years, their emotional intelligence score increased.[8]

But this approach is just one of many ways to help boost EI.

One method, co-designed by Dan, spends several sessions spread over a week on each of the EI competencies, explaining the particulars of that strength, having learners reflect on it in their work and life, and giving daily exercises to help them with mastery.[9] So, for example, with the Emotional Balance competence, one exercise has you track moments you become emotionally hijacked and what triggered that reaction—a "trigger log"—and reflect on how you reacted and what would be a more effective response. Then when one of your triggers comes along, you learn to pause, shift from a reactive posture to a better response, and try it out. Live sessions with others going through the course and facilitated by seasoned coaches give learners a chance to practice those better responses, and to hear about other ways to handle dicey situations like a heated conversation.

Two different meta-analyses (the method, remember, for pooling the results of many independent studies) assessed such EI development programs. The studies covered included a wide variety of occupations and work settings—from managers and executives in medium- and large-sized companies to professional cricketers to students in MBA programs.[10] All showed benefits—for instance, professional cricket players showed a jump of 13 percent in their EI from training while a comparison group had, on average, no change.

While most all of these training programs led to increased EI, more significantly there were positive bottom-line outcomes. For instance, emotional intelligence training for medical residents led to an increase in patient satisfaction scores. After a training for bank employees, customer satisfaction scores increased. Pharmaceutical representatives who received EI training outperformed a comparison group in sales revenue.[11]

EI training programs also have improved key drivers of organizational productivity, such as employee well-being and workplace relationships. For instance, when a group of employees in a defense contracting organization went through an EI training program, their job satisfaction significantly increased. When midlevel managers at a large retail marketing chain went through EI training, their job satisfaction, stress levels, and general health all improved. Project managers given such EI training showed improvements in teamwork and conflict management—key skills for their task.[12] Such training programs have led to enhanced coaching skills, boosted employability and reemployment, reduced workplace incivility, and a better institutional climate.[13]

Ingredients of an Effective EI Training Program

A consultant delivered the same training program for the top executives and managers at two different companies. The program had been effective in other settings, and it had a positive impact in one of these companies. But it didn't work in the other. Why?

The trainer believed it came down to how the CEOs behaved. In the company where it failed, the CEO came in at the beginning of the first session, told the participants how important EI was, and then turned around and left, never to return. In the successful program, the CEO actively participated in the training along with his team.

When top leaders model the importance of EI training in such ways, they send a strong message of support. We've found that a shift to an EI-positive culture can be stronger if an influential leader actively endorses it. This was true, for example, with the head of Progressive's Customer Relations Management division (or CRM, where insurance was sold, a mainstay of the business), and with the CEOs of both BL Companies and MD Anderson Cancer Center, each of whom was an EI champion. And this vocal support need not come from on high: at Amazon Web Services a self-proclaimed "EI evangelist" created a groundswell of interest from the ground up.

In the past, MD Anderson's leadership training efforts focused only on midlevel leaders like department heads, but a new president, who openly talked about the importance of an EI culture, began a training effort around emotional intelligence and wanted everyone to participate.[14]

At MD Anderson's Leadership Institute, the first-level program for frontline workers has a focus on self-awareness, while the training for supervisors and managers covers relationship management. The third-level course is primarily for department heads and focuses on how to manage emotions while having difficult conversations. Their leadership courses for division heads and institutional leaders emphasize modeling EI and emotional contagion—how feelings spread from leaders outward.

Elements of EI also are infused in many other training programs at MD Anderson. In the course called "Holding Difficult Conversations," the trainers will ask, "How might you use EI in this conversation?" Even though there's no formal requirement for executives to take the EI courses, more than 90 percent of the organization's leaders have participated in them.

Design That Works

To be sure, there also are programs that are strong on hype but lack validated results. And too many programs are poorly designed and implemented. When we looked at the most successful EI training programs, we found that they usually had the following five ingredients:

1. *Highly motivated participants.* Increasing our EI requires considerable time and effort. Without a high degree of commitment and motivation, most of us will drop out before any change can occur. Successful programs increase and sustain engagement in a variety of ways. In one the participants received an email twice a week for four weeks, encouraging them to apply a different part of the course each time.[15]

2. *Ten or more hours of training, spaced out over time, with periodic booster sessions.* Dosage is important—the more hours of training, the better; it should be delivered over time when possible. One of the best programs, involving 54 senior managers from a private company, consisted of 30 hours of training spread over seven weekly sessions of 95 minutes each. In addition, five hours of online training was required between each in-person session.[16]

3. *Ongoing practice and reinforcement.* Training sessions are important, but mastery in emotional intelligence requires repeated feedback and rehearsal in between those sessions— and for long after the formal training ends. From a neural perspective, EI training entails a different model of learning than that of our school days. Unlike cognitive skills like budgeting or planning logistics, emotional intelligence is a behavioral skill. Such soft skills are strengthened in the same way as a skill like your golf game: through models, supportive trials, and lots of practice.

4. *Social support.* Feeling supported by others also makes a big difference. Coaching offers a powerful learning path at the top of the house, but learning teams make more sense at other levels. At BL Companies, all participants become part of an application group that meets once a month, offering a place where employees can practice their skills and receive support

for the on-the-job learning plans they developed during their
training.

5. *Active modeling and support of key organizational leaders.* As
we've seen, when a top executive participates in an EI training program, he or she models how important they consider
that training to be. This has a compelling effect on others
throughout the organization who are inclined to take the
program themselves, validating their commitment. On the
other hand, top executives who are openly dismissive of such
training undermine that appeal. Tacit or explicit support of
EI training by respected top executives gives such programs
a tangible boost.

Not all training programs need to be alike, and not all need to incorporate every one of the five ingredients. But the more ingredients they
do incorporate, the more likely it is that they will work. While effective training programs can help you perform at more optimal levels if
you're motivated and they are well run, the real payoff comes when the
whole organization is moving in that direction. An organization's emphasis on development for high performance works best when the overall
culture supports its value. We find, for instance, a great advantage in
having a champion of this approach from the business side rather than
this coming from human resources. When a top executive—particularly
the CEO—repeatedly states its value, people will more eagerly engage;
leaders set norms.

EI Training That Sticks

One promising approach to EI training is Richard Boyatzis's Intentional
Change Theory (ICT), which incorporates all of the five ingredients. He
has used this learning sequence with his executive MBAs at the Weatherhead School of Management at Case Western for more than thirty years.
Impressively, his team found that the EI competencies MBA students

strengthened while at Case were still strong—as seen by that person's work associates—as long as seven years later.[17]

This EI approach begins by helping individuals to identify their "ideal selves," a strong inner motivator. A trainer or coach might ask, "Ideally, how would you like to see yourself in five years?"

Next, the program assesses for each participant a diagnosis of strengths and limits across the full spectrum of EI. For this the program uses the Emotional and Social Competence Inventory (ESCI), that 360-degree assessment instrument that renders scores on all twelve EI competencies that set star performers apart from average ones.[18]

While there are perhaps a dozen or more different measures of EI, each with its own strengths, this particular variety, the 360-degree view, has been found the best predictor of workplace excellence.[19] It tells you how your strengths and limits are seen by those who know you well and whose opinions you value. For instance, a study of one hundred leaders of family businesses found strong relationships between the leader's EI ratings and their effectiveness—but only using the "other" ratings, not self-report.[20] Those anonymous evaluations from trusted people give you a diagnostic profile that can help you spot where to start working on getting better.

In the third step, the trainers or coaches help the executives to connect their profile to their aspirations, circling back to step one. This connects their deep motivation with their EI learning challenge, by asking them questions like "Enhancing which competence would help you get to your ideal self?" For example, for greater presence, executives often work on their listening habits, key to empathy. Research at the University of California, Berkeley, finds that people in positions of power often cut off others before they have a chance to finish their thought—a poor listening habit that we can learn to change for the better.[21]

The final step is to practice the learned behaviors repeatedly until they become second nature. For better listening, the participants might become mindful of the many chances to practice this, which can occur with a teenager or spouse over the dinner table as well as with a direct report at work.

Such repeated practice, as we've noted, seems to drive the new learning into the brain's basal ganglia, where it becomes an automatic habit rather than a behavior change we have to think about. The good news for EI training from this "neuroplasticity" is that we can acquire new habits at any point in life—it's never too late to upgrade this skill set.

The late Florida State University psychologist Anders Ericsson once told Dan he was upset at the widespread belief that there's something magical about ten thousand hours of practice. His research, on which that popular myth was based, actually showed that the hours of practice to the point of mastery varies greatly, and depends on the specific skill you're mastering. It might take the lead violinist in a symphony orchestra ten thousand or so hours to learn to play so well. But compare the number of hours to mastery of another skill, memory for a long string of digits: this takes just several hundred hours.

In general, there's a dose-response relationship here, where the more hours of practice you put in, the greater your mastery of a given skill. So when you are in the optimal state, the degree to which you can display your talents depends partly on how well and how long you have honed them. No matter a person's inherent abilities, practice holds the key to mastery. Small improvements gradually add up.

So it is with EI. Richard Boyatzis has for years had his MBA students get a 360-degree assessment of their EI strengths and limitations on the ESCI, and pick a competency to work on improving. Their work here can't be tracked in hours, but rather in how many times they practice the new behavioral sequence that will replace a dysfunctional EI habit, one that did not help them.

Coaching

While training for individual contributors and first-time leaders tends to be done by courses, training at top levels is more often through one-on-one coaching. Recall that when the Conference Board surveyed its corporate members on the focus of coaching for their leaders, emotional intelligence emerged as the number one topic addressed in the vast majority of these engagements (though the EI competencies often went under different names). While that Conference Board survey was done pre-Covid, the organization returned to these findings as the pandemic seemed to be lifting, to emphasize the continued need for empathy in particular and emotional intelligence in general for leaders.[22]

Far down on the list of common coaching topics: strategic thinking and business competencies. The report says that EI skills like empathy and self-mastery are more needed than ever.

Anyone working on improving their emotional intelligence will be helped by ongoing feedback—not just "one and done" courses or off-sites, where they are exposed to a method or motivation to enhance this skill set, but then left to their own devices. If it's an executive at the top of the house, they are more likely to be given a coach, essentially an ongoing tutorial. If the person is a midlevel manager, their need may be just as great, but costs make it unlikely their organization will consider a coach.

Coaching for EI—or "soft skills," more generally—has become widespread among top executives, yet this developmental path alone may not be sufficient to boost an organization to its optimal level of performance. One reason, as the team expert Vanessa Druskat notes, is that while those in the C-Suite have often gotten there because they have a high achievement drive, they may still be so competitive that they seek "wins" for their unit at the expense of the overall organization's success.

To ensure that this top group operates as a winning team, and so promotes the organization's overall goals, Druskat urges having the C-suite group apply the same norms in their work together that typify high-performing teams. "Individual coaching," she has found, "is not enough" to improve a team's EI. She adds, "Building highly effective group norms offers a complementary path of development."

Individual EI coaching and team EI are two separate learning paths. Team-building among C-suite members means they don't hold back what they tell others as might be the case if they lack that feeling of psychological safety.

She envisions the next step for development going beyond coaching for the individual's goals alone, to also building EI norms for interactions among the top team. And, of course, her approach works with any team at any level—Amazon Web Services, for instance, as of this writing, is exploring using Druskat's team learning approach to take EI to scale throughout the division.

Boosting team EI could be synergistic with coaching individuals for the same skill set. "Highly emotionally intelligent people interact in ways that make the other person feel good," Druskat observes. "If you're on a high-EI team, it helps increase your individual EI. The team becomes a learning experience for the individual that brings out the best in everyone." As people feel safer, they are more open in what they share.

In sum, screening new hires for EI can be difficult, while training for EI can be far more effective. There are many methods for developing EI, but the best share in common several points. They motivate and encourage participants; they offer enough training hours; training is ongoing rather than onetime; participants have social support from each other or workmates; and the organization's leaders model EI and encourage people to develop further strengths in these soft skills.

As we will see, all of that can happen most powerfully when an organization embraces the importance of EI.

13

Building an EI Culture

The company had been booming, growing for years, but a recession led to the first layoffs in the company's history. So BL Companies' CEO, Carolyn Stanworth, met with all the remaining employees. Rather than give them a pep talk, acting as though it was no big deal or ignoring it, she began by sharing with them her own feelings of sadness.

Then she opened it up for others to speak about their feelings and concerns. When it looked like most of the group was ready to move on, she began to talk about how the company would look going forward.

As she did so, her own mood shifted from sadness and regret to optimism and excitement about the future. While there was lingering anxiety, gradually the collective mood shifted toward enthusiasm about the company's future—an emotional contagion built on reality: facing the sad facts, but then looking beyond.

BL Companies, a midsize architectural and engineering firm, has outperformed its competitors for more than a decade. But that wasn't always true. Fifteen years ago, BL had higher employee turnover and struggled with significant growth. So what changed?

In the intervening years, BL instituted a leadership program that includes emotional intelligence development, which at the time was unique for large organizations and particularly for companies in its industry. BL Companies did more than just try to develop its leaders' emotional intelligence: they changed the culture. The company adopted an EI approach to hiring and performance review. Perhaps crucially, the

CEO let people know she cared about having an emotionally intelligent culture.

Result: BL's leaders have grown significantly in the skills that underlie EI, such as relationship-building, teamwork, and empathy. These changes have in turn led to improvements in the company's diversity, engagement, and retention statistics; employee well-being; client lifetime value; and ultimately its overall performance and growth.[1]

Today, BL Companies isn't alone. Organizations as diverse as the MD Anderson Cancer Center (the world's number one for oncology), Progressive (better known as Progressive Insurance), and Amazon are investing in their employees' emotional self-management and interpersonal skills. Amazon has teams across the company that are bringing EI training to employees.

When an organization's leaders and employees are skilled at managing their own emotions and those in their relationships with others, researchers find that the company and its people benefit, seeing better performance in every sense: profit and growth, retention and loyalty, higher motivation, and a better emotional climate and overall well-being. We call such organizations *emotionally intelligent*.

Here we share our current thinking on how leaders can develop these strengths in their companies—how to recruit for them, train for them, model them, and bake them into the company's culture. Most crucial: developing an emotionally intelligent organization calls for senior leaders who model and champion an EI culture.

While well-designed and well-implemented training programs are crucial, an organization needs to go beyond EI training to bring about the most dramatic benefits. An emotionally intelligent organization incorporates EI into its DNA for recruitment, hiring, performance management, and promotion.

Reviewing Performance for EI

Despite the value of soft skills, most companies still focus on hard skills in reviewing how leaders perform. This focus misses valuable soft skills like managing your own emotions well and showing empathy. But at BL Companies, the annual performance reviews give equal weight to hard and soft skills. Managers look at *how* employees did their jobs as well as what they accomplished. "If you get the job done, but you stomp all over other people in the process, you're not going to be rewarded for that behavior in your raise and bonus," says CEO and president Carolyn Stanworth.

A competence model (as we've seen in Chapter 3) reflects the specific skill set found in the most outstanding performers. It creates a picture that people at a given company can aspire to become. Including EI in the organization's leadership competency model signals that these skills matter. It's a constant incentive to everyone to take EI seriously. Even more important, this lets the organization make the development of EI a formal part of the annual performance review process.

So, for example, MD Anderson's leadership model, which they introduced for selection, training, performance management, and promotion, includes EI competencies "teaming" and "active listening" for all employees. "Teaming" at MD Anderson refers to high levels of collaboration from all team members, valuing everyone's contributions, encouraging diversity, and balancing a given member's goals with those of the team. "Active listening" means paying full attention to the other person, acknowledging differences in perspective, and seeking to empathize with him or her.

Performance review discussions can not only show that EI matters, but even more helpful, can identify additional EI training and development that would seem to be effective for a given leader.

Employees' performance reviews can also be used to gauge their *managers'* EI. At Progressive, an employee's performance review includes a question about whether they feel valued, respected, engaged—which can speak to their boss's level of emotional leadership.

It Takes a Leader

BL Companies' response to the pandemic showed how their CEO, Carolyn Stanworth, reinforces the values of empathy and caring for others.

She said, "It's been a really hard year. A lot of people's spouses were losing their jobs with the pandemic. And our employees have done everything we've asked them to do and more. So we decided to give everyone a three-thousand-dollar 'appreciation bonus' in addition to their regular year-end bonus. And we did this right before Thanksgiving so they would be able to use it to buy presents for the holidays. It cost the company about a million dollars, but it was worth it. If you show employees that you appreciate them, they will give back ten times as much."

Stanworth believes that the most important part of her role is to be "leader of the culture," and that the values and norms she reinforces every day make the company an "emotionally intelligent" organization. Her continual endorsement of the value of EI has been a driver of programs like training and performance review that feature this set of personal skills.

In our work we've found that when what was traditionally called "HR," or human resources, tries to impose soft skills alone, it rarely goes very far. On the other hand, an influential leader's enthusiastic statement of EI values and modeling of EI behaviors establishes the norms and culture for the rest of the company—even better when the whole leadership team takes on this role. We've seen this at BL Companies and Progressive's Customer Relations Management, or CRM, division, which handles insurance sales and their agents.

Take a more high-profile example, when Satya Nadella became the third CEO in Microsoft's history. On his first day as CEO, Nadella sent a company-wide memo proposing that empathy—a word then little heard at Microsoft—would be a key skill going forward, as well as a growth mindset.[2] Nadella linked these EI "soft skills" to business strategy, arguing that empathy with customers—sensing their unmet and unstated needs—along with openness to further development, were sources of innovation.

Nadella urged his leadership team to be empathic to shift the company culture toward trust. When an economic downturn led tech companies to lay off thousands of employees, Nadella demonstrated empathy in action. In contrast to other tech firms where, for example, thousands of people were fired out of the blue via Twitter, Nadella pledged that at Microsoft it would be done differently: "As we go through this process, we will do so in the most thoughtful and transparent way possible." He softened the blow by paying higher-than-usual severance, and for six months after leaving, having people's health insurance and stock vesting continue.

In a similar way, EI has taken root in the company culture at Progressive, thanks to the vocal support of former CRM division head John Murphy (who has since been promoted to president of the company's Claims division). Emotional intelligence training, originally designed for leaders in the CRM division, spread in pockets to other groups, including IT and Claims. While EI remains a cultural signature of the CRM division—where EI was talked about, supported, and developed while Murphy was leader there—its appeal has spread more widely throughout the company.

Such a leader from the business side of a company—in short, someone outside HR—who champions EI tends to be critical to building an emotionally intelligent organization. We've seen this with CEOs at BL Companies and at MD Anderson, and with key senior executives—for example, at American Express Financial Advisors (now Ameriprise Financial) with the senior executive overseeing all the company's advisors.

Sometimes the EI champion can be a leader further down in the organization. Starting in Amazon Web Services, the company's highly profitable cloud-computing division, enthusiasm for emotional intelligence has grown in a grassroots fashion. Engineer, strategist, and self-proclaimed "EI evangelist" Rich Hua has gathered a team of more than six hundred others who share enthusiasm for EI, and who have provided EI training for more than 300,000 other employees so far.

While the EI team at Amazon began as an ad hoc group, it has now become officially recognized, with its own budget line, with Hua as worldwide head. Called the EPIC Leadership program (EPIC stands for Empathy, Purpose, Inspiration, and Connection), the training itself is EI-focused.

EPIC gets an increasing number of senior executives from far-flung parts of the company asking for emotional intelligence training for their entire group, which can number in the thousands. One advantage of this bottom-up approach over top-down policy: those who actively spearhead EI training are likely to be more motivated and engaged than those who do so because they are told to from above.

Guidelines for Leaders

"There was a big snowstorm and many employees lost power but our offices did not," as BL Companies' CEO Carolyn Stanworth tells the story. "So employees would bring in food for those who had lost power. Then we encouraged our employees to take some of it with them when they finally could leave so that their family members at home would have food to eat as well." She added, "To me, the things we care about come out in those stories."

Stanworth sees stories as an effective way to convey that the company values EI. Her story about how they handled hardships faced by employees, for instance, conveys the importance of empathy and teamwork.

For an EI champion, making EI values explicit goes beyond simply stating them. At best it means explicitly demonstrating EI's value to your organization, particularly linking it to existing business imperatives such as your mission and performance goals, and showing the impact it has made in your own work.

Some tips for leaders:

Show that EI matters for the bottom line. An "Emotional Competence" team at what is now Ameriprise Financial did research revealing that financial advisors had difficulty talking with clients about buying life insurance—preparing for your death, or even thinking about it, can be awkward or even off-putting.

After implementing a pilot training program in emotional competence for some advisors and their managers, the company found that the advisors who had been through the program with their managers generated 11 percent more growth in sales revenue during a fifteen-month period than did advisors whose management team did not go through the training. This translated into $200 million more in sales revenue for the company (this figure would be over $320 million in today's values).

Model EI. Leaders who are EI champions also need to walk the talk of EI. There are three behaviors that seem to make the difference, changing the tone of the organization's culture as a whole:

Self-regulation. A company's founder frequently got angry—and it impacted everybody. As one executive who had reported to him put it, "He would rip into you. He was fine about it and could move on in five minutes. But the other people in the group couldn't. So we found ourselves trying to gauge where he was emotionally before sharing information with him, and that isn't a good thing. If there is an issue an employee has and they need your help and they can't approach you right away, it just multiplies by the time it gets to you."

"Self-regulation" is technical jargon for managing your own emotions and what you say and do. For example, don't blow up at people. Research shows that when a boss explodes in anger at someone, that person feels alienated and prefers to distance himself from the boss afterward (though this may take the form of passive resistance if that person still has to work with the boss). Over-the-top anger from a boss kills the connection.

Emotional transparency. When the leader of a business died, the second in command talked to his staff about his own grief, with his eyes tearing up. This opened up a conversation about the emotions staff were feeling. And the leader's vulnerability came across as a strength, a mark of authenticity, rather than a weakness. A combination of self-awareness and empathy, being emotionally transparent, means giving people a window onto your own feelings.

Emotional presence. BL Companies' CEO Carolyn Stanworth started meeting virtually with all of the 365-plus employees every Friday for an hour at noon when the pandemic started, and then kept her schedule open for the rest of the afternoon so that she could respond immediately to the emails she always received from employees after the meeting. In doing so, she models empathy, putting herself in her employees' shoes and sensing how disappointed or anxious they would be if she put off answering them.

Be available emotionally. This means being empathetic toward your people, showing an underlying respect but still having clear boundaries—creating a norm for them to do the same. A case in point, for our digital age: The former president of the CRM division at Progressive, John Murphy, wanted to connect as much as possible with the company's 7,000 or so agents across the country. Pre-Covid he would go into the field and talk to managers, cultivating relationships, which in his view are the fuel that keep people in the game. If he has a tough ask, it goes easier if he has a good connection. He'd send handwritten notes and videos an agent might find useful. With the onset of Covid, though, Murphy couldn't visit each one, so he created a Facebook page as a way to share in the lives of the agents. While there were just a handful of agents on the page at first, attendance grew to a large majority.

The page is about people's lives, not their work: people post their anniversaries, the birth of kids, and other such details of their lives. With the advent of the Covid lockdowns and as fears of the virus spread, the Facebook page emerged as a place where agents could share their anxieties and show their gratitude, such as being glad to have a job in a difficult economy. Murphy sent messages—for example, congratulation on a wedding anniversary, and other such personal wishes. The Facebook page served to bring together the company's far-flung agents.

The importance of leaders in building an emotionally intelligent organization was summed up well by CEO Stanworth. When we commented that managing emotions seemed to be a big part of her job, she immediately responded, "It *is* the job."

Emotional Intelligence Throughout

Initiating a sustained culture shift toward emotional intelligence takes patience. For most companies it takes years; for some, decades. Despite the benefits, many companies are reluctant to focus on something as intangible and "soft" as emotions. Also, leaders sometimes resent the implication that their emotional intelligence isn't where it should be and resist training on that score.

At Progressive Insurance's CRM division, when the then-new division president, John Murphy, endorsed emotional intelligence almost two decades ago, he met with resistance. When emotional intelligence assessments were required for top-tier leaders, those same executives pushed back initially. As one of those involved in leadership development put it, "The culture wasn't ready. It was hard for leaders to hear they weren't where they wanted to be on emotional intelligence."

But Murphy persisted. He dedicated his annual leadership meetings with regional managers to emotional intelligence, emphasizing the value of self-awareness, self-management, and empathy in their relationship-based business, insurance sales. Over the years the number of field agents who have undergone development for emotional intelligence grew from just 200 or so to around 5,000 of the 7,000 agents.

"In the early years the culture was tactical and transactional," says Murphy. "Now there's been a culture shift to relational, due to the increasing emotional intelligence level of our leaders." Murphy sees emotional intelligence as the secret sauce for nourishing and sustained connections, both among his own people and with their clients. "Relationships," as he puts it, "are the heart of everything we do."

The EI Organization: An Ideal Type

As we were exploring the research and reflecting on how emotional intelligence can boost organizational performance, we came up with a tentative diagnostic list of what might be distinguishing signs. We were inspired in part by the group norms that Druskat and Wolff found in high-performing teams, and adapted their insights to the organizational level.

In generating this list we drew on such research findings as well as our own extrapolations to piece together what an emotionally intelligent organization would look like. At this point we need to speculate, because the exact research we would need for a more definitive look has not been done—precisely the situation we were in a quarter century ago with emotional intelligence in the workplace. Only after decades of research on how emotional intelligence boosts individual performance, leadership, and teams have we been able to write this book. What follows is an aspirational vision of what the ideal emotional intelligent organization might look like.

As with individual and team EI, the emotionally intelligent organization exhibits self-awareness. This means an understanding of the emotions, needs, and motives that course through the networks of people who make up the organization. Reading the emotional climate at the organization level most often takes the form of climate surveys in teams and within larger business units. On the one hand, sterling readings—individual or team—are celebrated or otherwise rewarded and encouraged. On the other, when such assessments reveal problem areas, the organization explores underlying causes and acts to fix them. This means the organization creates or has in place processes for looking into systemic sources of stress. It also requires the organization to recognize how its own policies and practices impact employees emotionally, for better or for worse.

Another sign of self-awareness at this level: knowing the organization's strengths—what it has been good at doing—as well as its limits, which identify areas where growth and development will be needed. This includes sensitivity to the emotions and needs of employees throughout the organization, and communicating to specific internal groups in a timely, empathic, and caring way.

Self-awareness makes the next step, self-management, possible. For an EI organization, this means managing feelings within the outfit itself—for instance, establish norms for the appropriate expression of emotion. Such norms should be modeled by leaders at every level in their own emotional expression, and violations of this norm need to be named and dealt with. Such violations might include, for instance, rudeness, yelling at people, or other such signs of anger or panic run amok. On the positive side, leaders can model effectiveness under pressure—for instance, by staying positive and optimistic when facing setbacks or challenges.

Along with helpful norms for emotional expression, an EI organization would become aware of how it might be increasing stress in employees, and find ways to lessen those stressors. Common systemic stresses include routinely expecting people to do too much with too little time or too few resources. One sign of such stress might be high turnover rates—people tend to flee too-high stress. Another source of systemic stress for minorities could be implicit bias against those groups—and again higher turnover by such groups would be another indicator. Climate surveys can help here, signaling where pressure and stress points might be found.

Another organizational strategy for systemic stresses might be to help individuals become more resilient—that is, able to recover more quickly from the stress of a setback. But this approach requires the organization not do so in a way that "blames the victim" by putting the onus on people more vulnerable to stress—rather than fixing aspects of the organization that create that stress in the first place.

Clarity about expectations and goals offers another path for managing internal upsets. A lack of clarity about goals creates confusion, which hampers drive and motivation. Conversely, an organization's clarity about its goals helps the individual marshal the energy that lets him or her go beyond just meeting their own KPIs, to helping with larger aims. Here articulating a shared sense of meaning in the organization's purpose can inspire and guide people at every level.

Along with clear goals, organizations can encourage their people to connect and collaborate. This could mean a norm as simple as encouraging sharing of information, but it often goes beyond, to create events, for instance, where workers and leaders can get to know each other as people: a weekly after-hours meet-up at a local eating joint, for instance, or a weekend off-site. This bonding can include having rituals and celebrations and the like to raise everyone's spirits. Celebrating wins is an obvious move, but these spirit-raising events can happen throughout the year.

Then there's fostering that sense of belonging. Just as Vanessa Druskat (and Google) found this feeling of belonging in a safe space as essential to top team performance, the same holds for organizations. That psychological sense of belonging goes far beyond just, for example, going by numbers and ratios to meet goals for diversity, equity, and inclusion; the feeling of truly belonging is a mental reality that makes DEI work. Lacking that sense of belonging, numbers alone that seem to show an ideal ratio of a minority group to the overall workforce are meaningless.

Then there are the ways people in a workplace can help each other with a shared self-awareness of the emotional climate. This shared awareness allows another key step: helping each other manage disturbing feelings like grief at the death or departure of a workmate, or the loss of friends when a company has to let large numbers of people go. Rather than ignore the unsettled feelings such normal losses bring, an EI organization can collectively recognize them and talk through their emotional reactions, helping one another manage those feelings—think of Carolyn Stanworth at BL Companies holding an open meeting to talk about the feelings aroused by downsizing because of poor market conditions.

Then there is the challenge of a hybrid workweek, with people working remotely, asynchronous communication, virtual meetings, side conversations over Slack, and tribes or subcultures forming that are invisible to senior leaders. EI can help communicate culture and climate when leaders seize any opportunity to remind everyone that how they manage themselves and their relationships matters more than ever—and model this themselves.

A more positive side of helping manage emotions better can be seen in people coaching each other—learning together how to do better. While this should always be part of a leader's role, such coaching can happen peer to peer, too.[3]

Finally, there's what an organization can learn from its failures—an inevitable part of organizational life. Sadly, too many outfits play a "blame game," simply finding a person or lapse to pin the failure on, and stopping there. An EI organization would use that setback as a learning opportunity, seeing what went wrong, but also going beyond to anticipate how to handle such a challenge going into the future. That lets the organization be more agile in confronting changing demands. Even better, it can make it a "learning organization," one that continually takes lessons from its own operations that will let everyone there keep learning how to improve.

Then there are a set of norms in an EI organization that make it skilled in handling other organizations, from those in its supply chain that it depends on to keep operating smoothly, to customers, to competitors, to regulators and beyond. This ability starts with organizational-level empathy: understanding how other entities see this one, what they feel and need, what motivates them and the like. This can include monitoring how this organization impacts the local community and the environment. It also requires ongoing communication with all the external groups that matter to it, in ways that are not just timely and accurate, but also caring.

Finally, there's skillfully managing emotions in these relationships, just as the emotionally intelligent leader or team does. At the organizational level this might mean forming alliances with key organizations. The marketing and communications functions are critical here: the organization's messaging should spread compelling, even inspiring, themes that elevate both sender and recipient. Should conflicts with other entities arise, the EI organization would manage them constructively. And, ideally, the operations of the organization would contribute to sustainability—for itself, for other entities, and for the larger environment.

In short, forward-looking organizations bring emotional intelligence into the DNA of their culture. Data shows that being an emotionally intelligent organization enhances performance as shown by many metrics: profit and growth, retention and loyalty, more positive motivation and engagement. Such organizations incorporate "soft skills" like EI into their performance reviews along with the usual hard measures. They offer EI training and encourage employees at every level to go through it.

EI in the DNA means leaders model and advocate it. The most powerful alliance entails a business leader who endorses EI and a people department that offers ways to improve this skill set. But if this idea is new to an organization it will take time to bring the essential changes— and it takes persistence and patience. Leaders can take specific steps to move an organization in this direction. These include showing how EI matters for the organization's goals and bottom line; modeling EI by managing well their own emotions and relationships; being open about their own feelings; and empathizing with what people are going through.

As we'll see in Part IV, these people skills will be essential in the skill set that we will all need to face whatever challenges and crises lie in the years ahead.

PART IV

The Future of Emotional Intelligence

14

The Crucial Mix

We've seen what the basics of emotional intelligence involve, how they help boost us into our optimal state, and how this matters in work life. Now we look beyond emotional intelligence per se to envision what other abilities EI could synergize to help us better handle whatever challenges lie ahead for humanity.

A seed for this larger lens was planted years ago when Dan gave a talk on EI to top leaders at Salesforce and then had dinner with Marc Benioff, founder and CEO. Marc urged Dan to write about how emotional intelligence was synergistic with creativity, hard skills, and a strong sense of purpose. He called them "the four Qs": EQ, IQ, CQ (for creativity), and SQ (spiritual intelligence, or purpose).

Along the same lines, Tim Cook, CEO of Apple, gave a similar recipe of talents when he described the set of abilities that he looks for in hiring someone.[1] Cook, who at the time was receiving an honorary degree at the University of Naples Federico II in Italy, said people he's hired at Apple have done very well there if they are equipped with this particular mix of skills:

- *Technical expertise in their field of choice.* This cognitive skill set includes a wide *curiosity*—asking lots of questions—a trait named essential for the future by our Consortium member Claudio Fernández-Aráoz, several years earlier.[2] As we'll see, a wide net of information-gathering that builds on current expertise can be a first step in innovation.

- A deep sense of *purpose*, caring about the world around us, and wanting to leave the world better than when we found it. That mission—a reason bigger than just oneself—acts as a driver for people's best work. A company needs a similar mission to draw out its employees' sense of purpose, a vision about enhancing the lives of people. Lacking this, no amount of money would make a job worth doing.
- *Innovative collaboration.* Working well on a team. Apple's uncanny history of product innovation, CEO Cook said, depends on people developing new ideas together rather than an individual coming up with a creative insight. Creativity means "thinking differently" about a problem, not being caught up in easy, standard solutions, but looking at it "from different angles."

We've reflected on Benioff's and Cook's thinking, and added to it. In particular, it seems to us that in addition to these skill sets, a *systems* lens will also be essential for meeting whatever challenges the future may hold.

Emotional Intelligence, Of Course

Various aspects of EI get highlighted anew in different decades, and no doubt will matter more and more in the future. Different dimensions of a given competence may loom larger in days to come than they have in the past—for instance, as we saw with adaptability, a talent for agility in meeting changing demands and calm in the face of ambiguity and uncertainty rather than, say, juggling multiple tasks, might become the most germane parts of adaptability for leaders in the days ahead.

The predicted earthquake in jobs, driven by the advent of AI-created text, may well mean drastic change in who does what. But as AI puts some of us out of work, assists others in what we do already, and creates new job possibilities, the need for person-to-person excellence remains—and likely will be all the more valuable.

Then there's workplace changes as fundamental as who comes into work and how often. A hybrid workplace depends on virtual communication, whether by email or videoconference. While our brains developed their social radar for face-to-face interactions, we foresee more and more virtual meetings. Perhaps because a virtual connection gives us fewer channels for sensing the feelings of the other person, we become all the more sensitive to whatever emotional cues come our way. Here again emotional intelligence adds an essential layer of effectiveness to whatever cognitive abilities you may have.

There's a good reason emotional intelligence will likely remain a distinguishing asset for leaders and organizations at large: as automation and chatbots mean more and more jobs are done by robots and AI, human work will escalate to higher-level tasks like design and creativity—even as routine work in fields like engineering gravitates to these nonhuman assistants. If every company has more or less the same technologies and hard skills, the difference will be greater in how those companies manage their people.

As a Conference Board global survey points out, "While automation is infiltrating the workplace, teams are still composed of people and recognition of the 'human touch' is needed more than ever."[3]

Then there's the unique outlook-shaping experiences of our younger generations—and leaders of the future.

Purpose

Do you remember duck-and-cover?

For those who don't, that was a drill school students practiced every month or so in the 1950s and 1960s: you stoop under your desk and put one hand over your eyes, the other over your neck. That, your teacher assured you, would protect you from a nuclear blast.

If you recall duck-and-cover, that marks you as a Baby Boomer. The exercise was ubiquitous during the height of the Cold War, as was talk of fallout shelters.

But if instead of duck-and-cover you recall "active shooter" drills in school, hiding in your classroom or running down the halls to escape, you are a member of Generation Z or the next generation, the youngest of whom are still doing this drill in schools, while the oldest are entry-level in many companies.

A generation's shared trauma can lead to a collective sense of purpose. For instance, hidden in this difference between Boomers and Gen Z lies a gap between the realistic fears of younger consumers and entry-level workers—as well as their older peers, Generation X—but which may elude the Boomers who are still running corporations.

First, consider some telling differences between these older and younger groups. The two generations have lived through very different shared trauma. For those born in the decades after the end of World War II, these include not just the Cold War but the accompanying fears of nuclear destruction. Headlines magnified nuclear terror by telling of ever-more-destructive bombs and their delivery systems. Many homes had fallout shelters.

But if you were born since 1980 or so, your cohort's generational trauma—apart from school shootings—has centered on fears of environmental meltdown. We are in the midst of a steady drumbeat of alarming ecological news: huge wildfires from Australia to California, record-setting heat waves in Europe and Antarctica, and hundreds of blocks in cities and entire towns inundated by waters from a huge hurricane. That unnerving drumbeat continues in the daily news.

The difference between the two age cohorts is telling, especially when it comes to finding a sense of purpose in combating the momentum of climate change. Those of the older generation lived through economic boom times and few hints of troubles with Mother Nature. Today's younger generations are keenly alert to environmental dangers. Many of them are discovering a heartfelt sense of meaning in finding ways to slow down, if not reverse, what they perceive as a planet-wide death march.

A Gallup poll put numbers to this age gap: 70 percent of Americans between 18 and 34 are worried about the impacts of global warming, while among those 55 and older the rate is just 56 percent. The relationship between age and environmental concern: the younger the group, the more they care about the environment.

The generation gap grows even bigger if you ask what may be the most telling question, whether you think climate change will become a problem for you during your lifetime.

For the youngest, Gen Z, the environment tops the list of issues they want corporations to address. If younger consumers and talented younger employees find an urgent purpose in doing the right thing for the environment, then companies would do well to embrace such goals. But to loosen the pressure on companies for quarterly results, investor expectations would need to change. That might allow for more environment-enhancing missions, like reducing an organization's carbon footprint.

Companies are increasingly seeking a larger mission, some driven by activists and investors. But consumers are increasingly playing a role in this trend. Companies would do well to find that second purpose in doing what they can to combat the planetary drift toward warming. While that strategy was largely a bust in former times when relatively few consumers cared about the climate, there are signs that the time for this is now. The difficulty is aligning what consumers say they want with what investors want. Managing that ambiguity demands equanimity from a leader, yet another instance where EI matters.

For Gen Z the environment tops the list of issues they want corporations to address. Declaring environmental concerns as vital to a corporation's mission could be of immense help in attracting and retaining talented young people, many of whom say they do not want to work for a company that does not align with their own sense of purpose. Plus, companies that are genuine "good guys" in the eyes of Gen Z and Millennials are more likely to win their loyalty as clients and customers in years to come.

Eco-anxiety seems to be shaping a new consumer style among the youngest, placing greater value, for example, on repurposing than on purchasing. An online survey of 1,338 people, reported in the *Journal of Environmental Psychology*, found that 46 percent felt strong anxiety about their environmental future, and these fears were strongest among the youngest surveyed.[4] A significant number of the very youngest with eco-fears espoused the more thrifty shopping ethos. Experts expect such worries to increase among the young as time goes on.

The timeworn assumption that eco-impacts are a problem of the commons, not of those who create the impacts, no longer serves us. More and more companies are putting their mission in terms of making the world a better place one way or another. Aligning that purpose with actions that both improve the planet and appeal to the values of young people seems a smart move.

A Bus Ride

It's been decades since that steamy summer day in Manhattan when Dan took a bus, the M101, up Third Avenue. He still remembers the bus driver, a jovial, outgoing African American of middle age who carried on an entertaining monologue commenting on places the bus passed by. He alerted us to sales going on, told us a bit of the history of buildings and stores, offered reviews of films playing at theaters whizzing by, and suggested we visit exhibits at nearby museums.

It wasn't the specifics of what he said, but the ebullient mood he transmitted. That bus was a cauldron of emotional contagion, all positive. On that muggy August day most passengers boarded in a sullen mood. But as they exited the bus that driver would smile and wish them a happy day—and their smiles in return showed their mood was already heading there.

Years later Dan learned from an obituary in the *New York Times* that the driver's name was Govan Brown. His obituary revealed that Brown had been pastor of a Black church on Long Island, and saw his passengers as part of his flock. He brought a greater purpose—tending to his flock—to what otherwise could be seen as a mundane job.

Govan Brown's sense of purpose stands in stark contrast to that of the New York City Transit agency of the Metropolitan Transportation Authority, his employer. That organization's mission might be summarized as simply getting passengers to their destinations efficiently—which has little or nothing to do with tending to the well-being of those passengers. The MTA's formal, rather dry mission statement: "enhance the quality of life and economic health of the region through the cost-efficient provision of safe, on-time, reliable, and clean transportation services."

But, surprisingly, such a mismatch of personal purpose and organizational mission may not matter that much. Simply being in touch with *your* purpose can matter greatly, more than the match itself.

Research by our Consortium colleague Signe Spencer at the Korn Ferry Institute applauds being "purposeful"—having clarity about your own purpose and, at best, finding some way in which your purpose can become compatible with whatever niche you have in your organization. Such purposefulness, her data shows, has a high correlation with both feeling engaged in one's work, and with commitment to your organization.[5]

For instance, take the counterintuitive advantage of a fossil fuel company hiring a climate change activist whose purpose revolves around ending carbon dioxide emissions: that's the vision and energy that might help that company open a division aiming at carbon reduction through alternative energy, which could prove a major strategy for that company's survival in the future.

In short, you need not have an exact match between your personal purpose and your organization's mission. Companies can benefit, it turns out, by welcoming people, like Govan Brown, whose burning purpose is not a cookie-cutter fit with that organization's mission.

Of course, not everyone will be as fortunate as Govan Brown, finding meaning in a job that, on the surface, may seem merely about taking people from here to there. A value conflict between your heart and your job can be a huge stress. Take the school nurse who was repeatedly asked by her principal to do things she felt violated her professional ethics. She quit.

That fit between our values and what we do speaks to the power of purpose, the sense that our efforts matter in what has meaning for us. Meaningful work helps us get into and stay in our optimal zone. Our inner compass—indicating what feels right and what feels off—points us there.

If you recall times you've been at your best, in your optimal state, you were engaged and enthused. Our richest experiences are most likely to come not when we are toiling toward someone else's imposed goals, but rather when we are doing what we love well, when we are working toward something bigger than just getting ahead.

Values like warmheartedness, friendship, belonging, and loyalty—in short, caring about other folks—are more likely to make someone both engaged with their work and a good organizational citizen than are valuing self-transformation and personal well-being. Such people-oriented values correlate well with purposefulness—and in turn with organizational commitment and engagement. Organizations whose purpose was to benefit or improve the world around them did better than those whose purpose was to improve their own position.

As Spencer put it, "Employees don't necessarily need to have their personal purpose aligned with their organization's stated purpose, but they do benefit from feeling that there is a connection between their work and a meaningful-to-them purpose."

The quest for money alone, without regard for ethics, morals, or meaning, can lead to a worsened sense of well-being. Many people find that having a purpose greater than personal profit and financial rewards is more rewarding.

Dan's bus trip with Govan Brown, which he recounted in the opening pages of *Emotional Intelligence*, struck a chord with Howard Gardner, the Harvard psychologist. He saw Brown as a prime example of what he and his research partners, William Damon at Stanford and the late Mihaly Csikszentmihalyi, then at Claremont Graduate University, called "good work": a mix of first-class performance, utter engagement, and a guiding ethical purpose. That combination makes someone excellent at work they enjoy and find deeply satisfying.

Indeed, Brown was an outstanding bus driver. When he retired, hundreds of his devoted passengers came to a party in his honor—the only time New York City Transit threw such a retirement event. By then he had gotten more than 1,400 letters of commendation—and not one complaint.

Purpose vs. Pay

Perhaps surprisingly, an organization's purpose can rise in priority even over pay when employees look for a best fit between their values and their job.[6] That creates a strategic reason for companies to be more purpose-driven: increasing numbers of young people say they want to work for a company that supports their own sense of purpose.

Research tilts to a life purpose as mattering more when it comes to life satisfaction. It's no secret that career success by objective standards like a high-level title or large paycheck does not guarantee happiness; there are all too many harried and unhappy high-level executives.

Data reported in the *Journal of Gerontology* showed that simply finding a sense of purpose and meaning in one's work led to life satisfaction more than having a high-status job. It's how you feel about your job—the subjective reality—that makes for high levels of satisfaction.

Take the nuns who ran an institution for people with severe developmental disabilities. Their job, for most people, would be tough: cleaning up messes constantly, having to remind people over and over to care for themselves in the most rudimentary ways. Burnout rates among staff in such places are notoriously high.

Yet when Cary assessed the nuns who operated such a place he found the burnout rate was virtually zero. The main reason? The nuns shared a sense of purpose, that they were serving God. One nun, for instance, told him she loved every minute of her work, even the most menial, unpleasant parts like cleaning up after a resident had an accident. The meager salary didn't matter, she added, because she believed the most meaningful rewards would come when she entered heaven.

As we reported in Chapter 1, on people's best days, when they felt they have made progress, their motivation was internal. They were doing their work because they loved it, not because of some reward they might get. It wasn't money or promotion that drove them, but rather enjoyment of the work itself. They were the opposite of apathetic or disengaged.

Putting a Man on the Moon

Legend has it that way back in the 1960s, a janitor working at NASA, on being asked what he did, said, "I'm helping to put a man on the moon." Like that bus driver, this janitor saw a larger purpose in what otherwise might seem a mundane role.[7]

While money and status might be lures for a given job, our sense of purpose will be a stronger force in how engaged we feel once on that job, and so how hard we work at it. Large studies find only a marginal connection between salary and how satisfied people are with their work.[8]

When it comes to ranking jobs by how meaningful people find them, health care and social work—which explicitly help a greater good—rank high.[9] But as the NASA janitor's tale makes clear, people can find their own sense of meaning in what they do.

People who find meaning in what they do give all the signs of being in that optimal zone: they report better emotional and physical well-being and say they feel great engagement in their role; they thrive and grow. By the way, that role may have nothing to do with work as we think of it; great meaning can be found in raising children or caring for an aging parent.

This view of purpose as a prime motivator seems at odds with standard management practices that use rewards like bonuses, promotions, and salary to prod people to do their best. That standard assumption—that we work better in exchange for such reinforcements—has long been under attack by a rather subversive argument: that such rewards can actually *decrease* performance.

The rewards-performance connection was called into question by research decades ago that showed people were more motivated by passion and purpose than by the rewards they were offered.[10] Alfie Kohn's

1993 book, *Punished by Rewards: The Trouble with Gold Stars, Incentive Plans, A's, Praise, and Other Bribes* (the title says it all), made the case that grades, for instance, killed students' interest in their work. The bulk of research evidence supported his argument, which gained steam as others joined his view. As challenging as it was to the normal ways of thinking about what motivates students and workers, that view swept through many corners of the business and education worlds.

The strongest argument for this anti-reward view comes from mountains of data gathered on students, looking at the connection between grades (a reward or a punishment, depending) and achievement. Kohn reviewed findings by psychologists of the day like Edward Deci and Richard Ryan showing that having an inner drive to learn was a far better motivator than simply working hard for a good grade.[11] That same argument was taken to the workplace in Daniel Pink's book *Drive*, a business bestseller.[12] Pink argued rather persuasively that too many organizations follow an outmoded management practice, trying to goad workers to better performance via rewards in one form or another. It's far better when motivation comes from inside, and we feel we have made a choice rather than being told what to do; feel a sense of mastery, or at least that we are getting better; and finally, feel that what we do aligns with our sense of what matters to us.

In that Harvard Business School study when people kept diaries of their workday, standard management motivators backfired in how they impacted workers. The Harvard study backed Pink's conclusion: threats, harsh evaluations, too-tight deadlines, even the promise of rewards like bonuses all fall into the category of "extrinsic," or imposed motivators, and don't necessarily help performance, particularly in the long term.

Take a finding from that Harvard study of the inner reality of a workday: In a rebuttal to the common assumption that high pressure and fear increase a person's productivity, the data showed just the opposite. The days when people were most pleased with how they had done were highly positive, leaving them happy. Most telling, on those days they felt they were guided by what mattered to them most rather than driven by someone else's agenda for them.

The big paradox here: when people are self-motivated to do their work, they do it much better and enjoy it far more than when they do the same work under threat or pressure. Yet students still strive to get good grades; workers work harder to get a better salary or a promotion—at least that's the predominant idea when we look around us at the motivators life offers.

More recent research has led to a more nuanced understanding. There are times when outer rewards work just fine giving us a strong encouragement to pursue our work. But those rewards are most potent when they are synergistic with inner motivation, reinforcing what we do because we already enjoy it.[13]

Let's say you find meaning and purpose in what you do. Does that make you impervious to how other people see what you do—that is, you are so dedicated internally that you don't really care how others view your efforts? It turns out that how people who matter to you—teachers if you are in school, your boss at work, say—let you know how well you are doing can still make a difference to you.

So if you get some negative feedback—a poor grade, or bad performance review—that can set you back, even if your main motivator is how meaningful the task is for you.[14] On the other hand, even negative feedback can strengthen your inner motivation if it includes tips on how you can improve, you agree with the standards used to judge you, and you get that feedback in person and in a timely way.[15]

These three steps—showing how to improve, fair evaluation, and on-the-spot feedback—turn out to be an effective way to give anyone data on how well they are doing while helping them develop further strengths.

Big-*P* and Small-*p* Purpose

Laurie Santos, who has taught perhaps the most popular course in the history of Yale—on happiness—assigns Alfie Kohn's book to her students. Santos says when her super-high-achieving students read that book they often express uncertainty as to the point of simply building more accolades, and ask, what's the purpose of their life?

Her answer: "It's smelling your coffee in the morning. Loving your kids. Having sex and daisies and springtime. It's all the good things in life."

What Santos lists here can be seen as "small-*p* purpose," the everyday pleasures that give us a boost. But a strong argument can be made that it is "big-*P* Purpose," the deeper inner motivations that move us, that truly gives our lives meaning and purpose.

Your sense of purpose revolves around the values that bring meaning to what you do. Purpose reflects your moral rudder or "true north," the deep outlooks you find most compelling that guide you in your most crucial decisions. This rings true particularly for the big-*P* Purposes in our life, the singular calling that resonates with us most strongly.

One of the rare survivors of the Nazi death camps—and a famous advocate for big-*P* Purpose—was Viktor Frankl, a Viennese psychiatrist. His parents, brother, and pregnant wife all perished there. When he was sent to Auschwitz, the first of four camps he survived, his overcoat had stitched into its lining the manuscript of a book he very much wanted to publish. The coat was taken from him the day he arrived, but the burning desire to one day publish that book stayed with Frankl over the four years of his incarceration.

The book Frankl sought to publish was *Man's Search for Meaning*, which later became an international bestseller, and a moral compass for generations of readers. In it he argues that by finding a sense of meaning and purpose in life we can survive even the worst of hells—and he offers his own years in four camps and near death as evidence.[16]

Frankl's thesis: that a purpose in life helps us overcome even the worst. As Frankl put it, quoting a favorite line from the German philosopher Friedrich Nietzsche, "Whoever has a *why* to live can bear almost any *how*."

Giving up operating from a self-centered set of values—like minimizing pain and maximizing pleasure—allows us to follow a more values-driven agenda, making choices premised on who we want to be instead of merely how we feel.[17]

Many companies are putting their mission face forward when recruiting entry-level folks, like Gen Z college grads. "What they want to hear about is how we're solving cancer or what we are doing for river blindness," reports Tracey Franklin, vice president of talent recruitment at Merck. "They believe they can actually change the world, and want to work for a company who does change the world."[18]

As climate warming increases, an organization with environmental sustainability as a core purpose will very likely attract more talented younger leaders. Beyond sustainability, consider regeneration, operating in ways that actually help the planet regain its splendor.[19]

Of course our values and mission may morph as life goes on.

At the fiftieth year reunion of his college class, Dan asked about a hundred classmates how many of them were engaged in some sort of activity that was to help others, not just in their self-interest. Nearly every hand went up.

That reflects what we heard from another Consortium member, Kathy Kram, an emeritus professor at Boston University's Questrom School of Business, who with other academic retirees was engaged in research on so-called "retirement." They were finding that fewer and fewer people actually retire anymore, at least in the sense of not working at all. Rather, they found, people in the last stage of life talk about the change in their sense of purpose. When you leave the job you've held for so long it's natural to mourn the loss of your work identity. But then, they find, this leaves you wide open to find a new purpose, a pursuit that has meaning for you.

At the end of a career, purpose looms larger for many, if only because they now count their life in how many years they might have left, rather than how long since they were born. What their legacy might be takes on more import. As people retire from their day job, and mourn the loss of that identity, the question emerges: How can I use my skills and talents for a meaningful purpose?

"People go from being tenants—living for a mission defined by their job—to architects of their sense of meaning," as Kram put it. "You can use your expertise to help a cause you believe in. And your days can have more joy and less toil."[20]

The Purpose of Emotional Intelligence

Bus driver Govan Brown embodies a sometimes overlooked sign of high-level emotional intelligence: He left each person he connected with feeling better. His very being had a nutritious impact on everyone he contacted—he was an urban saint, spreading ripples of good feeling in a city that sorely needs them.

The first two parts of emotional intelligence—focusing on ourselves so we can better manage our disturbing emotions, and marshaling more positive ones like resilience—creates a calmer view, a mindset that sees the upside potential in ourselves and everyone else and lets us keep going toward our goals. When our inner world has that balance, we can tune in to each person with empathy and, once attuned more effectively connect with them. If all this goes right, the other person will come away from our interaction in a more positive state—one that moves them toward their optimal zone.

So Govan Brown's contagiously warm treatment of his bus passengers bespeaks a purpose of emotional intelligence: *to put ourselves and anyone with whom we connect closer to the optimal state.*

Some key points: Emotional intelligence will be necessary, but not sufficient in itself, for meeting the challenges just over the time horizon, not to mention far into the future. A synergistic mix of capabilities will power better responses to the crises, challenges, and opportunities humanity will confront. For one, a strong sense of purpose will fuel the necessary drive for solutions. Younger people seem particularly drawn to causes and organizations that see their purpose in terms of a greater good. Finally, as we'll see in the next chapter, two more synergistic skill sets include an understanding of systems and the spirit of innovation.

15

Innovation and Systems

Two biologists, François Jacob, from Paris, and Sydney Brenner, a South African (each of whom later won a Nobel Prize), were spending a day off from their lab at the California Institute of Technology (Caltech) lolling on a nearby beach.[1] For months they had been stumped by failed attempts to reproduce in vivo a ribosome, the chemical messenger that emerges from RNA to instruct a gene to make a given protein—a key to genetic activity.

Despite their fussing with the complex biochemistry involved, even when they captured the right molecules the mixture fell apart. They knew that in nature there was certain to be a chemical glue that would hold the ribosome together—but they were flummoxed. What could it be?

Brenner, musing on the beach, was certain the suspect was a simple chemical, one that was ubiquitous in everything biological. Then out of the blue it came to him, and sand flying, he bolted upright and shouted, "It's the magnesium!"

And it was.

They went back to their lab and added magnesium to the ribosome mix. When they got the proportions right, the chemical messenger held together—a small triumph in the long march toward today's genomic science. Genetic science (like every other scientific field) has been formed via a staggering number of such creative insights—small wins—each building on previous knowns but combining them in unique ways.

We see a particular kind of mental agility as having crucial value for innovation—and the ability to innovate will only take on increasing import as we head into a future packed with unheralded changes and challenges, opportunities and obstacles. Mental agility, in the form of altering our mental state, turns out to be a key to creative insight.

That moment of insight by the sea embodies the classic three stages of creativity. *First* there's the immersion in the problem itself—here, fruitless tinkering with the biochemistry of the ribosome. In the *second* stage the mind goes into neutral, wandering off where it will; this stage ends with "illumination," the creative insight—that's what happened on the beach. Finally there's the *third* stage, execution, where the hard work of putting the insight into action—making it useful—goes on.

Each of these stages in a creative arc demands a different brain state. The first activates neocortical regions for curiosity and wide information-gathering. The second stage, sometimes called "incubation," turns that activity off and instead engages a neural network called the "default mode network," or DMN, which takes over when our mind is not focused on a particular task.[2] In this mode creative insights are more fertile, with novel ideas arising seemingly out of nowhere. In the third stage we execute on the insight and turn it into a useful form, which again requires task-focused neocortical activity.

In short, creativity requires the mental agility to shift your brain state out of the get-it-done mode to the daydreamy receptive DMN state where your mind floats free and where novel elements are more likely to combine in never-seen-before ways—*It's magnesium!*

Then comes another shift, to the task-focused neural activity needed for execution, where we hammer the creative insight into a useful form. For Brenner and Jacob this meant the arduous work of trying to find the right proportion of magnesium. Each needs the other—the creative insight guides the execution stage, and the trial-and-error during execution finally yields the right way to make that insight a reality.

A brain scan comparing people who readily came up with creative ideas and those who struggled to have such fresh ideas revealed key differences in how their brains operate.[3] Analysis of which brain regions were more strongly connected to each other revealed that the more creative group had greater connectivity between key parts of the prefrontal cortex (the left inferior frontal gyrus, among others) and the DMN. Their more fluid creativity seems linked to the DMN and its talent for imaginative thought, and the brain's executive centers.

The brain states during incubation and execution operate on very different clocks. The DMN, the home of incubation, can't be hurried, while execution watches the clock. At a high-end fashion company an executive complained to Dan about a perennial tension between the creative designers and the CEOs of their division, each a famous brand. That tension might be inevitable: design genius hinges on insights during incubation, which can't be programmed on a schedule, while the CEO must execute on fresh designs three or four times a year no matter what, starting production well before the designs are made public. The two operate on entirely different timelines, a recipe for trouble.

The three-stage formulation of the creative process dates back at least to the seventeenth century, when mathematician and philosopher Blaise Pascal proposed these stages of creativity. Science finds his model still holds up. The first step in a creative act often begins with curiosity, where you explore broadly and gather information widely, all bearing in some way on the problem needing a creative solution.

Curiosity

Francis Bacon, the story goes, was journeying through London on a snowy day when he suddenly wondered if the cold could preserve a dead chicken. Bacon, the seventeenth-century philosopher and early developer of the scientific method, investigated this by stuffing snow into a dead chicken. But in doing so he got chilled, caught pneumonia, and died.

This perhaps apocryphal story was told by another seventeenth-century philosopher, Thomas Hobbes, as a cautionary tale, a warning about the downsides of too much curiosity. Its modern parallel might be falling for clickbait, conspiracy theories, and what scientists actually call "bullshit."

On the other hand, researchers find, a healthy curiosity can make us more creative. It all comes down to how we handle our innate habit of being "infovores," hunting for information that helps us find the meaningful patterns that can help us make sense of life's uncertainties. While a wide-ranging curiosity can yield much data that has little immediate use, we have a natural tendency to fill in gaps in our understanding, a tendency that drives our search for what's surprising and perhaps might be useful.

This drive seems to have a basis in the brain's operations. Uncertainty, or a gap in information, activates circuitry in the prefrontal cortex that in turn triggers positive feelings and energizes memory.[4]

This healthy curiosity has benefits for creativity, exposing us to a wider range of novel facts, ideas, and ways of seeing that can help us find insights or new solutions to vexing problems. But the kind of curiosity we bring matters. The worst might be a morbid curiosity, which has us explore, for example, grisly crimes, or the mental itch that drives us to pursue questionable theories and doomscroll. The best has been called "joyous exploration," a wide-ranging interest joined with real pleasure in learning and in deep reflection.[5]

Incubation

At a dinner, Dan was seated across the table from Maya Lin—famous for designing the Vietnam Veterans Memorial. Soon, Maya told him, she was going to Paris to create an installation. But, she continued, she has no idea what it would be; the place would speak to her.

Sitting next to Dan was Ian Cheng, who has created an entirely new art form merging AI, video game technology, cognitive science, and free-floating imagination.[6] Cheng explains that during his creative moments he lets his unconscious mind show him what to do next.

In a sense Lin and Cheng are saying the same thing, from a brain perspective, describing a mental maneuver that we see as increasingly vital in the future: being open to creative insight, the seed of all innovation.

A novelist writes about how she gets her inspirations: "There are times when finding material to work with is really hard. When ideas aren't flowing, I try to let my mind wander without the distractions that accompany my computer (Twitter! Instagram! Email!)."[7]

She praises "unplugged moments"—not listening to some podcast, multitasking, or otherwise immersing yourself in someone else's thoughts. Better, she finds, is taking a quiet walk. The DMN takes over in such downtimes: lolling on a beach, taking a bath or shower, during the boredom of a commute. At such times we're more readily able to let go of focusing on some problem, and (with luck) solutions bubble up from the mind's depths into an Aha! moment, the illumination. Good ideas arise seemingly out of nowhere. The Roman philosopher Cicero is credited with noting, "Only the person who learns to relax is able to create, and for them ideas reach the mind like lightning."

When Harvard researchers analyzed hundreds of people's diary entries made during the workweek, they found that creative thinking was rare on days with urgent time pressure, and far more common on days with low time pressure.[8] The very rare exception—people coming up with breakthrough ideas under high pressure—occurred when people were under the gun on a project so important, all other distractions were kept at bay so they could concentrate on finding a solution. That suspension of other responsibilities may have allowed time to dip into the DMN.

Execution

Mending a horse's ailing hooves is one of the perennial challenges for farriers, who tend to the health of hooves. At their worst, hoof ailments cause bone loss severe enough to be fatal to a horse.

"I'd been using Velcro, nails, all the usual ways to put a horse's cracked hoof back together," said the late Doug Ehrmann, a seasoned farrier. "None of them worked."

Ehrmann had a history of creative inventions in his world of farriers, including a half-dozen patents. These patentable ideas, he said, come out of nowhere, in the middle of the night. One night he had a crucial insight about ailing hooves: "I saw that the remedy had to be something you nail into the hoof—and these years people had been shying away from anything nailed, favoring sealers like Velcro and glue."

Ehrmann couldn't recall whether he or his business partner came up with the idea to use zinc for the DE Hooftap they were going to sell to farriers. The hooftap is an antimicrobial zinc-coated, slightly curved inch of narrow steel with three hooklike points for holding the device in place. Zinc, Ehrmann and his partner knew, wouldn't rust, a real problem when you are trying to heal a horse's hoof—you just can't get a horse to keep its hooves dry.

But once they started to distribute these to farriers, they received reports that the taps were healing hoof disease, an effect they hadn't expected. As Ehrmann delved into the properties of zinc, he found that the metal halts the progression of an infection.

While the zinc-coated taps would not cure an infected hoof, the hooftap encourages new cell growth that restores the wall to health. So as Ehrmann and his partner executed on the zinc insight, they stumbled on a new reason for its use and a fresh way to market the hooftap.

This fine-tuning typifies the execution phase, where the new and novel concept gets road-tested by use, and the need for niggles, nudges, and adjustments makes it better and better.

Ehrmann held the patent on DE Hooftaps, a remedy that seems a miracle cure for a host of hoof troubles, from laminitis to split toes. A $2 million racehorse had chronic split toes—which could have ended its racing career—but was cured by DE Hooftaps. A professor at Cornell University College of Veterinary Medicine—the Harvard Medical School of veterinary medicine—has been using the DE taps with horses he treats.

As Howard Gardner, the Harvard psychologist, points out, two features make a new idea a creative act: a novel combination of elements, and usefulness.[9] The incubation stage elicits that novel combination, while the execution stage revolves around usefulness.

While getting a novel and useful insight may seem the hard part of the creative arc, creatives themselves often argue that the toughest phase is executing on that. Execution means you coax the novel idea into a useful form. This takes not just the relevant technical skills, but also discipline, focus, and the ability to inspire others to join you—in short, emotional intelligence.

Getting execution right may be as simple as reframing the invention to signal its use—*DE Hooftaps help healing*—or as challenging as finding just the right ratio of magnesium to use, which took lots of experimentation.

As with magnesium in genetic science, creating that final reality can take endless troubleshooting and problem-solving, and overcoming unforeseen challenges. As the Harvard study of a good day found, "Small steps forward shared by many people can accumulate into excellent execution."[10]

The singular enemy of the mental agility necessary for innovations: rigidity. At one of the world's largest petroleum companies, an investigation by *Bloomberg Businessweek* discovered, management's reluctance to use windfall oil profits to research innovative and more sustainable ways to operate led to deep dissatisfaction, particularly in its IT division.[11] As a result, many talented tech experts decided to quit the company.

Or take what happened with the BlackBerry, the brand that dominated the early market for smartphones. In those years many companies gave their employees a BlackBerry, taking advantage of its superior security and well-designed keyboard. The co-CEOs of BlackBerry focused the company's R&D on improving such technical elements—and failed to notice that corporations had begun to let their employees bring their own Android and Apple phones to work. Even as their market share plummeted, the engineer duo of co-CEOs staked the company's future on the same old, rigid focus. These days it's hard to find a BlackBerry anywhere.

The history of listings on the New York Stock Exchange tells the story of companies that have been adept at this form of adaptation, and those that have not. Almost all the companies listed a century ago no longer exist. They've largely been replaced by companies powered by innovative thinking that have brought to market once-novel products and services that in many cases put their old rivals out of business. These companies will in turn either die or innovate. The future will only bring more pressures and opportunities for companies to survive, even thrive, through creativity and innovation.

It's the System

"There are elections today on my island," a woman from the Caribbean tells Dan, "and I can vote down there. There are two parties, and either one will pay my plane fare down so I can vote."

But there's a catch, she adds. "They expect you to vote for them if they pay your airfare. And both parties are corrupt."

Whoever wins the election, she explains, will fill the government with their cronies, and those in power will get rich on bribes. On her island the wealthy get richer while the poor stay in shacks.

That predicament, with a moneyed power class and an impoverished underclass, typifies all too many nations these days. While corruption adds another layer to the problem, the economic basis for the growing gap between rich and poor was pinpointed by the research in Thomas Piketty's *Capital in the Twenty-First Century* that documented an inexorable trend over centuries for owners to grow richer and workers relatively poorer.

While charity by the wealthy can help the plight of the poor a bit, the need is far greater than philanthropy alone can fix. As that woman from the Caribbean says, the whole system is rife with troubles. One answer, which seems highly unlikely, is a radical change in the system.

Organizational Awareness, an EI competence, bespeaks a systems perspective. Usually described in terms of understanding the dynamics within a family or organization, this awareness applies to any level of system. That includes economic and political systems, as in that woman's insights about her island home—empathy on a global scale.

We all are exposed to such systems dynamics in our extended family of origin, the people around us when we grew up. Who influenced whom? Was there an uncle or aunt who had an outsize influence on one or another parent? A sibling whose opinions counted more than those of other brothers or sisters? Then as a teenager, who among your friends was the strongest influence on you and your peers—the "cool kid"?

In other words, there almost always is one or a few people who are far more influential than other family members or those in a friendship circle. So it is with organizations, which in their fundamental dynamics are a kind of family, with subterranean social networks. Being able to understand who influences whom lies at the heart of the Organizational Awareness competence.

Being able to name who the members of a given social network might be suggests you have organizational awareness, the ability to read the social systems at work. Those who are able to create a cascade of changes, for example, do not have to hold a titled position to be effective—but they need to move those in their social network and beyond toward that change.[12]

So at the heart of organizational awareness lies the ability to read the emotional currents and power relationships in a group, and so know who influences whom.[13] This means understanding the sense in which an organization is a social system—this capacity depends on systems thinking.

Along with networks of influence, this sensitivity lets you pick up the unspoken rules and guiding values that operate in that social reality, recognize the personal networks that matter, and so find the right person to make key decisions—even build a coalition to get things done.

Global crises like climate warming, the rich-poor gap, political corruption, and the like all indicate a greater need for systems thinking if we are to face these challenges.

The turbulent realities ahead in systems like climate, the economy, and society at large demand we focus on the wider web that offers us both opportunity and sets limits on our choices. This systemic awareness lets us understand how the dynamics of technological evolution, of economic cycles, of cultural and social fashions, and of the inexorable environmental warming will impact our goals and how to get there.

Here's a systemic dilemma that impacts each of us all our lives: Our environmental surround constantly feeds us a mix of air pollution, toxic chemicals, contaminants in our water and food, radiation, pharmaceutical compounds, heavy metals, particulates, and the like. These chemicals slowly accumulate in our body to produce a lifetime exposure that, in turn, speeds diseases like cancers, asthma, dementia, and heart disease, not to mention the ravages of aging.[14]

To be sure, at any one moment this deadly mix arrives in small doses; it's their buildup in our bodies over a lifetime that matters most. Each year as many as 12 million people, one estimate has it, die prematurely from the cumulative impacts of these exposures—about 20 percent of all deaths and a third of premature deaths (among those in people ages 30–69). That's more than deaths from infections, violence, or tobacco.

While genetic susceptibilities certainly matter here, evidence suggests that our daily exposure to this long list of environmental toxins has an even larger impact on our health. Enter the new science of *exposomics*, the study of the multitude of ways these exposures damage our biology.

The culprit here: us. Since the 1950s, for example, hundreds of thousands of newly synthesized industrial chemicals have been added to the mix of our exposures, with virtually no understanding of their adverse health impacts (at least in the U.S.; European countries have been more alert to these dangers). We just blithely use these chemicals in our clothes and cosmetics, spread them on our crops, and deploy them in the vast array of material goods we use daily.

We are oblivious to the biological costs, which mount up slowly as the total of such chemicals or their derivatives that we carry in our bodies. They increase inflammation, cell death, and organ damage, trigger cancer and chronic diseases like diabetes, and age our bodies faster. They also disrupt our endocrine function, make us more susceptible to allergies and infections, and interfere with cognition.

Despite all this, the biological pathways to any of these troubles are opaque; we can't know for sure that what we are exposed to "causes" any of these problems. So the causes continue to harm us in a multitude of ways—with no "smoking gun" to show exactly how they harm us.

Given that such exposures matter enormously for our collective health, what can we do to protect ourselves? That's where the mix of capacities—emotional intelligence, a strong sense of purpose, innovation, and systems thinking—becomes essential. Creating transparency about these chemicals will require strong collective resolve, if only because so many products contain toxic ingredients that those who sell them to us will resist identifying publicly. Innovations in how we spot and post publicly such ingredients will be needed. A larger systems view would allow us to survey the wide range of exposures we get from all parts of our environmental surround. Doing all this with emotional intelligence will up the odds that this perhaps uncomfortable and even confrontational process of discovery and transparency will go more smoothly.

In undertaking such gargantuan tasks, we would do well to consider the critical difference between concern and influence. Our radius of concern can range from the people we love and are most concerned about (our circle of caring), to concerns for dangerous drivers, to planetary climate warming. But then there's your circle of influence—the people and issues where we can actually have an impact.[15] Our influence depends greatly on the position we hold—a congressman in the U.S. or the CEO of a global food company has a larger sphere of influence than, say, the driver of a truck for that company.

It makes sense, then, to focus our efforts where we can matter (or, as the philosopher-clown Wavy Gravy has said, "Put your good where it will do the most"). The converse of this: trying to change what we can't—because it lies outside our sphere of influence—dissipates our energy and wastes our time.

On the other hand, while individually we may not make that big a difference, as an aggregate a network of people doing the same small action can add up to a major effect. Elections are the obvious case in point and so are shareholders voting en masse to change a corporate strategy, or consumers boycotting a product.

We can expand our circle of influence by forming alliances or partnerships with those who have more power in a given domain. We may not be highly effective toward a given goal, but might know (and be able to partner with) others who are. The Dalai Lama advises doing whatever we can toward the goals that matter to us, even if we may not live to see those goals achieved: at least we do our part in moving the ball that much further down the field.

AS WE WRITE THIS, THE POPULATION OF EARTH HAS JUST REACHED 8 billion people. Can our planet survive carrying all those people? That's an open question at this point. As the Dalai Lama points out, we are essentially all the same—but, as he repeatedly says, "We must learn to live together."

This will, no doubt, require deep rethinking of systems we've long taken for granted. As we complete this book the president of Columbia University's business school, no less, notes that even the foundations of our economic give-and-take are open to question, as he says, in light of "climate change, issues of social justice, and what globalization means for societies." He adds that "all of these are raising profound questions about what the future can be."[16]

Going into the uncertainties of the future—a hotter planet, more people competing for fewer resources, widening gaps between rich and poor, growing polarities of beliefs and ideology, to name a few clear trends—managing our own emotions looms as step one in dealing with the crises we are certain to confront. That will let us better make sound decisions in the face of tough situations, stay motivated and goal-focused, and maintain positive relationships. Collaboration and teamwork will, no doubt, be essential.

"You can plan for a hundred years but you don't know what will happen the next moment," a wise Indian yogi once told Dan. The old song "Que Sera, Sera" tells us "the future's not ours to see." Innovations yet to come, for instance, may be major game changers. In short, no one knows.

With these cautions in mind, we realize as we look ahead to how emotional intelligence might matter, we head into the fog of the future. A disclaimer: we have no idea what's in that thick cloud, but these have been our best guesses as to what skill sets, along with emotional intelligence, could possibly help us navigate whatever storms we meet ahead.

Acknowledgments

First, a heartfelt thanks to Ania Wieckowski, our erstwhile editor at the *Harvard Business Review*. Her queries and challenges led us to see that what we had to say was best argued in this longer book rather than in a shorter *HBR* article. Ania, perhaps inadvertently, guided us on our way.

We appreciate too the members of the Consortium on Research for Emotional Intelligence in Organizations (CREIO), whose findings over the years have both confirmed and helped us think through our message—and whose research we cite repeatedly.

Dan thanks Jonathan Dahl for permission to use some of Dan's columns from *Korn Ferry Briefings* and a few of his blogs from kornferry.com in this book. Dan feels grateful, too, to Marc Benioff, CEO at Salesforce, who encouraged him to write what eventually evolved into this book.

Many others contributed insights, data, or other reflections that have informed our thinking, including: Richard Boyatzis, Michael Stern, R. J. Sadowski, George Kohlreiser, Richard Davidson, Diana and Jonathan Rose, Bill George, Ronald Humphrey, Signe Spencer, Ruth Malloy, Matt Lippincott, Richard Hua, Elizabeth Lesser, Emma Bena, and Bilal Ghalib.

Cary thanks Rob Emmerling, who made it possible for Cary to devote full time to this project by ably assuming the helm at CREIO. Cary also thanks Cornelia Roche, whose many contributions in their previous work informed this book. His gratitude also to Lara Delmolino Gatley and the other administrative staff at the Rutgers Graduate School for Applied and Professional Psychology who continue to provide support for Cary's projects.

Special appreciation goes to our editor at HarperCollins, Hollis Heimbouch, who set us free to think through the issues and points we raise here.

We thank our wives. Dan, as always, appreciates his wife Tara Bennett-Goleman's intuitive genius in emotional intelligence, her warm-hearted advice, and all he has learned from her over the years. Cary thanks his wife, Deborah, a model of emotionally intelligent leadership, who was always there for him with loving-kindness and support every step of the way.

Notes

Introduction | Your Optimal Zone

1. The description of the match and the quotes in the next four paragraphs are from David Waldstein, "How Ajla Tomljanovic Faced Down Serena Williams and 24,000 Others," *New York Times*, September 3, 2022.

2. By design the Consortium brings together practitioners of all persuasions who are trying out applications of emotional intelligence in organizations like businesses and schools, with academic researchers who can apply their methodological skills to such studies. See www.eiconsortium.org. As of this writing Rob Emmerling has stepped into the director's role.

3. According to the Georgetown University Health Policy Institute Center on Children and Families, anxiety and depression increased 27 percent for anxiety and 24 percent for depression from 2016 to 2019. There was a 21 percent increase in behavior and conduct problems between 2019 and 2020.

1 | Optimal You

1. A similar inner landscape has been mapped by other psychologists. Martin Seligman, who spearheaded the "positive psychology movement," calls it "flourishing," which shares several points in common with what we are calling the optimal state. See Martin Seligman, *Flourish* (New York: Atria, 2012).

2. Alice Isen et al., "Positive Affect Facilitates Creative Problem Solving," *Journal of Personality and Social Psychology* 52, no. 6 (1987): 1122–31, https://doi.org/10.1037/0022-3514.52.6.1122.

3. B. Frederickson and C. Branigan, "Positive Emotions Broaden the Scope of Attention and Thought-Action Repertoires," *Cognition and Emotion* 19 (2005): 313–32.

4. Susie Cranston and Scott Keller, "Increasing the 'Meaning Quotient' of Work," *McKinsey Quarterly*, January 1, 2013.

5. These are soft numbers. We need more hard-nosed research to determine actual percentages for amount of time in an optimal state and how much more productive people are while in it. Think of these estimates as hypotheses for further testing.

6. The recipe for a good day: Teresa Amabile and Steven Kramer, "The Power of Small Wins," *Harvard Business Review*, May 2011.

7. Teresa Amabile and Steven Kramer, *The Progress Principle* (Boston: Harvard Business Review Press, 2011).

8. Ibid., 54.

9. Shannon Watts interviewed in *Tricycle*, Spring 2022, 85.

10. See, for example, Amy Arnsten and P. S. Goldman-Rakic, "Noise Stress Impairs Prefrontal Cortical Cognitive Function in Monkeys: Evidence for a Hyperdopaminergic Mechanism," *Archives of General Psychiatry* 55 (1998): 362.

11. Mihaly Csikszentmihalyi, *Beyond Boredom and Anxiety* (San Francisco: Jossey-Bass, 1975).

12. See, e.g., Steven Kotler, "Create a Work Environment That Fosters Flow," *Harvard Business Review*, October 2019.

13. Mihaly Csikszentmihalyi and Isabella Selega Csikszentmihalyi, eds., *Optimal Experience: Psychological Studies of Flow in Consciousness* (New York: Cambridge University Press, 1988).

14. Charles Duhigg, *The Power of Habit* (New York: Random House, 2014).

15. C. J. Fullagar and E. K. Kelloway, "Flow at Work: An Experience Sampling Approach," *Journal of Occupational and Organizational Psychology* 82 (2010): 595–615, doi:10.1348/096317908X357903.

16. S. Engeser and F. Rheinberg, "Flow, Performance and Moderators of Challenge-Skill Balance," *Motivation and Emotion* 32 (2008): 158–72, https://doi.org/10.1007/s11031-008-9102-4.

2 | Emotional Intelligence and the Bottom Line

1. This academic debate about emotional intelligence and workplace performance continues: Marie T. Dasborough et al., "Does Leadership Still Need Emotional Intelligence? Continuing the Great EI Debate," *Leadership Quarterly* (2021), https//doi.org/10.1016/j.leaqua.2021.101539.

2. See J. C. Rode, M. Arthaud-Day, A. Rawaswami, and S. Howes, "A Time-Lagged Study of Emotional Intelligence and Salary," *Journal of Vocational Behavior* 101 (2017): 77–89, https://www.researchgate.net/publication/316816644_A_time -lagged_study_of_emotional_intelligence_and_salary.

3. B. Kidwell, D. M. Hardesty, B. R. Murtha, and S. Sheng, "Emotional Intelligence in Marketing Exchanges," *Journal of Marketing* 75 (2011): 78–95.

4. R. E. Boyatzis, K. Rochford, and K. Cavanagh, "The Role of Emotional and Social Intelligence Competencies in Engineer's Effectiveness and Engagement," *Career Development International* 22 (2017): 70–86, doi:10.1108/CDI-08-2016-0136.

5. Business Wire, "MDRT Study Finds Americans Deem Emotional Intelligence the Most Trustworthy Quality in an Advisor," https://www.businesswire.com /news/home/20200507006157/en/MDRT-Study-Finds-Americans-Deem -Emotional-Intelligence-the-Most-Trustworthy-Quality-in-an-Advisor.

6. Ibid.

7. J. Grobelny, P. Radke, and D. Paniotova-Maczka, "Emotional Intelligence and Job Performance: A Meta-analysis," *International Journal of Work Organisation and Emotion* 12 (2021): 1–47, doi:10.1504/IJWOE.2021.10037977.

8. See D. L. Van Rooy and C. Viswesvaran, "Emotional Intelligence: A Meta-analytic Investigation of Predictive Validity and Nomological Net," *Journal of Vocational Behavior* 65, no. 1 (2004): 71–95, doi:10.1016/S0001-8791(03)00076-9; D. L. Joseph and D. A. Newman, "Emotional Intelligence: An Integrative Meta-analysis and Cascading Model," *Journal of Applied Psychology* 95 (2010): 54–78, doi:10.1037 /a0017286; E. H. O'Boyle Jr., R. H. Humphrey, J. M. Pollack, T. H. Hawver, and P. A. Story, "The Relation Between Emotional Intelligence and Job Performance: A Meta-analysis," *Journal of Organizational Behavior* 32 (2011): 788–818, doi:10.1002 /job.714; D. L. Joseph, J. Jin, D. A. Newman, and E. H. O'Boyle, "Why Does Self-Reported Emotional Intelligence Predict Job Performance? A Meta-analytic Investigation of Mixed EI," *Journal of Applied Psychology* 100, no. 2 (2015): 298– 342, https://doi.org/10.1037/a0037681; C. Miao, R. H. Humphrey, and S. Qian, "Emotional Intelligence and Job Performance in the Hospitality Industry: A Meta-analytic Review," *International Journal of Contemporary Hospitality Management* 33 (2021): 2632–52, https://doi.org/2610.1108/IJCHM-2604-2020-0323.

9. D. L. Joseph and D. A. Newman, "Emotional Intelligence: An Integrative Meta-analysis and Cascading Model," *Journal of Applied Psychology* 95 (2010): 54–78, doi:10.1037/a0017286.

10. W. Schaufeli, A. B. Bakker, and M. Salanova, "The Measurement of Work Engagement with a Short Questionnaire," *Educational and Psychological Measurement* 66, no. 4 (2006): 701–16.

11. J. K. Harter, F. L. Schmidt, and T. L. Hayes, "Business-Unit-Level Relationship Between Employee Satisfaction, Employee Engagement, and Business Outcomes: A Meta-analysis," *Journal of Applied Psychology* 87 (2002): 268–79, doi:10.1037/0021-9010.87.2.268. See also B. L. Rich, J. A. LePine, and E. R. Crawford, "Job Engagement: Antecedents and Effects on Job Performance," *Academy of Management Journal* 53 (2010): 617–35. They found a strong link between worker engagement and performance in a study of 245 firefighters and their supervisors.

12. Gallup, *State of the Global Workplace: 2022 Report*, https://www.gallup.com/workplace/349484/state-of-the-global-workplace.aspx#ite-393245.

13. M. d. C. Pérez-Fuentes, M. d. M. M. Jurado, J. J. G. Linares, and N. F. O. Ruiz, "The Role of Emotional Intelligence in Engagement in Nurses," *International Journal of Environmental Research and Public Health* 15 (2018): 1915, doi:10.3390/ijerph15091915.

14. L. Wang, "Exploring the Relationship Among Teacher Emotional Intelligence, Work Engagement, Teacher Self-Efficacy, and Student Academic Achievement: A Moderated Mediation Model," *Frontiers in Psychology* 12 (2022):810559, doi:10.3389/fpsyg.2021.810559.

15. Y. Brunetto, S. T. Teo, K. Shacklock, and R. Farr-Wharton, "Emotional Intelligence, Job Satisfaction, Well-being and Engagement: Explaining Organisational Commitment and Turnover Intentions in Policing," *Human Resource Management Journal* 22 (2012): 428–41.

16. Maggie was a subject in Cary's ten-year follow-up study of how new professionals in human service settings recovered from early career burnout. See Cary Cherniss, *Beyond Burnout: Helping Teachers, Nurses, Therapists, and Lawyers Overcome Stress and Disillusionment* (New York: Routledge, 1995).

17. C. Miao, R. H. Humphrey, and S. Qian, "A Meta-analysis of Emotional Intelligence and Work Attitudes," *Journal of Occupational and Organizational Psychology* 90 (2017): 177–202, doi:10.1111/joop.12167.

18. Ibid.

19. Gallup, *State of the Global Workplace: 2022 Report*.

20. See T.-Y. Park and J. D. Sha, "Turnover Rates and Organizational Performance:

A Meta-analysis," *Journal of Applied Psychology* 98 (2013): 268–309, doi:10.1037/a003072.

21. See M. Riketta, "Attitudinal Organizational Commitment and Job Performance: A Meta-analysis," *Journal of Organizational Behavior* 23 (2002), doi:10.1002/job.141. This meta-analysis combined 111 separate samples. Also see Miao, Humphrey, and Qian, "A Meta-analysis of Emotional Intelligence and Work Attitudes."

22. Dennis W. Organ, *Organizational Citizenship Behavior: The Good Soldier Syndrome* (Lexington, MA: Lexington Books, 1988).

23. T. M. Nielsen, G. A. Hrivnak, and M. Shaw, "Organizational Citizenship Behavior and Performance," *Small Group Research* 40, no. 5 (2009): 555–77, doi:10.1177/1046496409339630.

24. C. Miao, R. H. Humphrey, and S. Qian, "Are the Emotionally Intelligent Good Citizens or Counterproductive? A Meta-analysis of Emotional Intelligence and Its Relationships with Organizational Citizenship Behavior and Counterproductive Work Behavior," *Personality and Individual Differences* 116 (2017): 144–56, https://doi.org/10.1016/j.paid.2017.04.015. This meta-analysis combined 56 studies, a total of 11,542 employees.

25. The meta-analysis for counterproductive work behavior (CWB) covered 17 samples and 3,914 employees.

26. For instance, one meta-analysis with over 19,000 participants found a link between emotional intelligence and mental, psychosomatic, and physical illness. A. Martins, N. Ramalho, and E. Morin, "A Comprehensive Meta-analysis of the Relationship Between Emotional Intelligence and Health," *Personality and Individual Differences* 49, no. 6 (2010): 554–64, doi:10.1016/j.paid.2010.05.029. See also K. V. Keefer, J. D. A. Parker, and D. H. Saklofske, "Emotional Intelligence and Physical Health," in C. Stough, D. H. Saklofske, and J. D. A. Parker, eds., *Assessing Emotional Intelligence: Theory, Research, Applications* (New York: Springer, 2009), 191–218; and G. Matthews, M. Zeidner, and R. D. Roberts, "Emotional Intelligence, Health, and Stress," in C. L. Cooper and J. C. Quick, eds., *Handbook of Stress and Health: A Guide to Research and Practice* (London: Wiley, 2017), 312–26.

27. When people had to perform a public speaking task in the laboratory, cortisol levels were lower for those who had higher EI. M. Mikolajczak, O. Luminet, C. Fillée, and P. de Timary, "The Moderating Impact of Emotional Intelligence on Free Cortisol Responses to Stress," *Psychoneuroendocrinology* 32 (2007): 1000–1012, https://doi.org/10.1016/j.psyneuen.2007.07.009.

28. Keefer, Parker, and Saklofske, "Emotional Intelligence and Physical Health." See also the review by S. Laborde, F. Dosseville, and M. S. Allen, "Emotional Intelligence in Sport and Exercise: A Systematic Review," *Scandinavian Journal of Medicine and Science in Sports* (2015), e-pub ahead of print.

29. H. S. Friedman and M. L. Kern, "Personality, Well-being, and Health," *Annual Review of Psychology* 65 (2014): 719–42.

3 | Emotional Intelligence, Redux

1. Peter Salovey and John D. Mayer, "Emotional Intelligence," *Imagination, Cognition and Personality* 9, no. 3 (1990): 185–211, https://doi.org/10.2190/DUGG-P24E-52WK-6CDG.

2. Cliff Lansley, "What Scientists Who Study Emotional Intelligence Agree On," Emotional Intelligence Academy, April 2021, https://www.eiagroup.com/.

3. Cary Cherniss, "Emotional Intelligence: Toward Clarification of a Concept," *Industrial and Organizational Psychology: Perspective on Science and Practice* 3, no. 2 (2010), 110–26.

4. David C. McClelland, "Testing for Competence Rather than for Intelligence," *American Psychologist* 28 (1973): 1–14.

5. Lyle M. Spencer and Signe M. Spencer, *Competence at Work: Models for Superior Performance* (New York: Wiley, 1993).

6. See, e.g., Jonas W. B. Lang and Harrison Kell, "General Mental Ability and Specific Abilities: Their Relative Importance for Extrinsic Career Success," *Journal of Applied Psychology* 105, no. 9 (2020): 1047–61.

7. Jared S. Allen et al., "What Matters More for Entrepreneurship Success? A Meta-analysis Comparing General Mental Ability and Emotional Intelligence in Entrepreneurial Settings," *Strategic Entrepreneurship Journal* 15, no. 3 (2020): 352–76.

8. This difference is one bit of evidence among many that suggest different brain systems operate each of these human abilities; the search for those networks is underway. See, e.g., Chunlin Li et al., "Large-Scale Morphological Network Efficiency of the Human Brain: Cognitive Intelligence and Emotional Intelligence," *Frontiers in Aging Neuroscience*, February 24, 2021, https://doi.org/10.3389/fnagi.2021.605158.

9. Cherniss, "Emotional Intelligence."

4 | Self-Awareness Applied

1. George Mumford, interviewed in *Tricycle*, Summer 2003, 103.

2. Richard Huskey et al., "Flexible and Modular Brain Network Dynamics Characterize Flow Experiences During Media Use: A Functional Magnetic Resonance Imaging Study," *Journal of Communication* 72, no. 1 (February 2022): 6–32, https://doi.org/10.1093/joc/jqab044.

3. Daniel Goleman and Richard Davidson, *Altered Traits: Science Reveals How Meditation Changes Your Mind, Brain, and Body* (New York: Avery, 2018).

4. See, e.g., James Wagner, "For the Mets, Deep Breaths, a Little Chatter and a Lot of Wins," *New York Times*, June 26, 2022.

5. J. D. Rooks et al., "'We Are Talking About Practice': The Influence of Mindfulness vs. Relaxation Training on Athletes' Attention and Well-Being over High-Demand Intervals," *Journal of Cognitive Enhancement* 1 (2017): 141–53, https://doi.org/10.1007/s41465-017-0016-5.

6. Self-awareness definition: From KeyStepMedia, *Emotional Self-Awareness: A Primer* (Florence, MA: MoreThanSound, 2017), 34.

7. See, e.g., Amishi Jha et al., "Mindfulness Training Modifies Subsystems of Attention," *Cognitive, Affective, & Behavioral Neuroscience* 7 (2007): 109–19, https://doi.org/10.3758/CABN.7.2.109. The evidence for this effect has become stronger over the years.

8. David Fessell and Cary Cherniss, "Coronavirus Disease 2019 (COVID-19) and Beyond: Micropractices for Burnout Prevention and Emotional Wellness," *Journal of the American College of Radiology* 17 (2020), doi:10.1016/j.jacr.2020.03.013.

9. Matthew Killingsworth and Daniel Gilbert, "A Wandering Mind Is an Unhappy Mind," *Science*, November 12, 2010, 32.

10. J. G. Randall et al., "Mind-Wandering, Cognition and Performance: A Theory-Driven Meta-analysis of Attention Regulation," *Psychological Bulletin* 140, no. 6 (2014): 1411–31, doi:10/1037/a0037428.

11. Michael Mrazek et al., "Mindfulness Training Improves Working Memory Capacity and GRE Performance While Reducing Mind Wandering," *Psychological Science* 24, no. 5 (2013): 776–81, doi:10.1177/0956797612459659.

12. For more detail on mindfulness research, see Goleman and Davidson, *Altered Traits*, 2018.

13. Clifford Nass in an NPR interview, as quoted in *Fast Company*, February 2, 2014.

14. Amishi Jha et al., "Short-Form Mindfulness Training Protects Against Working Memory Degradation over High-Demand Intervals," *Journal of Cognitive Enhancement* 1 (2017): 154–71, https://doi.org/10.1007/s41465-017-0035-2.

15. Mind and Life Education Research Network, "Contemplative Practices and Mental Training: Prospects for American Education," *Child Development Perspectives* 6, no. 2 (2012): 146–53, https://doi.org/10.1111/j.1750-8606.2012.00240.x.

16. Amishi Jha et al., "The Effects of Mindfulness Training on Working Memory Performance in High-Demand Cohorts: A Multi-study Investigation," *Journal of Cognitive Enhancement* 6 (2022): 192–204, https://doi.org/10.1007/s41465-021-00228-1.

17. Mark Connor was a subject in Cary Cherniss's research. See C. Cherniss, *Beyond Burnout: Helping Teachers, Nurses, Therapists, and Lawyers Overcome Stress and Disillusionment* (New York: Routledge, 1995).

18. Susie Cranston and Scott Keller, "Increasing the 'Meaning Quotient' of Work," *McKinsey Quarterly*, January 1, 2013.

19. Daniel Kahneman, *Thinking, Fast and Slow* (New York: Farrar, Straus & Giroux, 2013).

20. Oprah Winfrey, *The Path Made Clear* (New York: Flatiron Books, 2019), 14.

21. The EI course: https://www.keystepmedia.com/emotional-intelligence/.

22. Marc Brackett, *Permission to Feel* (New York: Celadon Books, 2020).

5 | Manage Yourself

1. Gabriele Gratton et al., "Dynamics of Cognitive Control: Theoretical Bases, Paradigms, and a View for the Future," *Psychophysiology* 55 (2018), https://doi.org/10.1111/psyp.13016.

2. L. Pruessner, S. Barnow, D. V. Holt, J. Joormann, and K. Schulze, "A Cognitive Control Framework for Understanding Emotion Regulation Flexibility," *Emotion* 20, no. 1 (2020): 21–29, https://doi.org/10.1037/emo0000658.

3. See, e.g., Chai M. Tyng et al., "The Influences of Emotion on Learning and Memory," *Frontiers in Psychology* (2017), https://doi.org/10.3389/fpsyg.2017.01454.

4. Walter Mischel, *The Marshmallow Test: Mastering Self-control* (New York: Little, Brown, 2018).

5. Philip K. Peake, "Predicting Adolescent Cognitive and Self-Regulatory Competencies from Preschool Delay of Gratification," *Developmental Psychology* 26, no. 6 (1990): 978–86.

6. Angela Duckworth et al., "What *No Child Left Behind* Leaves Behind: The Role of IQ and Self-control in Predicting Standardized Achievement Test Scores and Report Card Grades," *Journal of Educational Psychology* 104 (2012): 439–51.

7. Leah S. Richmond-Rakerd et al., "Childhood Self-control Forecasts the Pace of Midlife Aging and Preparedness for Old Age," *PNAS* 118, no. 3 (2021): e2010211118, https://doi.org/10.1073/pnas.2010211118.

8. V. M. Dotson et al., "Depression and Cognitive Control across the Lifespan: A Systematic Review and Meta-analysis," *Neuropsychology Review* 30 (2020): 461–76, https://doi.org/10.1007/s11065-020-09436-6.

9. Ulrike Zetsche et al., "Shedding Light on the Association between Repetitive Negative Thinking and Deficits in Cognitive Control—Meta-analysis," *Clinical Psychology Review* 63 (2018): 56–65.

10. As a boy he helped support his impoverished family by selling newspapers on the streets of Chicago, but he managed to go to college, then to law school, cofounded a business law firm (D'Ancona, Pflaum, Wyatt & Riskind)—and eventually became general counsel to the Hertz Corporation.

11. A. E. Poropot, "A Meta-analysis of the Five-Factor Model of Personality and Academic Performance," *Psychological Bulletin* 135 (2009): 322–38, http://dx.doi.org/10.1037/a0014996.

12. Patrick C. L. Heaven and Joseph Ciarrochi, "When IQ Is Not Everything: Intelligence, Personality and Academic Performance at School," *Personality and Individual Differences* 53 (2012): 518–22.

13. Angela Duckworth, *Grit: The Power of Passion and Perseverance* (New York: Scribner's, 2016).

14. Angela Lee Duckworth and Patrick D. Quinn, "Development and Validation of Short Grit Scale (Grit-S)," *Journal of Personality Assessment* 91, no. 2 (2009): 166–74. This is Duckworth's most-cited article on grit. Duckworth notes the similarity to McClelland's achievement motive, but claims grit applies to harder-to-reach and more long-term goals.

15. Teresa Amabile and Steven Kramer, *The Progress Principle: Using Small Wins to Ignite Joy, Engagement, and Creativity at Work* (Boston: Harvard Business Review Press, 2011).

16. Suniya S. Luthar, Nina L. Kumar, and Nicole Zillmer, "High-Achieving Schools Connote Risks for Adolescents: Problems Documented, Processes Implicated, and Directions for Interventions," *American Psychologist* 75, no. 7 (2020): 983.

17. Emily Esfahani Smith, "Teen Anguish in the Pandemic," *New York Times*, May 9, 2021, Week in Review, 8.

18. Reported in the American Institute of Stress, https://www.stress.org/stress-level -of-americans-is-rising-rapidly-in-2022-new-study-finds.

19. KeyStepMedia, *Building Blocks of Emotional Intelligence, Achievement Orientation: A Primer* (Florence, MA: MoreThanSound, 2017), 24.

20. Angela Duckworth and James J. Gross, "Self-control and Grit: Related but Separable Determinants of Success," *Current Directions in Psychological Science* 23, no. 5 (2014), https://doi.org/10.1177/0963721414541462.

21. Colin O'Brady quoted in Alex Tzelnic, "Extremely Still," *Tricycle*, Spring 2022, 58.

22. Carol Dweck, *Mindset: Changing the Way You Think to Fulfill Your Potential* (New York: Avery, 2016).

23. Daeun Park et al., "The Development of Grit and Growth Mindset During Adolescence," *Journal of Experimental Child Psychology* 198 (2020), https://doi .org/10.1016/j.jecp.2020.104889.

24. Martin Seligman, *Learned Optimism* (New York: Vintage, 2006).

25. KeyStepMedia, *Building Blocks of Emotional Intelligence, Positive Outlook: A Primer* (Florence, MA: MoreThanSound, 2017), 23.

26. Susan David, *Emotional Agility* (New York: Avery, 2016).

27. Adaptability definition from KeyStepMedia, *Building Blocks of Emotional Intelligence: The Twelve Crucial Competencies* (Florence, MA: MoreThanSound, 2017).

28. The EI online competence course: see https://courses.keystepmedia.com/.

6 | From Burnout to Resilience

1. Ed Yong, "Why Health-Care Workers Are Quitting in Droves," *The Atlantic*, November 16, 2021.

2. See, e.g., https://www.kornferry.com/insights/this-week-in-leadership/workplace -stress-motivation.

3. Infinite Potential, *The State of Workforce Burnout 2023*, https://infinite-potential.com.au/the-state-of-burnout-2023.

4. https://www.stress.org/stress-level-of-americans-is-rising-rapidly-in-2022-new-study-finds.

5. Emotional self-control or emotional balance: KeyStepMedia, *Building Blocks of Emotional Intelligence, Emotional Self-control: A Primer* (Florence, MA: More-ThanSound, 2017).

6. The classic formulation: R. S. Lazarus and S. Folkman, "Transactional Theory and Research on Emotions and Coping," *European Journal of Personality* 1, no. 3 (1987): 141–69, https://doi.org/10.1002/per.2410010304.

7. Connie (not her real name) was part of a study of new professionals conducted by Cary and a team of researchers. See Cherniss, *Beyond Burnout*.

8. S. Toppinen-Tanner et al., "Burnout Predicts Hospitalization for Mental and Cardiovascular Disorders: 10-Year Prospective Results from Industrial Sector," *Stress & Health* 25, no. 4 (October 2009): 287–96, cited in C. Maslach and M. P. Leiter, "Understanding the Burnout Experience: Recent Research and Its Implications for Psychiatry," *World Psychiatry* 15, no. 2 (2016): 103–11, https://doi.org/10.1002/wps.20311.

9. Hannah Seo, "Stress Might Age the Immune System, New Study Finds," *New York Times*, June 17, 2022, https://www.nytimes.com/2022/06/17/well/mind/stress-aging-immune-system.html.

10. https://www.kornferry.com/insights/this-week-in-leadership/workplace-stress-motivation.

11. See P. M. Le Blanc et al., "Take Care! The Evaluation of a Team-Based Burnout Intervention Program for Oncology Care Providers," *Journal of Applied Psychology* 92 (2007): 213–27, doi:10.1037/0021-9010.92.1.213. See also Maslach and Leiter, "Understanding the Burnout Experience"; W. Schaufeli and D. Enzmann, *The Burnout Companion to Study and Research: A Critical Analysis* (London: Taylor & Francis, 1998). For reviews, see C. L. Cordes and T. Dougherty, "A Review and Integration of Research on Job Burnout," *Academy of Management Review* 18 (1993): 621–56; R. T. Lee and B. E. Ashforth, "A Meta-Analytic Examination of the Correlates of the Three Dimensions of Job Burnout," *Journal of Applied Psychology* 81 (1996): 123–33; W. B. Schaufeli and B. P. Buunk, "Burnout: An Overview of 25 Years of Research and Theorizing," in *The Handbook of Work and Health Psychology*, edited by M. J. Schabracq, J. A. M. Winnubst, and C. L. Cooper (Chichester, England: Wiley, 2002), 383–425.

12. https://www.kornferry.com/insights/this-week-in-leadership/workplace-stress -motivation.

13. For more detail on neural networks and emotion, and a new method for assessing brain area and emotions, see David J. Anderson, *The Nature of the Beast: How Emotions Guide Us* (New York: Basic Books, 2022). Anderson notes there may well be multiple pathways for fear in the brain, some of which do not involve the amygdala.

14. See Joseph Ledoux, "Rethinking the Emotional Brain," *Neuron* 73 (2012): 653– 76. Ledoux, whose earlier work drew a strong connection between fear and the amygdala, later questioned his findings and argued for using animal models to study emotions in the brain, as per Anderson, *The Nature of the Beast*.

15. Judy Lief, "Unraveling Anxiety," *Lion's Roar*, March 2022, 47.

16. Marc Brackett, *Permission to Feel: The Power of Emotional Intelligence to Achieve Well-being and Success* (New York: Celadon Press, 2019).

17. Kostadin Kushlev, "Do Happy People Care About Society's Problems?," *Journal of Positive Psychology* 15, no. 4 (2020): 467–77.

18. Maslach and Leiter, "Understanding the Burnout Experience."

19. American Psychological Association, "Stress in America," annual survey, 2021, https://www.apa.org/news/press/releases/stress/2021/decision-making-october -2021.pdf.

20. M. L. Jordano and D. R. Touron, "Priming Performance-Related Concerns Induces Task-Related Mind-Wandering," *Consciousness and Cognition* 55 (2017): 126–35, doi:10.1016/concog.2017.08.002.

21. See, e.g., Steven J. Spencer et al., "Stereotype Threat and Women's Math Performance," *Journal of Experimental Social Psychology* 35, no. 1 (1999): 4–28.

22. Stacey Schaefer, "Purpose in Life Predicts Better Emotional Recovery from Negative Stimuli," *PLoS ONE* 8, no. 11 (2013).

23. Goleman and Davidson, *Altered Traits*.

24. Uta Klusmann et al., "Is Emotional Exhaustion Only the Result of Work Experiences? A Diary Study on Daily Hassles and Uplifts in Different Life Domains," *Anxiety, Stress, & Coping* 34, no. 2 (2021): 173–90, doi:10.1080/106158 06.2020.1845430.

25. Han Liu and Richard Boyatzis, "Focusing on Resilience and Renewal from Stress: The Role of Emotional and Social Intelligence Competencies," *Frontiers in Psychology*, June 2021, https://doi.org/10.3389/fpsyg.2021.685829.

26. See https://www.keystepmedia.com/shop/psi/#.Y8bk2eLMJ_Q.

27. Fessell and Cherniss, "Coronavirus Disease 2019 (COVID-19) and Beyond."

7 | Empathy

1. Jean Decety, "The Neurodevelopment of Empathy," *Developmental Neuroscience* 32 (2010): 257–7.

2. James Shaheen in conversation with Jacqueline Stone and Donald S. Lopez Jr., "How to Read the Lotus Sutra," *Tricycle*, Spring 2020, 66. Such "skillful means" hinge on cognitive empathy.

3. See, e.g., C. Zahn-Waxler and M. Radke-Yarrow, "The Origins of Empathic Concern," *Motivation and Emotion* 14 (1990): 107–30, https://doi.org/10.1007 /BF00991639.

4. KeyStepMedia, *Building Blocks of Emotional Intelligence, Empathy: A Primer* (Florence, MA: MoreThanSound, 2017), 23.

5. When most of us masked our faces: Sarah D. McCrackin et al., "Face Masks Impair Basic Emotion Recognition," *Social Psychology* 54 (2022), https://econtent .hogrefe.com/doi/10.1027/1864-9335/a000470.

6. "Physician, Care for Yourself," *Lion's Roar*, March 2020, 23.

7. See, for example, Rebecca A. Rudd and Livia M. D'Andrea, "Compassionate Detachment: Managing Professional Stress While Providing Quality Care to Bereaved Parents," *Journal of Workplace Behavioral Health* 30, no. 3 (2015): 287– 305, doi:10.1080/15555240.2014.999079.

8. H. Riess et al., "Empathy Training for Resident Physicians: A Randomized Controlled Trial of a Neuroscience-Informed Curriculum," *Journal of General Internal Medicine* 27 (2012): 1280–86, https://doi.org/10.1007/s11606-012-20 63-z.

9. BusinessSolver, "2022 State of Workplace Empathy," https://www.businessolver .com/resources/state-of-workplace-empathy#gref.

10. Jamil Zaki, "Making Empathy Central to Your Company's Culture," *Harvard Business Review*, May 30, 2019, https://enterprisersproject.com/sites/default/files /empathy_culture.pdf.

11. Erik C Nook et al., "Prosocial Conformity: Prosocial Norms Generalize Across Behavior and Empathy," *Personality and Social Psychology Bulletin* 42, no. 8 (August 2016): 1054–62, doi:10.1177/0146167216649932.

12. Tracy Brower, "Empathy Is the Most Important Leadership Skill According to Research," *Forbes*, September 19, 2021.

13. See, e.g., the classic analysis: Scott Speier et al., "Leadership Run Amok," *Harvard Business Review*, June 2006.

14. Amabile and Kramer, *The Progress Principle*.

15. Rob Cross and Andrew Parker, *The Hidden Power of Social Networks: Understanding How Work Really Gets Done in Organizations* (Boston: Harvard Business Review Press, 2004).

16. Jamil Zaki, "Integrating Empathy and Interpersonal Emotion Regulation," *Annual Review of Psychology* 71 (2020): 517–40, https://doi.org/10.1146/annurev-psych-010419-050830.

17. Sigal Barsade et al., "Emotional Contagion in Organizational Life," *Research in Organizational Behavior*, December 2018, doi:10.1016/j.riob.2018.11.005.

18. Ed Yong, "Why Health-Care Workers Are Quitting in Droves," *The Atlantic*, November 16, 2021.

19. Patricia L. Lockwood et al., "Distinct Neural Representations for Prosocial and Self-Benefitting Effort," *Current Biology* (2022), doi:10.1016/j.cub.2022.08.010, https://www.cell.com/current-biology/fulltext/S0960-9822(22)01287-8.

20. Tania Singer and Olga M. Klimecki, "Empathy and Compassion," *Current Biology* 24, no. 18 (2014): 875–78, https://doi.org/10.1016/j.cub.2014.06.054.

21. L. Ramarajan, S. G. Barsade, and O. R. Burack, "The Influence of Organizational Respect on Emotional Exhaustion in the Human Services," *Journal of Positive Psychology* 3 (2008): 4–18.

22. K. Schabram and Y. T. Heng, "How Other- and Self-Compassion Reduce Burnout through Resource Replenishment," *Academy of Management Journal* 65, no. 2 (2022): 453–78. doi:10.5465/amj.2019.0493.

23. Le Blanc et al., "Take Care!" See also C. Maslach, W. B. Schaufeli, and M. P. Leiter, "Burnout," *Annual Review of Psychology* 52 (2001): 397–422.

24. Richard Boyatzis, in *Organizational Awareness: A Primer* (Florence, MA: MoreThanSound, 2017), 36.

25. Vinson Cunningham, "Blacking Out," *The New Yorker*, July 20, 2020, 64.

26. George Packer, *Last Best Hope: America in Crisis and Renewal* (New York: Farrar, Straus & Giroux, 2021).

27. See, e.g., https://www.benjerry.com/whats-new/2022/06/americans-agree-on -issues.

8 | Manage Your Relationships

1. https://www.trustacrossamerica.com/documents/index/Return-Methodology.pdf.

2. KeyStepMedia, *Building Blocks of Emotional Intelligence. Coach and Mentor: A Primer* (Florence, MA: MoreThanSound, 2017), 24.

3. Conference Board, *Global Executive Coaching Survey 2018*, https://www.con ference-board.org/topics/executive-coaching/global-executive-coaching-survey -2018-report.

4. Anthony Jack et al., "Visioning in the Brain: An FMRI Study of Inspirational Coaching and Mentoring," *Social Neuroscience* 8, no. 4 (2013): 369–84, doi:10 .1080/17470919.2013.808259.

5. Richard Boyatzis et al., *Helping People Change: Coaching with Compassion for Lifelong Learning and Growth* (Boston: Harvard Business Review Press, 2021).

6. C. Cherniss, "Instrument for Observing Supervisor Behavior in Educational Programs for Mentally Retarded Children," *American Journal of Mental Deficiency* 91 (1986): 18–21.

7. Peter Senge, in KeyStepMedia, *Building Blocks of Emotional Intelligence, Influence: A Primer* (Florence, MA: MoreThanSound, 2017), 38.

8. See Ken Burns's documentary on Franklin for more on how Franklin influenced others in the service of his country.

9. KeyStepMedia, *Building Blocks of Emotional Intelligence, Influence: A Primer* (Florence, MA: MoreThanSound, 2017), 24.

10. https://motivationalinterviewing.org/understanding-motivational-interviewing.

11. The lesson in influence: https://www.keystepmedia.com/emotional-intelligence/.

12. Blake Mycoskie, "The Founder of TOMS on Reimagining the Company's Mission," *Harvard Business Review*, January–February 2016.

13. KeyStepMedia, *Building Blocks of Emotional Intelligence, Inspirational Leadership: A Primer* (Florence, MA: MoreThanSound, 2017), 5.

14. Daniel Goleman, "Leadership That Gets Results," *Harvard Business Review*, March–April 2000.

15. Dr. Albert Bourla, *Moonshot: Inside Pfizer's Nine-Month Race to Make the Impossible Possible* (New York: HarperBusiness, 2022).

16. Cary Cherniss and Cornelia W. Roche, *Leading with Feeling: Nine Strategies of Emotionally Intelligent Leadership* (New York: Oxford University Press, 2020).

17. Amy Gallo, *HBR Guide to Dealing with Conflict* (Boston: Harvard Business Review Press, 2017).

9 | The Many Names for Emotional Intelligence

1. Raffaella Sadun et al., "The C-Suite Skills That Matter Most," *Harvard Business Review*, July–August 2022, 42–50.

2. Ibid.

3. Amy Lui Abel and Rebecca L. Ray, *Global Executive Coaching Survey 2018*, Conference Board, March 2019, https://www.conference-board.org/topics/executive-coaching/global-executive-coaching-survey-2018-report.

4. Jeremy Hunter, "Is Mindfulness Good for Business?" *Mindful*, April 2013, 54.

5. Sadun et al., "The C-Suite Skills That Matter Most," 47.

6. L. L. Baird, "Do Grades and Tests Predict Adult Accomplishment?," *Research in Higher Education* 23 (1985): 3–85, https://doi.org/10.1007/BF00974070. On the other hand another study found a higher correlation: Philip L. Roth and Richard L. Clarke, "Meta-Analyzing the Relation Between Grades and Salary," *Journal of Vocational Behavior* 53, no. 3 (1998): 386–400. School grades do not necessarily reflect IQ, but are also strongly influenced by factors such as motivation and conscientiousness.

7. P. L. Roth, C. A. BeVier, F. S. Switzer, and J. S. Schippmann, "Meta-Analyzing the Relationship Between Grades and Job Performance," *Journal of Applied Psychology* 81, no. 5 (1996): 548–56, https://doi.org/10.1037/0021-9010.81.5.548.

8. Jeffrey S. Zax and Daniel I. Rees, "IQ, Academic Performance, Environment, and Earnings," *Review of Economics and Statistics* 84, no. 4 (November 2002); 600–616. The overrating of IQ was in reference to claims made in Richard Hernstein and Charles Murray, *The Bell Curve* (New York: Free Press, 1994).

9. See, e.g., Bryan J. Pesta, "Discounting IQ's Relevance to Organizational Behavior: The 'Somebody Else's Problem' in Management Education," *Open Differential Psychology*, May 26, 2015, and Ken Richardson and Sarah H. Norgate, "Does IQ

Really Predict Job Performance?," *Applied Developmental Science* 19, no. 3 (2015): 153–69.

10. Signe Spencer and Heather Barnfield, "Emotional Intelligence: Why Now?," Korn Ferry Thought Leadership, 2021, https://www.kornferry.com/content /dam/kornferry-v2/pdf/institute/kfi-thought-leadership-emotional-intelligence -why-now.pdf.

10 | Leading with Emotional Intelligence

1. Dana Rubinstein, "The No. 1 Skill Eric Adams Is Looking For (It's Not on a Résumé)," *New York Times*, December 18, 2021.

2. Brookes Barnes et al., "Iger's Sudden Return to Disney Shocks a Discontented Kingdom," *New York Times*, November 21, 2022, https://www.nytimes .com/2022/11/21/business/media/disney-bob-iger.html.

3. D. Rosete and J. Ciarrochi, "Emotional Intelligence and Its Relationship to Workplace Performance Outcomes of Leadership Effectiveness," *Leadership and Organization Development Journal* 26 (2005): 388–99, https://www.emerald.com /insight/content/doi/10.1108/01437730510607871/full/html.

4. R. E. Boyatzis, D. Good, and R. Massa, "Emotional, Social, and Cognitive Intelligence and Personality as Predictors of Sales Leadership Performance," *Journal of Leadership and Organizational Studies* 19 (2012): 191–201, doi:10 .1177/1548051811435793.

5. R. Boyatzis, T. Brizz, and L. Godwin, "The Effect of Religious Leaders' Emotional and Social Competencies on Improving Parish Vibrancy," *Journal of Leadership & Organizational Studies* 18 (2011): 192–206, doi:10.1177/1548051810369676.

6. S. V. A. Araujo and S. Taylor, "The Influence of Emotional and Social Intelligence Competencies on the Performance of Peruvian Refinery Staff," *Journal of Cross Cultural Management* 19 (2012): 19–29, doi:10.1108/13527601211195600.

7. C. Miao, R. H. Humphrey, and S. Qian, *Journal of World Business* 53 (2018): 463–74, https://doi.org/10.1016/j.jwb.2018.01.003. Their analysis included 12 different studies and 2,764 participants. See also R. J. Emmerling and R. E. Boyatzis, "Emotional and Social Competencies: Cross-Cultural Implications," *Cross Cultural Management: An International Journal* 19 (2012): 4–18.

8. J. S. Allen, R. M. Stevenson, E. H. O'Boyle, and S. Seibert, "What Matters More for Entrepreneurship Success? A Meta-analysis Comparing General Mental Ability and Emotional Intelligence in Entrepreneurial Settings," *Strategic*

Entrepreneurship Journal 15 (2021): 352–76, https://doi.org/10.1002/sej.1377.

9. Cherniss, *Beyond Burnout.*

10. Mary Abbajay, "What to Do When You Have a Bad Boss," *Harvard Business Review*, September 7, 2018, cited in the McKinsey report, https://www.mckinsey.com/business-functions/people-and-organizational-performance/our-insights/the-boss-factor-making-the-world-a-better-place-through-workplace-relationships.

11. McKinsey Quarterly Five-Fifty, "Better Bosses," September 22, 2020, https://www.mckinsey.com/business-functions/people-and-organizational-performance/our-insights/five-fifty-better-bosses; https://www.mckinsey.com/business-functions/people-and-organizational-performance/our-insights/the-boss-factor-making-the-world-a-better-place-through-workplace-relationships.

12. C. Miao, R. H. Humphrey, and S. Qian, "Leader Emotional Intelligence and Subordinate Job Satisfaction: A Meta-analysis of Main, Mediator, and Moderator Effects," *Personality and Individual Differences* 102 (2016): 13–24, https://doi.org/10.1016/j.paid.2016.06.056.

13. Miao, Humphrey, and Qian, "A Cross-Cultural Meta-analysis."

14. Falahat N. Mohammad, Lau T. Chai, Law K. Aun, and Melissa W. Migin, "Emotional Intelligence and Turnover Intention," *International Journal of Academic Research* Part B, 6, no. 4 (2014): 211–20, doi:10.7813/2075-4124.2014/6-4/B.33.

15. Microsoft WorkLab, "Great Expectations: Making Hybrid Work *Work*," Annual Work Trend Index 2022 Report, https://www.microsoft.com/en-us/worklab/work-trend-index.

16. B. A. Scott, J. A. Colquitt, E. L. Paddock, and T. A. Judge, "A Daily Investigation of the Role of Manager Empathy on Employee Well-being," *Organizational Behavior and Human Decision Processes* 113 (2010): 127–40.

17. J. Skakon, K. Nielsen, V. Borg, and J. Guzman, "Are Leaders' Well-being, Behaviours and Style Associated with the Affective Well-being of Their Employees? A Systematic Review of Three Decades of Research," *Work & Stress* 24, no. 2 (2010): 107–39, doi:10.1080/02678373.2010.495262. See also F. Rasulzada, I. Dackert, and C. R. Johansson, "Employee Well-being in Relation to Organizational Climate and Leadership Style," in *Proceedings of the Fifth European Conference of the European Academy of Occupational Health Psychology, Berlin* (Nottingham, UK:

Institute of Work Health & Organisations, University of Nottingham, 2003), 220–24.

18. R. S. Vealey, L. Armstrong, W. Comar, and C. A. Greenleaf, "Influence of Perceived Coaching Behaviours on Burnout and Competitive Anxiety in Female College Athletes," *Journal of Applied Sport Psychology* 10 (1998): 297–318.

19. P. Moyle, "Longitudinal Influences of Managerial Support on Employee Well-being," *Work & Stress* 12 (1998): 29–49, https://doi.org/10.1080/0267 8379808256847.

20. Sigal Barsade and Olivia A. O'Neill, "Manage Your Emotional Culture," *Harvard Business Review*, January–February 2016.

21. This dilemma is especially acute for women leaders because they are expected to be both "warm and nice, as well as competent or tough." See Wei Zeng, Ronit Kark, and Alyson Meister, "How Women Manage the Gendered Norms of Leadership," *Harvard Business Review*, November 28, 2018, https://hbr.org/2018/11/how-women-manage-the-gendered-norms-of-leadership.

22. Nancy Rothbard, a professor at the Wharton School of the University of Pennsylvania who has studied emotions in the workplace, said that her research suggests that female and nonwhite leaders may face a steeper cost for emotional disclosures. Quoted in Rubinstein, "The No. 1 Skill Eric Adams Is Looking For (It's Not on a Résumé)."

23. K. Lanaj, R. E. Jennings, S. J. Ashford, and S. Krishnan, "When Leader Self-care Begets Other Care: Leader Role Self-compassion and Helping at Work," *Journal of Applied Psychology* 107, no. 9 (2022): 1543–60, https://doi.org/10.1037/apl0000957.

24. C. Cherniss, L. Grimm, and J. P. Liautaud, "Process-Designed Training: A New Approach for Helping Leaders Develop Emotional and Social Competence," *Journal of Management Development* 29 (2010): 413–31.

25. R. Gilar-Corbi et al., "Can Emotional Intelligence Be Improved? A Randomized Experimental Study of a Business-Oriented EI Training Program for Senior Managers," *PLoS ONE* 14, no. 10 (2019): e0224254, https://doi.org/10.1371/journal.pone.0224254.

26. Dina Denham Smith and Alicia A. Grandey, "The Emotional Labor of Being a Leader," *Harvard Business Review*, November 2, 2022.

27. One of the leaders Cary and his colleague Cornelia Roche studied. See Cherniss and Roche, *Leading with Feeling*.

28. G. Cummings, L. Hayduk, and C. Estabrooks, "Mitigating the Impact of Hospital Restructuring on Nurses: The Responsibility of Emotionally Intelligent Leadership," *Nursing Research* 54, no. 1 (2005): 2–12.

29. Leader EI was measured by having the nurses rate their leaders on the thirteen EI competencies in the Goleman-Boyatzis model. Then, based on their competency profile, they assigned the leaders to one or more of the leadership styles associated with emotionally intelligent leadership (visionary, coaching, affiliative, and/or democratic). See Daniel Goleman, Richard Boyatzis, and Annie McKee, *Primal Leadership: Realizing the Power of Emotional Intelligence* (Boston: Harvard Business Review Press, 2002).

30. R. E. Boyatzis, K. Thiel, K. Rochford, and A. Black, "Emotional and Social Intelligence Competencies of Incident Team Commanders Fighting Wildfires," *Journal of Applied Behavioral Science* 53 (2017):498–516, doi:10.1177/0021886317731575. Sixty critical incidents from interviews of fifteen incident commanders were analyzed for emotional and social intelligence competencies in incident management leadership.

31. Caruso's quote comes from Rubinstein, "The No. 1 Skill Eric Adams Is Looking For (It's Not on a Résumé)."

32. Quoted in Emma Goldberg, "When Your Boss Is Crying, but You're the One Being Laid Off," *New York Times*, August 24, 2022.

33. E. L. Carleton, J. Barling, A. M. Christie, M. Trivisonno, K. Tulloch, and M. R. Beauchamp, "Scarred for the Rest of My Career? Career-Long Effects of Abusive Leadership on Professional Athlete Aggression and Task Performance," *Journal of Sport and Exercise Psychology* (2016): 409–22.

34. Allie Caren, "Why We Often Remember the Bad Rather Than the Good," *Washington Post*, November 1, 2018, https://www.washingtonpost.com/science/2018/11/01/why-we-often-remember-bad-better-than-good/.

35. Shawn McClean, Stephen H. Courtright, Troy A. Smith, and Junhyok Yim, "Stop Making Excuses for Toxic Bosses," *Harvard Business Review* (2021), https://hbr.org/2021/01/stop-making-excuses-for-toxic-bosses.

36. J. A. Colquitt et al., "Justice at the Millenium: A Meta-Analytic Review of Organizational Behavior Research," *Journal of Applied Psychology* 86 (2001): 425–45.

37. For more details about the study, see C. Cherniss and C. W. Roche, "How Outstanding Leaders Use Emotional Intelligence," *Leader to Leader* 98 (Fall 2020):

45–50, https://doi.org/10.1002/ltl.20517. They collected 126 incidents from 25 leaders—12 men and 13 women—who came from a variety of organizations.

38. For more on this tactic for managing emotions, see Marilee Adams, *Change Your Questions, Change Your Life: 10 Powerful Tools for Life and Work,* 2nd ed. (San Francisco: Berrett-Koehler, 2009).

11 | Emotionally Intelligent Teams

1. See also Gerardo A. Okhuysen, David Lepak, Karen Lee Ashcraft, Giuseppe Labianca, Vicki Smith, and H. Kevin Steensma, "Theories of Work and Working Today," *Academy of Management Review* 38, no. 4 (2013): 491–502.

2. See Vipula Gandhi and Jennifer Robinson, "The 'Great Resignation' Is Really the 'Great Discontent,'" Gallup, July 22, 2021, https://www.gallup.com/workplace /351545/great-resignation-really-great-discontent.aspx.

3. N. C. Carpenter, D. S. Whitman, and R. Amrhein, "Unit-Level Counter-productive Work Behavior (CWB): A Conceptual Review and Quantitative Summary," *Journal of Management* 47 (2020): 1498–1527, https://doi.org/10 .1177/0149206320978812.

4. Spencer and Barnfield, "Emotional Intelligence: Why Now?"

5. They determined a team's effectiveness by looking at how well people worked together, as viewed by team members, their leaders, and executives who were familiar with the teams. They also looked at hard data on outcomes such as sales performance.

6. For more on the concept of psychological safety in groups, see A. Edmondson, "Psychological Safety and Learning Behavior in Work Teams," *Administrative Science Quarterly* 44, no. 2 (1999): 350–83, doi:10.2307/2666999.

7. "Guide: Understand Team Effectiveness," in *re:Work*, https://rework.withgoogle .com/print/guides/5721312655835136/. For a more detailed account of the study, see Charles Duhigg, "What Google Learned from Its Quest to Build the Perfect Team," *New York Times*, February 28, 2016, https://www.nytimes.com/2016/02/28 /magazine/what-google-learned-from-its-quest-to-build-the-perfect-team.html.

8. N. Campany et al., "What Makes Good Teams Work Better: Research-Based Strategies That Distinguish Top-Performing Cross-Functional Drug Development Teams," *Organization Development Journal* 25, no. 2 (2007): P179–P186.

9. V. U. Druskat and S. B. Wolff, "Building the Emotional Intelligence of Groups," *Harvard Business Review* 79, no. 3 (2001): 81–90.

10. For details of Druskat's team EI work see https://golemanconsultinggroup.com/.

11. Team EI: see https://golemanconsultinggroup.com/.

12. Vanessa Druskat et al., "The Influence of Team Leader Competencies on the Emergence of Emotionally Competent Team Norms," presented at the Annual Academy of Management Conference, San Antonio, TX, August 2011.

13. A. W. Woolley et al., "Evidence for a Collective Intelligence Factor in the Performance of Human Groups," *Science* 330 (2010): 686–88.

14. Duhigg, "What Google Learned from Its Quest to Build the Perfect Team."

15. A. Rezvani, P. Khosravi, and N. M. Ashkanasy, "Examining the Interdependencies Among Emotional Intelligence, Trust, and Performance in Infrastructure Projects: A Multilevel Study," *International Journal of Project Management* 36, no. 8 (2018): 1034–46, https://doi.org/10.1016/j.ijproman.2018.08.002.

16. F. Zhu, X. Wang, L. Wang, and M. Yu, "Project Manager's Emotional Intelligence and Project Performance: The Mediating Role of Project Commitment," *International Journal of Project Management* 39 (2021): 788–98.

17. E. S. Koman and S. B. Wolff, "Emotional Intelligence Competencies in the Team and Team Leader: A Multi-level Examination of the Impact of Emotional Intelligence on Team Performance," *Journal of Management Development* 27, no. 1 (2008): 5575.

18. A. Mazur, A. Pisarski, A. Chang, and N. M. Ashkanasy, "Rating Defence Major Project Success: The Role of Personal Attributes and Stakeholder Relationships," *International Journal of Project Management* 32 (2014): 944–57; A. C. Troth, P. J. Jordan, S.A. Lawrence, and H. H. Tse, "A Multilevel Model of Emotional Skills, Communication Performance, and Task Performance in Teams," *Journal of Organizational Behavior* 33 (2012): 700–22. Two other studies showing the positive link between team EI and team functioning include: P. J. Jordan, N. M. Ashkanasy, C. E. J. Hartel, and G. S. Hooper, "Workgroup Emotional Intelligence Scale Development and Relationship to Team Process Effectiveness and Goal Focus," *Human Resource Management Review* 12 (2002): 195–214; and J. W. Chang, T. Sy, and J. N. Choi, "Team Emotional Intelligence and Performance: Interactive Dynamics between Leaders and Members," *Small Group Research* 43 (2012): 75–104, doi:10.1177/1046496411415692.

19. *Forbes* reported in 2022 that women represent only "21% of Bachelor's degree recipients in engineering and engineering technology" despite recent gains. https://www.forbes.com/sites/markkantrowitz/2022/04/07/women-achieve-gains

-in-stem-fields/?sh=225ef085ac57. Women have reported engineering schools as a hostile environment; the Society of Women Engineers reported in 2019, "Over 32% of women switch out of STEM degree programs in college," https://alltogether.swe.org/2019/11/swe-research-update-women-in-engineering-by-the-numbers-nov-2019/.

20. A. G. Greenwald et al., "Implicit-Bias Remedies: Treating Discriminatory Bias as a Public-Health Problem," *Psychological Science in the Public Interest* 23 (2022): 7–40, doi:10.1177/15291006211070781; Jesse Singal, "What If Diversity Trainings Are Doing More Harm Than Good?" *New York Times*, January 17, 2023, https://www.nytimes.com/2023/01/17/opinion/dei-trainings-effective.html.

21. Michael Jacoby Brown, letter to the editor, *New York Times*, 1/27/23.

22. Singal, "What If Diversity Trainings Are Doing More Harm Than Good?"

23. https://ascent.net/stephen-kelner.

24. For more information on the program and its evaluation, see C. Cherniss, L. Grimm, and J. P. Liautaud, "Process-Designed Training: A New Approach for Helping Leaders Develop Emotional and Social Competence," *Journal of Management Development* 29 (2010): 413–31.

25. K. Holtz, V. Orengo Castella, A. Zornoza Abad, and B. González-Anta, "Virtual Team Functioning," *Group Dynamics: Theory, Research, and Practice* 24, no. 3 (2020): 153–67, doi:10.1037/gdn0000141.

26. "Guide: Understand Team Effectiveness," https://rework.withgoogle.com/print/guides/5721312655835136/.

27. P. M. Le Blanc et al., "Take Care! The Evaluation of a Team-Based Burnout Intervention Program for Oncology Care Providers," *Journal of Applied Psychology* 92 (2007): 213–27, doi:10.1037/0021-9010.92.1.213.

12 | EI Training That Works

1. Jamie Dimon, interviewed on the podcast *Coffee with the Greats*, July 15, 2021, https://cnb.cx/32N4W1C.

2. https://www.eeoc.gov/laws/guidance/employment-tests-and-selection-procedures.

3. David Noble et al., *Real-Time Leadership* (Boston: Harvard Business Review Press, 2023).

4. For more details, see the website of the Collaborative for Academic and Social Learning at https://casel.org/fundamentals-of-sel/what-does-the-research-say/.

5. See, e.g., R. Gilar-Corbi et al., "Can Emotional Intelligence Be Improved? A Randomized Experimental Study of a Business-Oriented EI Training Program for Senior Managers," *PLoS One* (2019), https://doi.org/10.1371/journal.pone.0224254.

6. The research on the results of training in emotional intelligence at Progressive is being done by Laura Gulliam, organizational development consultant. The research assesses the relative benefits of EI training either based on getting the Emotional and Social Competence Inventory (ESCI) and access to a website for self-directed emotional intelligence development, or getting assessed by the ESCI plus individual coaching.

7. Marshall Goldsmith commented on the Progressive study on the *M&M Show*, February 22, 2022.

8. Cherniss, Grimm, and Liautaud, "Process-Designed Training."

9. The Daniel Goleman Emotional Intelligence courses: see https://www.keystepmedia.com/.

10. The study with South African cricketers was a relatively small sample, but the training was done twice with different groups in two different years. Both times the trained group showed increases in EI of over 13 percent while the controls showed only a 2 percent improvement in one year and a decline of over 3 percent in the other year. See D. Crombie, C. Lombard, and T. Noakes, "Increasing Emotional Intelligence in Cricketers: An Intervention Study," *International Journal of Sports Science and Coaching* 6 (2011): 69–86. For the MBA study see the pathbreaking work of Richard Boyatzis and his colleagues at Case Western University's Weatherhead School of Management. A good summary can be found in R. E. Boyatzis and K. V. Cavanagh, "Leading Change: Developing Emotional, Social, and Cognitive Competencies in Managers During an MBA Program," in K. Keefer, J. Parker, and D. Saklofske, eds., *Emotional Intelligence in Education: The Springer Series on Human Exceptionality* (New York: Springer, 2018), 403–26.

11. J. W. Dugan et al., "A Longitudinal Study of Emotional Intelligence Training for Otolaryngology Residents and Faculty," *JAMA Otolaryngology Head Neck Surgery* 140 (2014): 720–26, doi:10.1001/jamaoto.2014.1169; M. Beigi and M. Shirmohammadi, "Effects of an Emotional Intelligence Training Program on Service

Quality of Bank Branches," *Managing Service Quality: An International Journal* 21 (2011): 552–67, doi:10.1108/09604521111159825; G. E. Gignac, R. J. Harmer, S. Jennings, and B. R. Palmer, "EI Training and Sales Performance During a Corporate Merger," *Cross Cultural Management 19* (2012): 104–16, doi:10.1108/13527601211195655.

12. R. Turner and B. Lloyd-Walker, "Emotional Intelligence (EI) Capabilities Training: Can It Develop EI in Project Teams?," *International Journal of Managing Projects in Business* 1 (2008): 512–34, doi:10.1108/17538370810906237; M. Slaski and S. Cartwright, "Emotional Intelligence Training and Its Implications for Stress, Health and Performance," *Stress and Health* 19 (2003): 233–39; N. Clarke, "The Impact of a Training Program Designed to Target the Emotional Intelligence Abilities of Project Managers," *International Journal of Project Management* 28 (2010): 461–68, doi:10.1016/j.ijproman.2009.08.004.

13. I. Kotsou, M. Mikolajczak, A. Heeren, J. Grégoire, and C. Leys, "Improving Emotional Intelligence: A Systematic Review of Existing Work and Future Challenges," *Emotion Review* 11 (2019): 151–65.

14. Most of the information on MD Anderson Cancer Center came from Courtney Holladay, associate vice president, Leadership Institute.

15. D. Nelis, I. Kotsou, J. Quoidbach, M. Hansenne, F. Weytens, P. Dupuis, and M. Mikolajczak, "Increasing Emotional Competence Improves Psychological and Physical Well-Being, Social Relationships, and Employability," *Emotion* 11 (2011): 354–66.

16. Gilar-Corbi et al., "Can Emotional Intelligence Be Improved?"

17. Boyatzis and Cavanagh, "Leading Change." A full presentation of the theory on which the program is based will appear in a forthcoming book by Richard Boyatzis on intentional change theory.

18. For information on how to obtain the ESCI, go to https://store.kornferry.com/en/search?search=ESCI.

19. The Emotional and Social Competence Inventory, for example, seems better at identifying workplace excellence than most other EI measures. R. E. Boyatzis, "The Behavioral Level of Emotional Intelligence and Its Measurement," *Frontiers in Psychology* 9 (2018), https://doi.org/10.3389/fpsyg.2018.01438.

20. Steve Miller, "Developing Next Generation Leadership Talent in Family Businesses" (PhD diss., Case Western Reserve University, 2014).

21. D. H. Gruenfeld, D. Keltner, and C. P. Anderson, "The Effects of Power upon Those Who Possess It: An Interpersonal Perspective on Social Cognition," in G. Bodenhausen and A. Lambert, eds., *Foundations of Social Cognition: A Festschrift in Honor of Robert S. Wyer, Jr.* (Hilldale, NJ: Erlbaum, 2003), 237–62.

22. Amy Lui Abel and Vivian Jaworsky, "COVID-19 Reset and Recovery: Coaching Leaders into the Future with Empathy and Emotional Intelligence," Conference Board, February 12, 2021.

13 | Building an EI Culture

1. Most of this information was provided by the company's president and CEO, Carolyn Stanworth.

2. Satya Nadella, *Hit Refresh: The Quest to Rediscover Microsoft's Soul and Imagine a Better Future for Everyone* (New York: HarperBusiness, 2017). Nadella recommended, for example, that his leadership team read Marshall Rosenberg, *Non-Violent Communication: A Language of Life* (Encinitas, CA: PuddleDancer Press, 2003).

3. For more on "peer coaching," see P. Parker, D. T. Hall, and K. E. Kram, "Peer Coaching: A Relational Process for Accelerating Career Learning," *Academy of Management Learning and Education* 7 (2008): 487–503.

14 | The Crucial Mix

1. Chloe Taylor, "Tim Cook Says He Uses 'a Very Good Formula' to Look for Apple Employees—These Are the Four Traits He Seeks Out," *Fortune*, October 3, 2022.

2. Claudio Fernández-Aráoz et al., "From Curious to Competent," *Harvard Business Review*, September–October, 2018.

3. Conference Board, "Key Themes and Trends Emerging in 2018," in *Global Executive Coaching Survey 2018*, https://www.conference-board.org/topics/executive -coaching/global-executive-coaching-survey-2018-report.

4. Lorraine Whitmarsh et al., "Climate Anxiety," *Journal of Environmental Psychology* vol. 83, October 2022, 101866

5. Guangrong Dai et al., "They Who Have a 'Why' to Live For: Purpose Facilitates Positive Employment Experience," Research Association for Interdisciplinary Studies, June 2020, doi:10.5281/zenodo.3909861.

6. Shawn Achor et al., "Nine Out of Ten People Are Willing to Work for Less Money for More Meaningful Work," *Harvard Business Review*, November 8, 2018.

7. A. M. Carton, "'I'm Not Mopping the Floors; I'm Putting a Man on the Moon': How NASA Leaders Enhanced the Meaningfulness of Work by Changing the Meaning of Work," *Administrative Science Quarterly* 63, no. 2 (2018): 323–69.

8. T. A. Judge et al., "The Relationship Between Pay and Job Satisfaction: A Meta-analysis of the Literature," *Journal of Vocational Behavior* 77, no. 2 (2010).

9. For example, "The Most and Least Meaningful Jobs," Payscale, http://www .payscale.com/data=packages/most-and-least

10. Alfie Kohn's seminal arguments have been borne out by further research, such as by Edward Deci. See, e.g., Edward Deci et al., "A Meta-Analytic Review of Experiments Examining the Effects of External Rewards on Intrinsic Motivation," *Psychological Bulletin* 125, no. 6 (1999).

11. Edward Deci and Richard Ryan, *Intrinsic Motivation and Self-determination in Human Behavior* (New York: Plenum Press, 1985). A summary of their work is in R. Ryan and E. Deci, "Self-determination Theory and the Facilitation of Intrinsic Motivation, Social Development, and Well-being," *American Psychologist* 55, no. 1 (2000): 68–78, https://doi.org/10.1037/0003-066X.55.1.68.

12. Daniel H. Pink, *Drive: The Surprising Truth about What Motivates Us* (New York: Riverhead Books, 2009).

13. Beth Hennessey et al., "Extrinsic and Intrinsic Motivation," in Cary L. Cooper, ed., *Wiley Encyclopedia of Management* (London: Wiley, 2014).

14. C. J. Fong et al., "A Meta-analysis of Negative Feedback on Intrinsic Motivation," *Educational Psychology Review* 31 (2019): 121–62, https://doi.org/10.1007 /s10648-018-9446-6.

15. C. J. Fong et al., "When Feedback Signals Failure but Offers Hope for Improvement: A Process Model of Constructive Criticism," *Thinking Skills and Creativity* (2018), https://doi.org/10.1016/j.tsc.2018.02.014.

16. Frankl tells this story in a posthumous book based on lectures he gave in Vienna just months after his liberation from a Nazi labor camp. Those forgotten lectures, rediscovered, have been published for the first time in English (and Dan had the

honor of writing an introduction). The book's title sums up Frankl's outlook: *Say Yes to Life in Spite of Everything* (Boston: Beacon Press, 2020).

17. T. B. Kashdan and P. E. McKnight, "Commitment to a Purpose in Life: An Antidote to the Suffering by Individuals with Social Anxiety Disorder," *Emotion* 13, no. 6 (2013): 1150–59, doi:10.1037/a0033278.

18. Tracey Franklin, quoted in Adam Piore, "Wanted: College Grads Seeking Adventure," *Newsweek*, June 28, 2019, 30.

19. Paul Hawken, *Regeneration* (New York: Penguin, 2021).

20. Kathy Kram, presentation at CREIO, Boston, May 3, 2019.

15 | Innovation and Systems

1. Sydney Brenner's creative insight on the ribosome: Siddhartha Mukherjee, *The Gene: An Intimate History* (New York: Scribner, 2013).

2. M. E. Raichle, "The Brain's Default Mode Network," *Annual Review of Neuroscience* 38 (2015): 433–47, https://doi.org/10.1146/annurev-neuro-0710 13-014030.

3. R. E. Beaty et al., "Creativity and the Default Network: A Functional Connectivity Analysis of the Creative Brain at Rest," *Neuropsychologia* 64 (2014): 92–98, doi:10.1016/j.neuropsychologia.2014.09.019.

4. M. J. Gruber and C. Ranganath, "How Curiosity Enhances Hippocampus-Dependent Memory," *Trends in Cognitive Science*, November 6, 2019, https://doi .org/10.1016/j.tics.2019.10.003.

5. T. Kashdan et al., "The Five-Dimensional Curiosity Scale," *Journal of Research in Personality* 73 (2018): 130–49.

6. Frank Rose, "Very Personal Computing: In Artist's New Work A.I. Meets Fatherhood," *New York Times*, August 27, 2021, https://www.nytimes.com /2021/08/27/arts/design/ian-cheng-shed-life-after-bob.html.

7. Melissa Dassori, "Inspiration versus Perspiration," Writersdigest.com, July 30, 2022.

8. Amabile and Kramer, *The Progress Principle*.

9. Howard Gardner, *Creating Minds* (New York: Basic Books, 2011).

10. Teresa Amabile and Steven Kramer, "The Power of Small Wins," in *Purpose, Meaning, and Passion* (Boston: Harvard Business Review Press, 2018), 120.

11. Kevin Crowley, "Exxon's Exodus: Employees Have Finally Had Enough of Its Toxic Culture," *Bloomberg Businessweek*, October 13, 2022, https://apple.news/AU93JES9cRIGbBO0CLCAzCw.

12. Julie Battilana and Tizania Cascario, "The Network Secrets of Great Change Agents," *Harvard Business Review*, July 1, 2013, https//hbr.org/2013/07/the-network-secrets-of-great-change-agents.

13. KeyStepMedia, *Organizational Awareness: A Primer* (Florence, MA: MoreThanSound, 2017), 23.

14. For more details, see Graham Lawton, "Our World Against Us," *New Scientist*, January 29, 2022, 44–47.

15. This distinction between circles of concern and of influence was made by Stephen Covey in *The 7 Habits of Highly Effective People* (New York: Simon & Schuster, 1989).

16. James S. Russell, "At Columbia's $600 Million Business School, Time to Rethink Capitalism," *New York Times*, January 6, 2023.

Index

Note: Page numbers in *italics* refer to figures.

work performance (*continued*)
   social skills for, 114–115
   in STEM occupations, 20–23
   stress sources, 68–70
   team performance, 153–154
   training programs and effect on,
     165

Work Trends Index 2022 Report
   (Microsoft), 129

"yet," 58
yogis, 40

Zaki, Jamil, 82

About the Authors

Daniel Goleman, a former science journalist for the *New York Times*, is the author of thirteen books and lectures frequently to professional groups and business audiences. He received the 2023 Centennial Medal from Harvard's Graduate School of Arts and Sciences for "excellence in communicating science" and for his influence on education, business, and society at large.

Cary Cherniss is Emeritus Professor of Applied Psychology at Rutgers University. He has published more than seventy scholarly articles and book chapters, as well as eight books, including *Leading with Feeling: Nine Strategies of Emotionally Intelligent Leadership* (with Cornelia Roche). He has consulted with many organizations in both the public and private sectors.

Goleman and Cherniss are founding members of the Consortium for Research on Emotional Intelligence in Organizations (CREIO) and served as cochairs for twenty-five years. Cherniss was also director of CREIO.